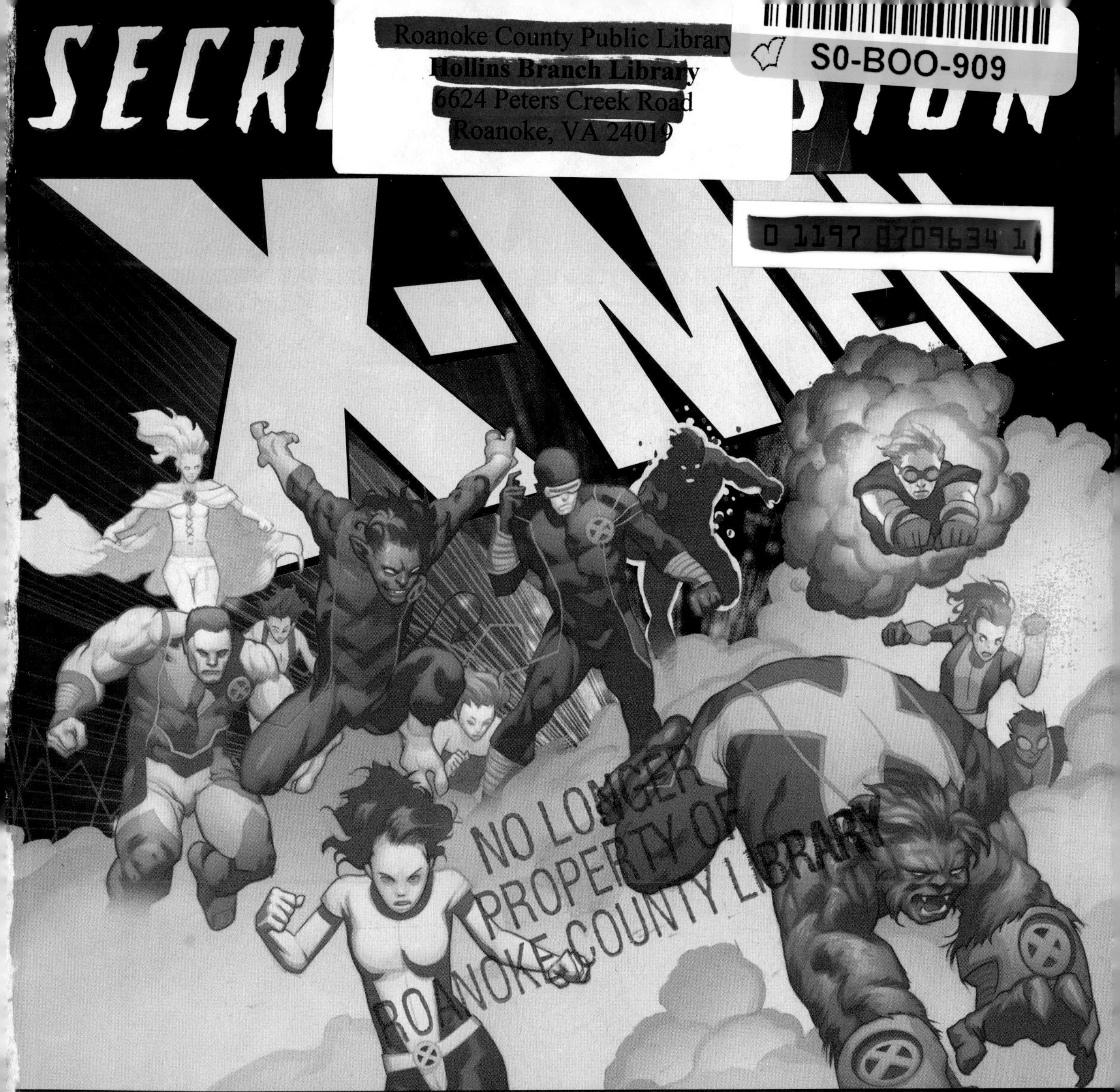
SECR
X-MEN

Writer: **MIKE CAREY**
Artists: **CARY NORD** & **M.A. SEPULVEDA** • Color Artist: **DAVE MCCAIG**
Letterers: **VC'S JOE CARAMAGNA** & **CHRIS ELIOPOULOS**
Cover Art: **TERRY DODSON, RACHEL DODSON** & **JUSTIN PONSOR**
Assistant Editors: **WILL PANZO** & **DANIEL KETCHUM** • Editor: **NICK LOWE**

FANTASTIC FOUR #250

Writer/Artist: **JOHN BYRNE** • Colorist: **CHRISTIE SCHEELE**
Letterer: **JOE ROSEN** • Editors: **TOM DEFALCO** & **JIM SALICRUP**
Color Reconstruction: **JERRON QUALITY COLOR**

Collection Editor: **JENNIFER GRÜNWALD** • Editorial Assistant: **ALEX STARBUCK**
Assistant Editors: **CORY LEVINE** & **JOHN DENNING**
Editor, Special Projects: **MARK D. BEAZLEY**
Senior Editor, Special Projects: **JEFF YOUNGQUIST**
Senior Vice President of Sales: **DAVID GABRIEL**
Production: **JERRY KALINOWSKI** • Book Design: **RODOLFO MURAGUCHI**

Editor in Chief: **JOE QUESADA** • Publisher: **DAN BUCKLEY**

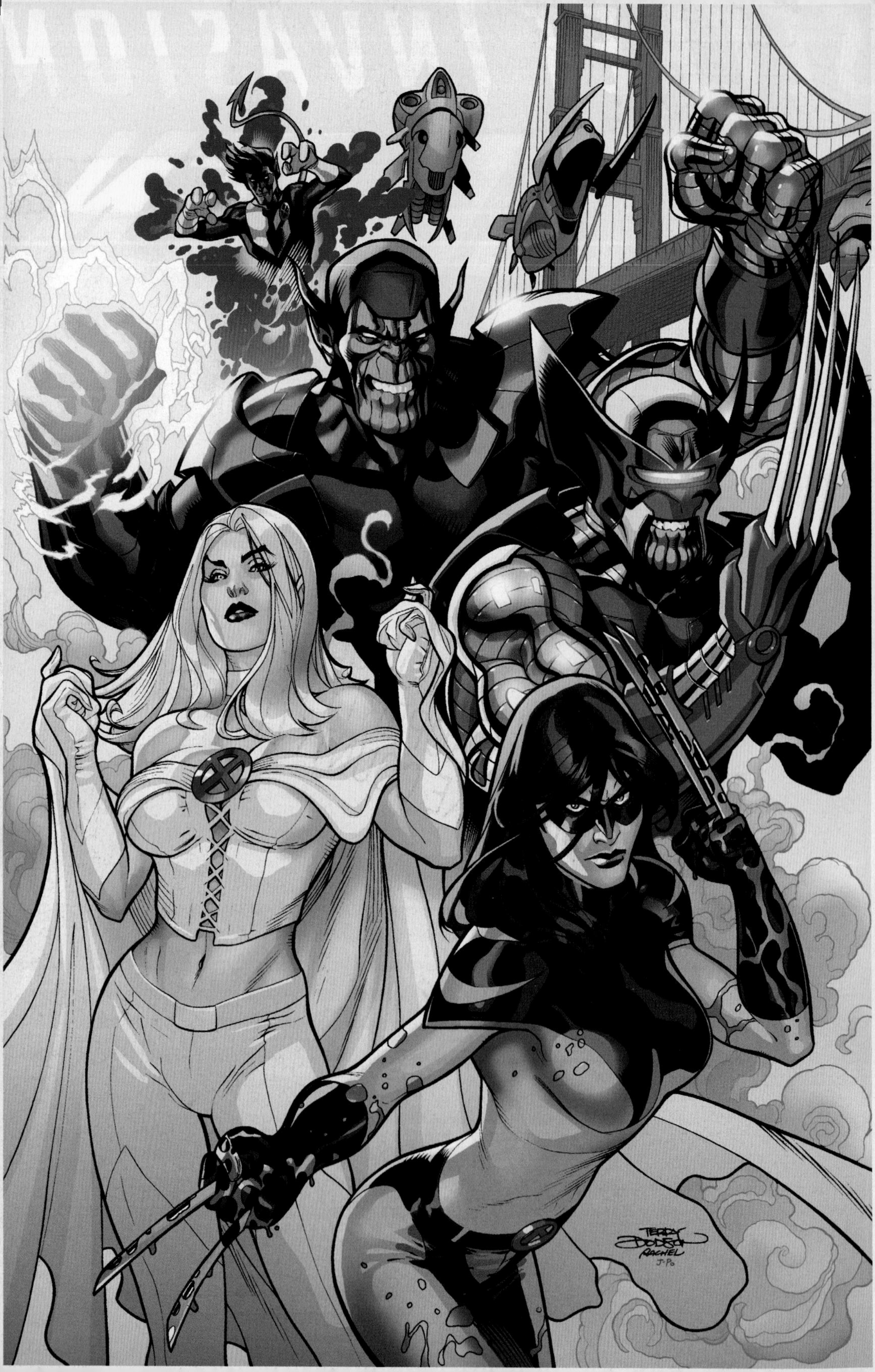
TERRY DODSON
RACHEL
J-Po

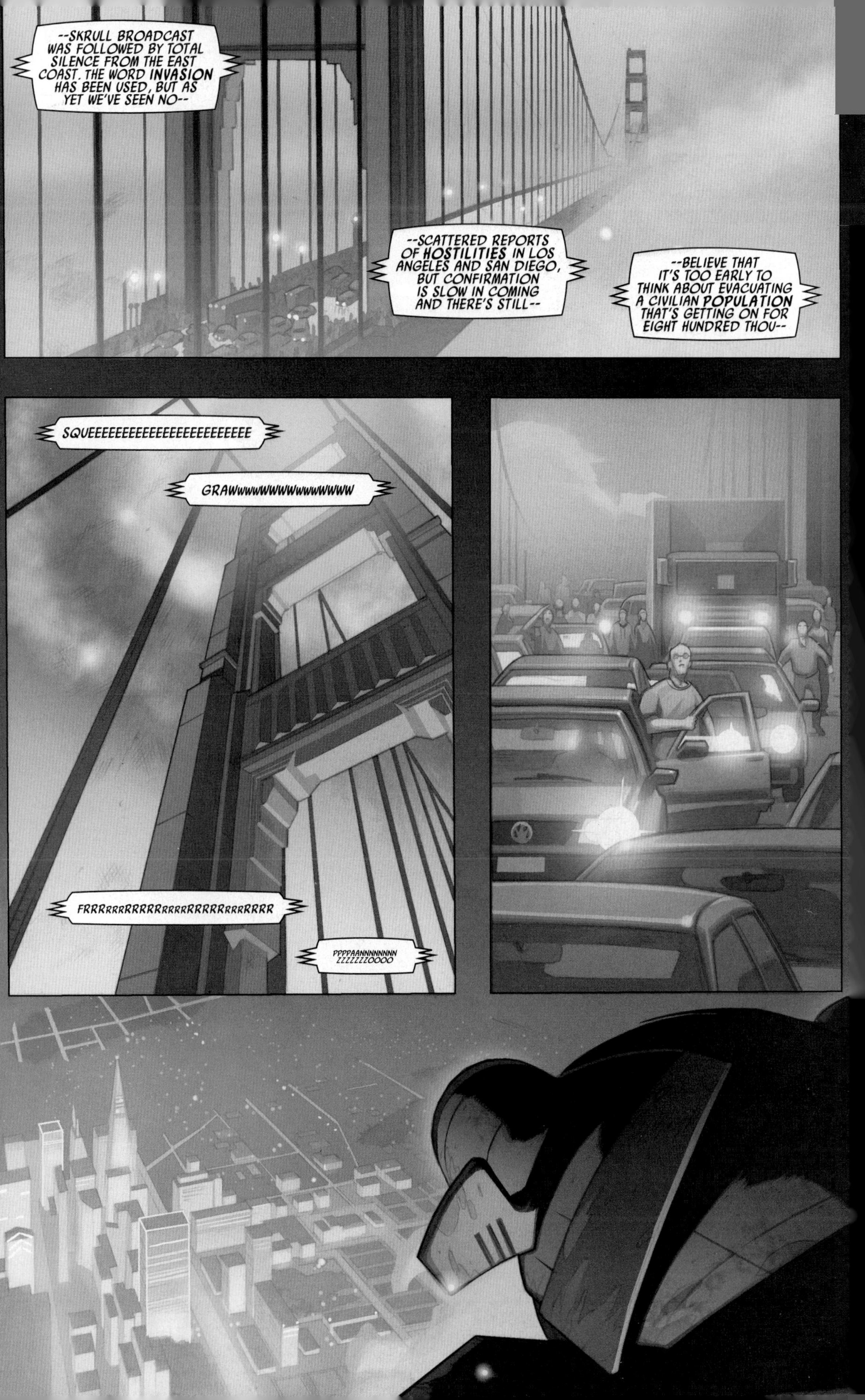
--SKRULL BROADCAST WAS FOLLOWED BY TOTAL SILENCE FROM THE EAST COAST. THE WORD **INVASION** HAS BEEN USED, BUT AS YET WE'VE SEEN NO--
--SCATTERED REPORTS OF **HOSTILITIES** IN LOS ANGELES AND SAN DIEGO, BUT CONFIRMATION IS SLOW IN COMING AND THERE'S STILL--
--BELIEVE THAT IT'S TOO EARLY TO THINK ABOUT EVACUATING A CIVILIAN **POPULATION** THAT'S GETTING ON FOR EIGHT HUNDRED THOU--
SQUEEEEEEEEEEEEEEEEEEEEEEEE
GRAWwwwWWWWwwwwWWWW
FRRRrrrRRRRRrrrrRRRRRrrrRRRR
PPPPAANNNNNNNNN ZZZZZZZOOOO

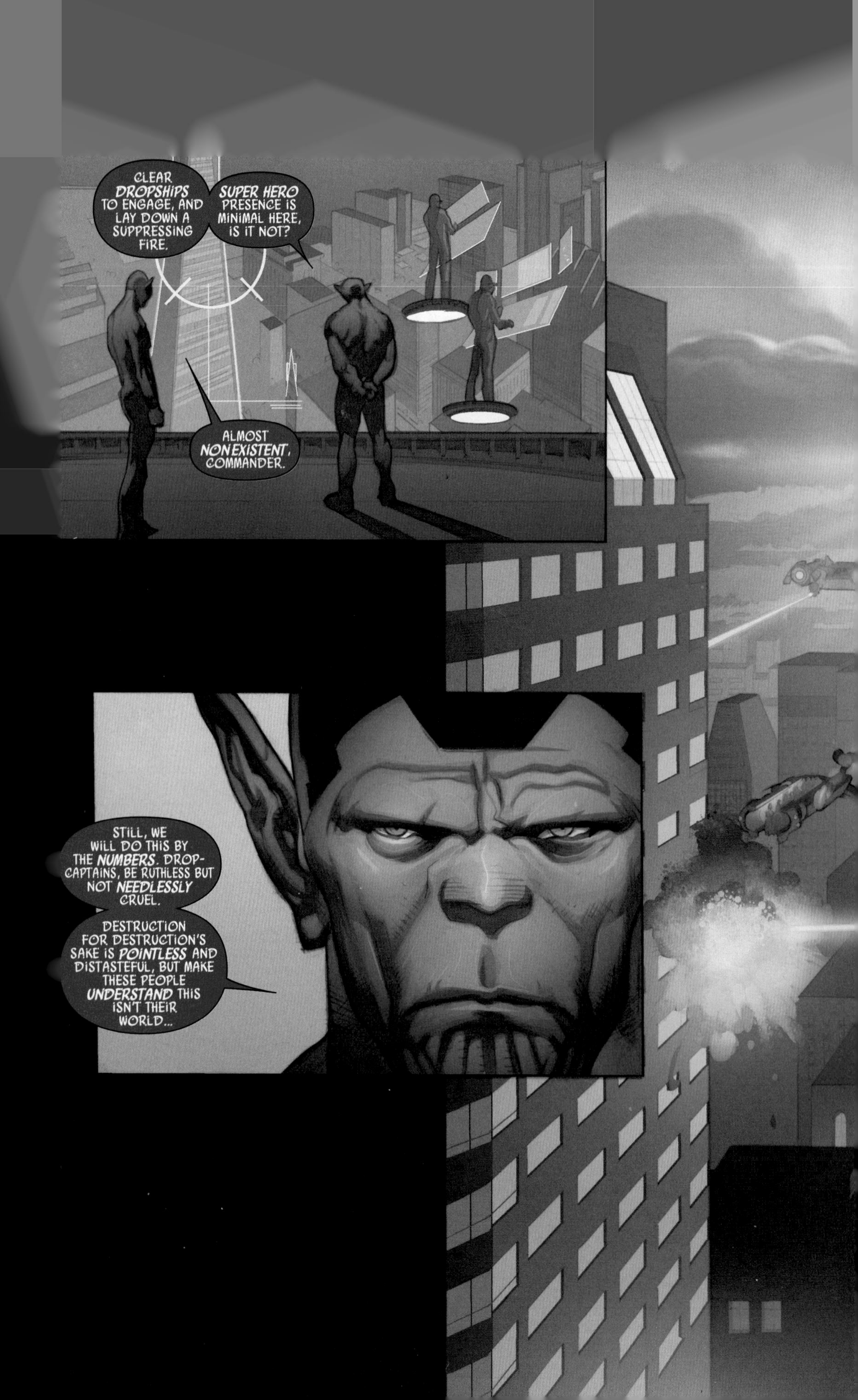
CLEAR DROPSHIPS TO ENGAGE, AND LAY DOWN A SUPPRESSING FIRE.
SUPER HERO PRESENCE IS MINIMAL HERE, IS IT NOT?
ALMOST NONEXISTENT, COMMANDER.
STILL, WE WILL DO THIS BY THE NUMBERS. DROP-CAPTAINS, BE RUTHLESS BUT NOT NEEDLESSLY CRUEL.
DESTRUCTION FOR DESTRUCTION'S SAKE IS POINTLESS AND DISTASTEFUL, BUT MAKE THESE PEOPLE UNDERSTAND THIS ISN'T THEIR WORLD...

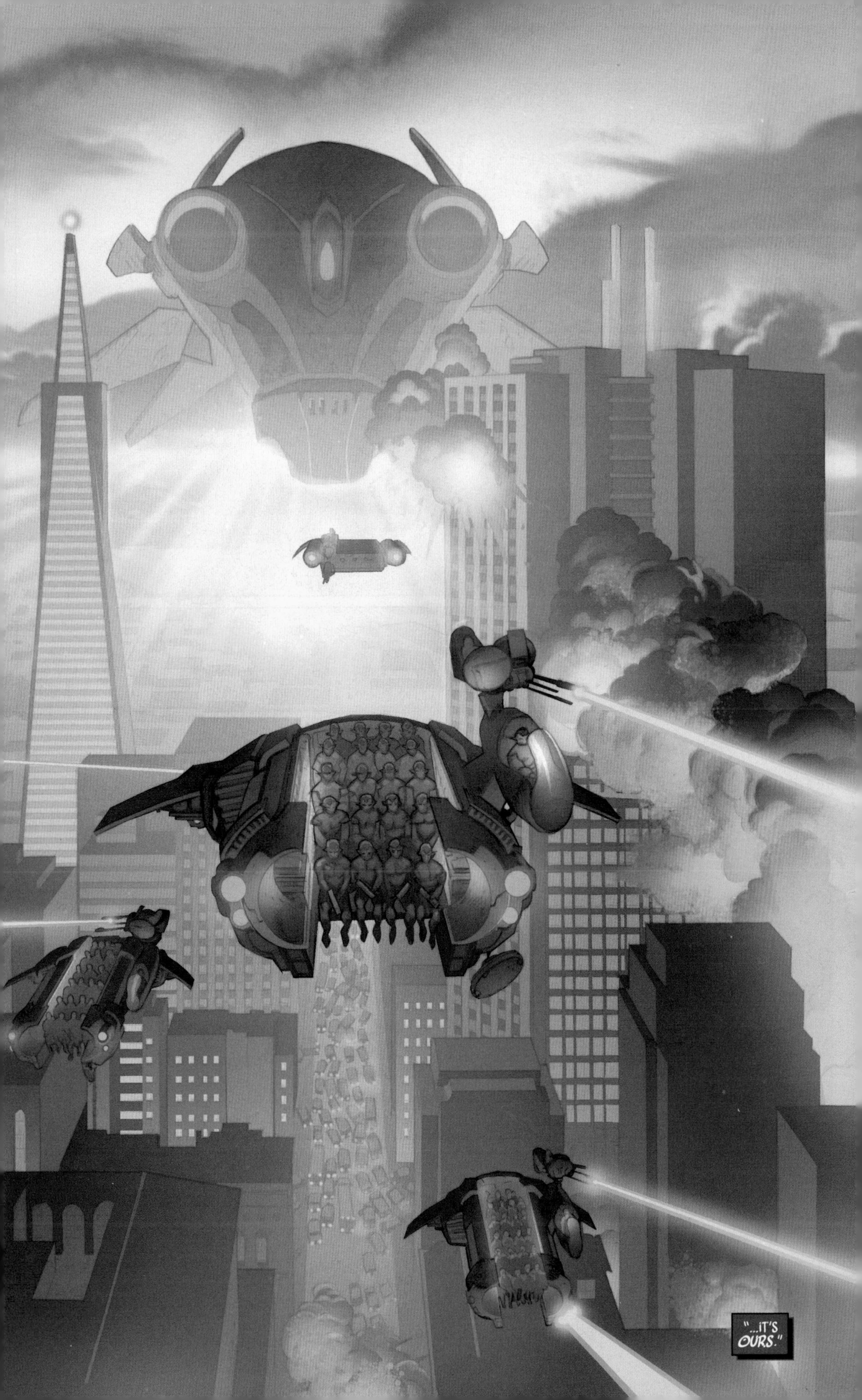
"...IT'S OURS."

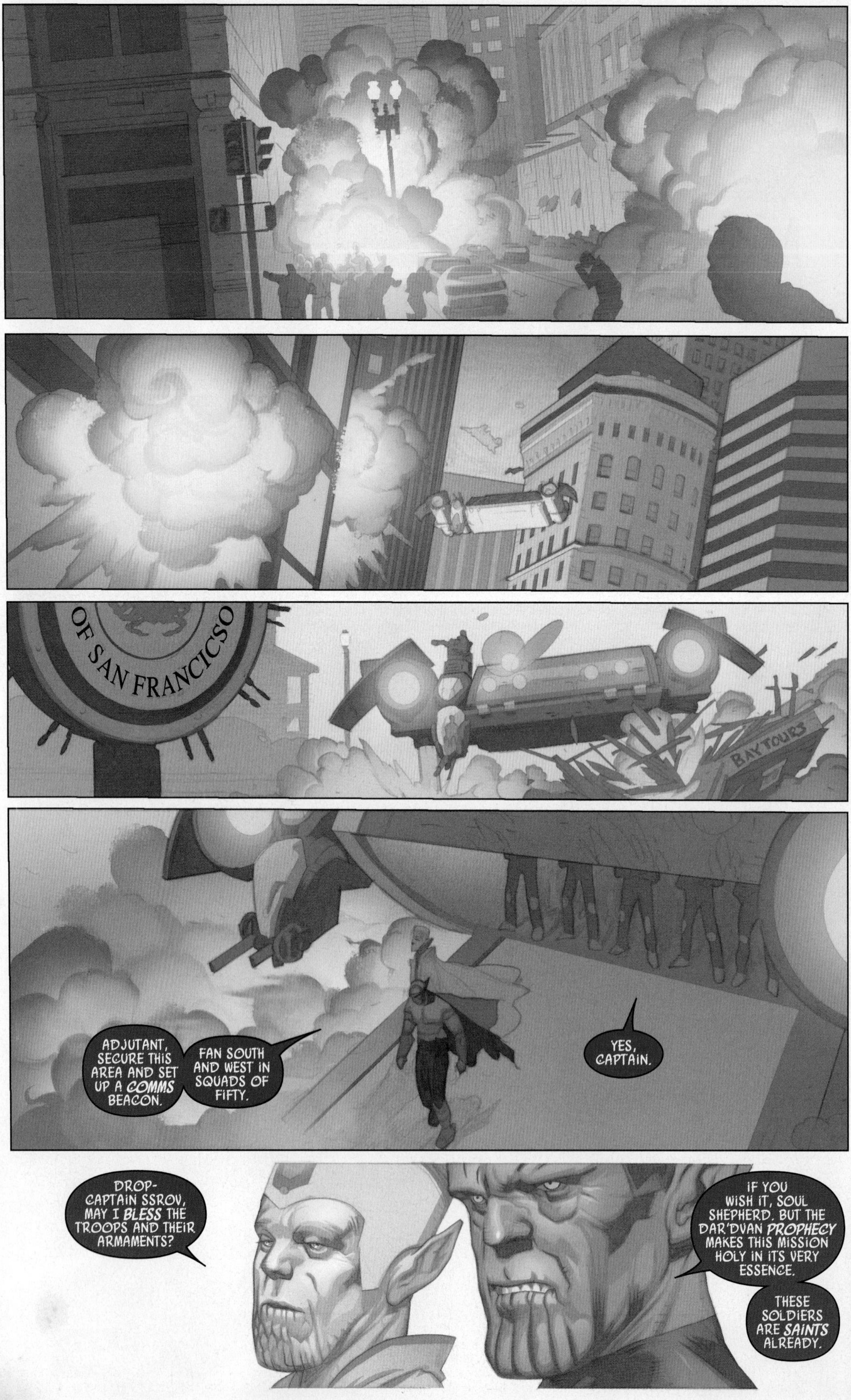
OF SAN FRANCICSO
BAY TOURS
ADJUTANT, SECURE THIS AREA AND SET UP A COMMS BEACON.
FAN SOUTH AND WEST IN SQUADS OF FIFTY.
YES, CAPTAIN.
DROP-CAPTAIN SSROV, MAY I BLESS THE TROOPS AND THEIR ARMAMENTS?
IF YOU WISH IT, SOUL SHEPHERD. BUT THE DAR'DVAN PROPHECY MAKES THIS MISSION HOLY IN ITS VERY ESSENCE.
THESE SOLDIERS ARE SAINTS ALREADY.

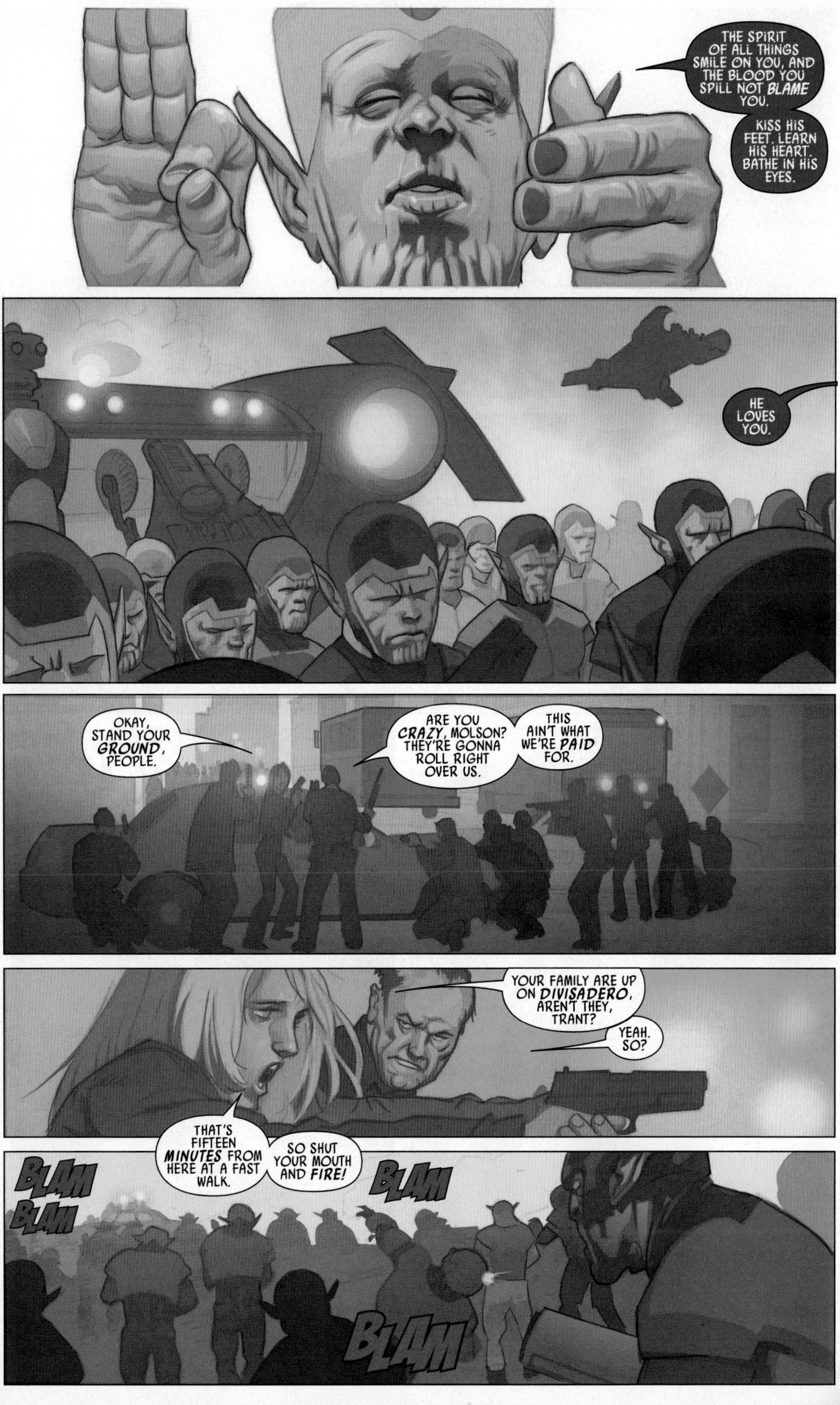
THE SPIRIT OF ALL THINGS SMILE ON YOU, AND THE BLOOD YOU SPILL NOT BLAME YOU.
KISS HIS FEET. LEARN HIS HEART. BATHE IN HIS EYES.
HE LOVES YOU.
OKAY, STAND YOUR GROUND, PEOPLE.
ARE YOU CRAZY, MOLSON? THEY'RE GONNA ROLL RIGHT OVER US.
THIS AIN'T WHAT WE'RE PAID FOR.
YOUR FAMILY ARE UP ON DIVISADERO, AREN'T THEY, TRANT?
YEAH. SO?
THAT'S FIFTEEN MINUTES FROM HERE AT A FAST WALK.
SO SHUT YOUR MOUTH AND FIRE!
BLAM
BLAM
BLAM
BLAM

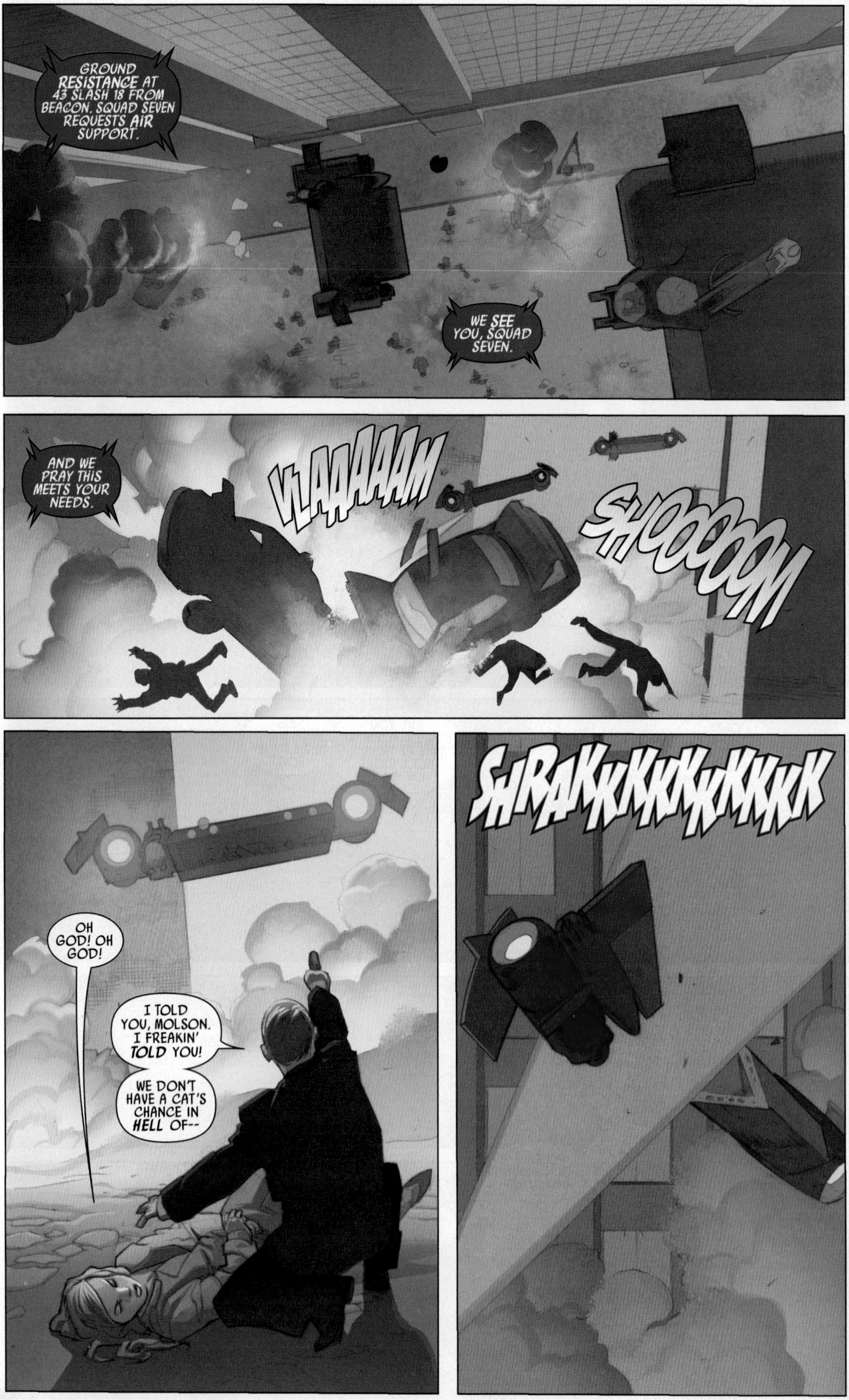
GROUND RESISTANCE AT 43 SLASH 18 FROM BEACON. SQUAD SEVEN REQUESTS AIR SUPPORT.
WE SEE YOU, SQUAD SEVEN.
AND WE PRAY THIS MEETS YOUR NEEDS.
VLAAAAAM
SHOOOOOM
OH GOD! OH GOD!
I TOLD YOU, MOLSON. I FREAKIN' TOLD YOU!
WE DON'T HAVE A CAT'S CHANCE IN HELL OF--
SHRAKKKKKKKKKK

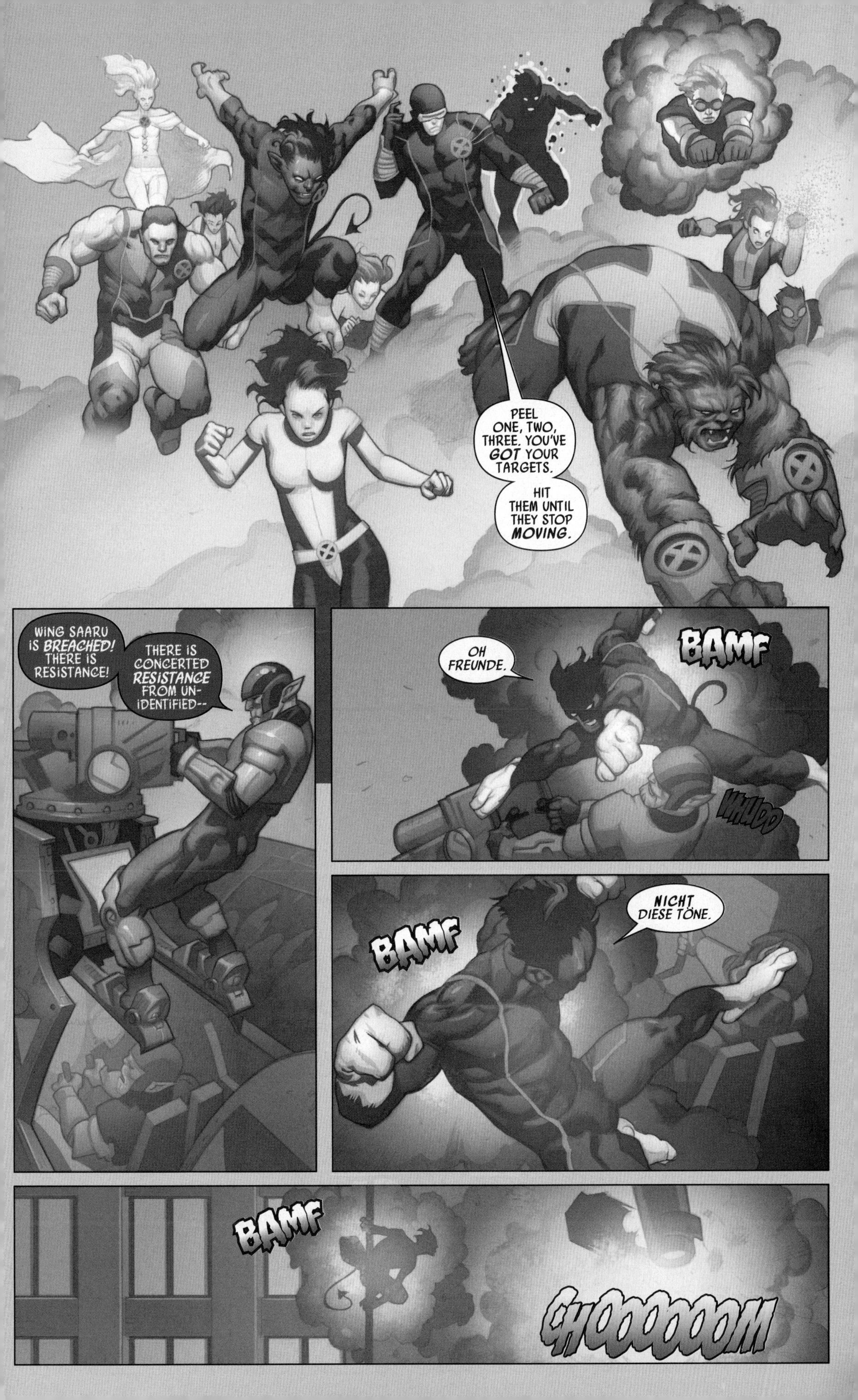
PEEL ONE, TWO, THREE. YOU'VE GOT YOUR TARGETS.
HIT THEM UNTIL THEY STOP MOVING.
WING SAARU IS BREACHED! THERE IS RESISTANCE!
THERE IS CONCERTED RESISTANCE FROM UN-IDENTIFIED--
OH FREUNDE.
BAMF
WHUDD
NICHT DIESE TÖNE.
BAMF
BAMF
CHOOOOOOOM

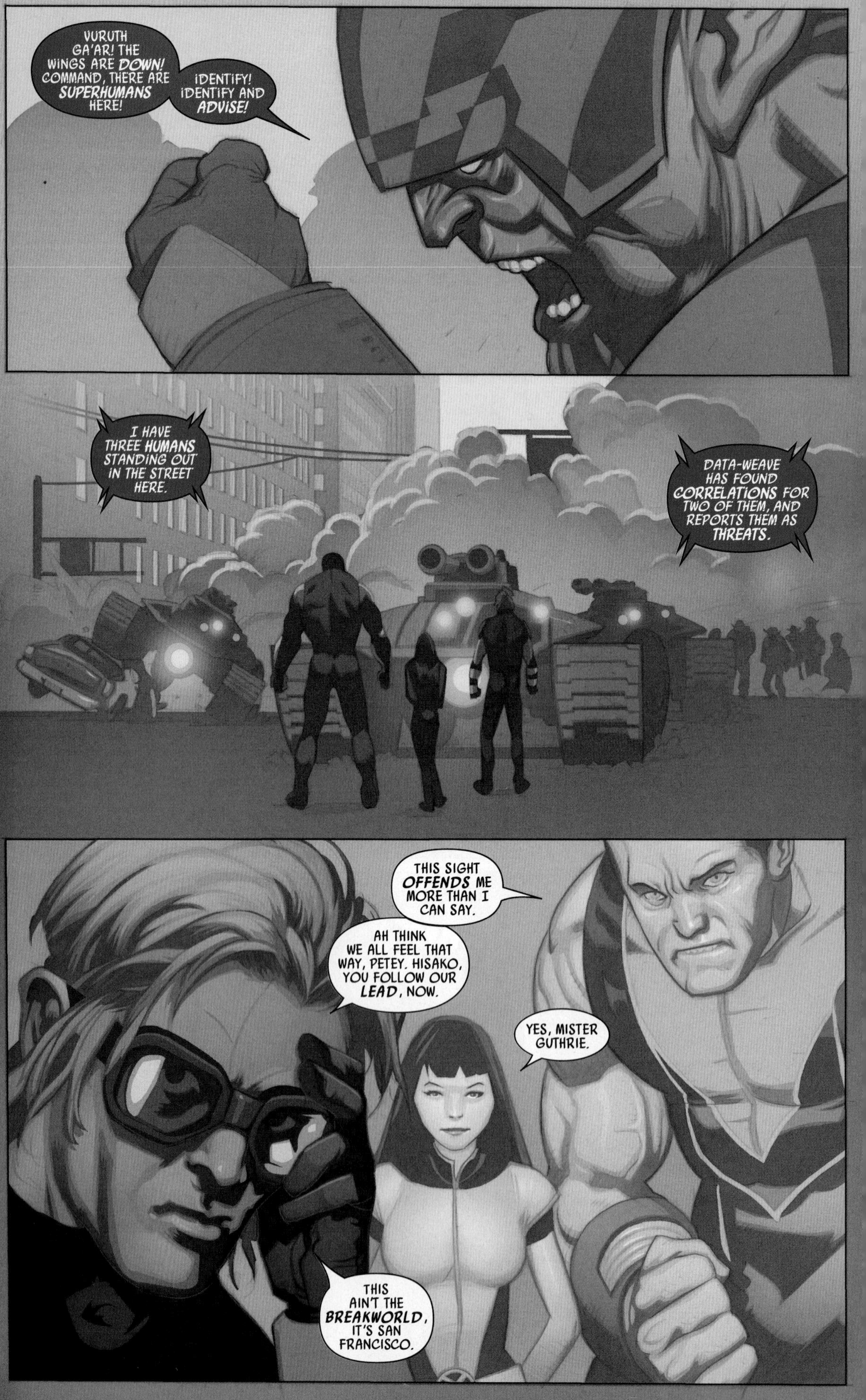
VURUTH GA'AR! THE WINGS ARE DOWN! COMMAND, THERE ARE SUPERHUMANS HERE!
IDENTIFY! IDENTIFY AND ADVISE!
I HAVE THREE HUMANS STANDING OUT IN THE STREET HERE.
DATA-WEAVE HAS FOUND CORRELATIONS FOR TWO OF THEM, AND REPORTS THEM AS THREATS.
THIS SIGHT OFFENDS ME MORE THAN I CAN SAY.
AH THINK WE ALL FEEL THAT WAY, PETEY. HISAKO, YOU FOLLOW OUR LEAD, NOW.
YES, MISTER GUTHRIE.
THIS AIN'T THE BREAKWORLD, IT'S SAN FRANCISCO.

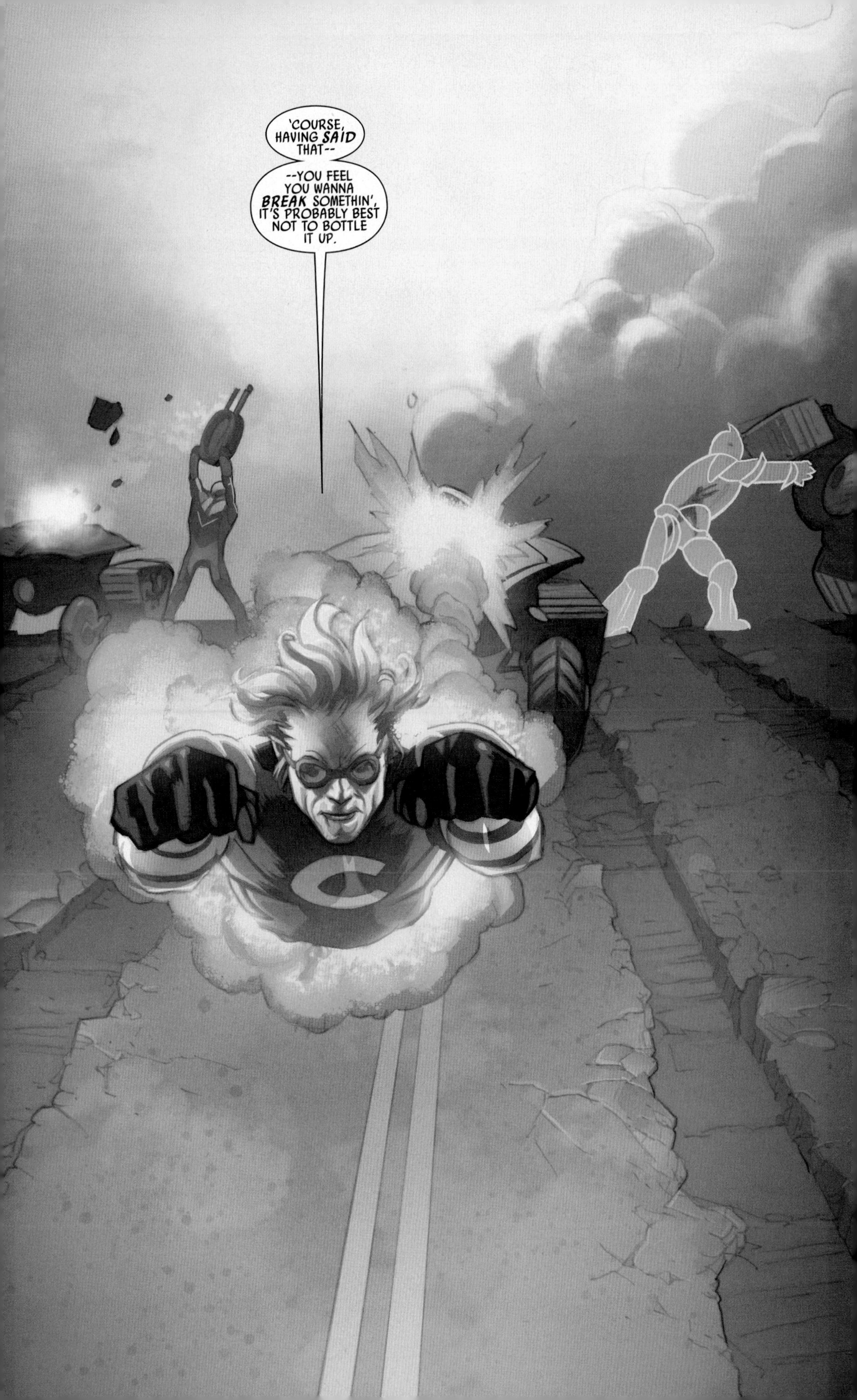
'COURSE, HAVING SAID THAT--
--YOU FEEL YOU WANNA BREAK SOMETHIN', IT'S PROBABLY BEST NOT TO BOTTLE IT UP.

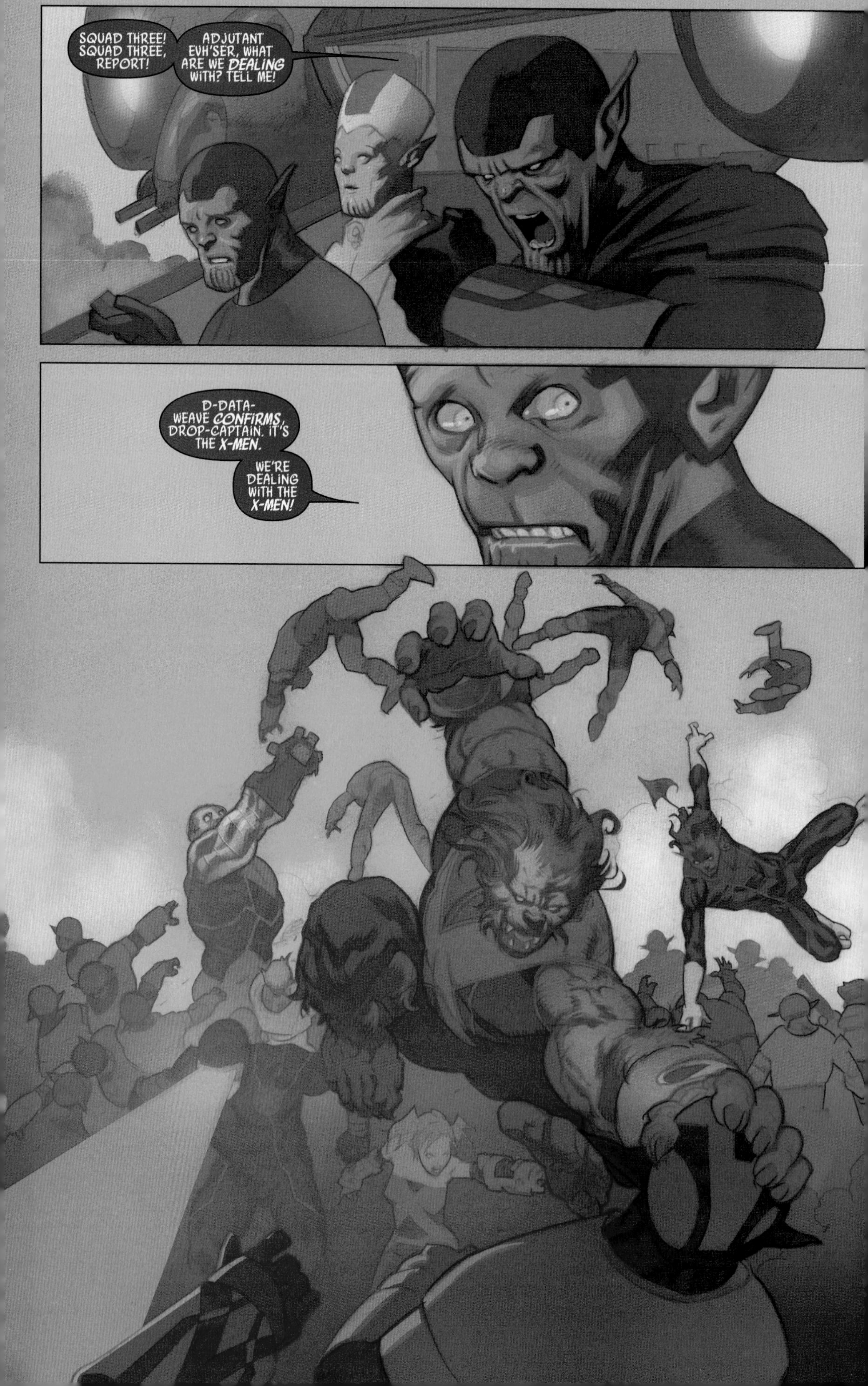
SQUAD THREE! SQUAD THREE, REPORT!
ADJUTANT EVH'SER, WHAT ARE WE *DEALING* WITH? TELL ME!
D-DATA-WEAVE *CONFIRMS*, DROP-CAPTAIN. IT'S THE *X-MEN*.
WE'RE DEALING WITH THE *X-MEN!*

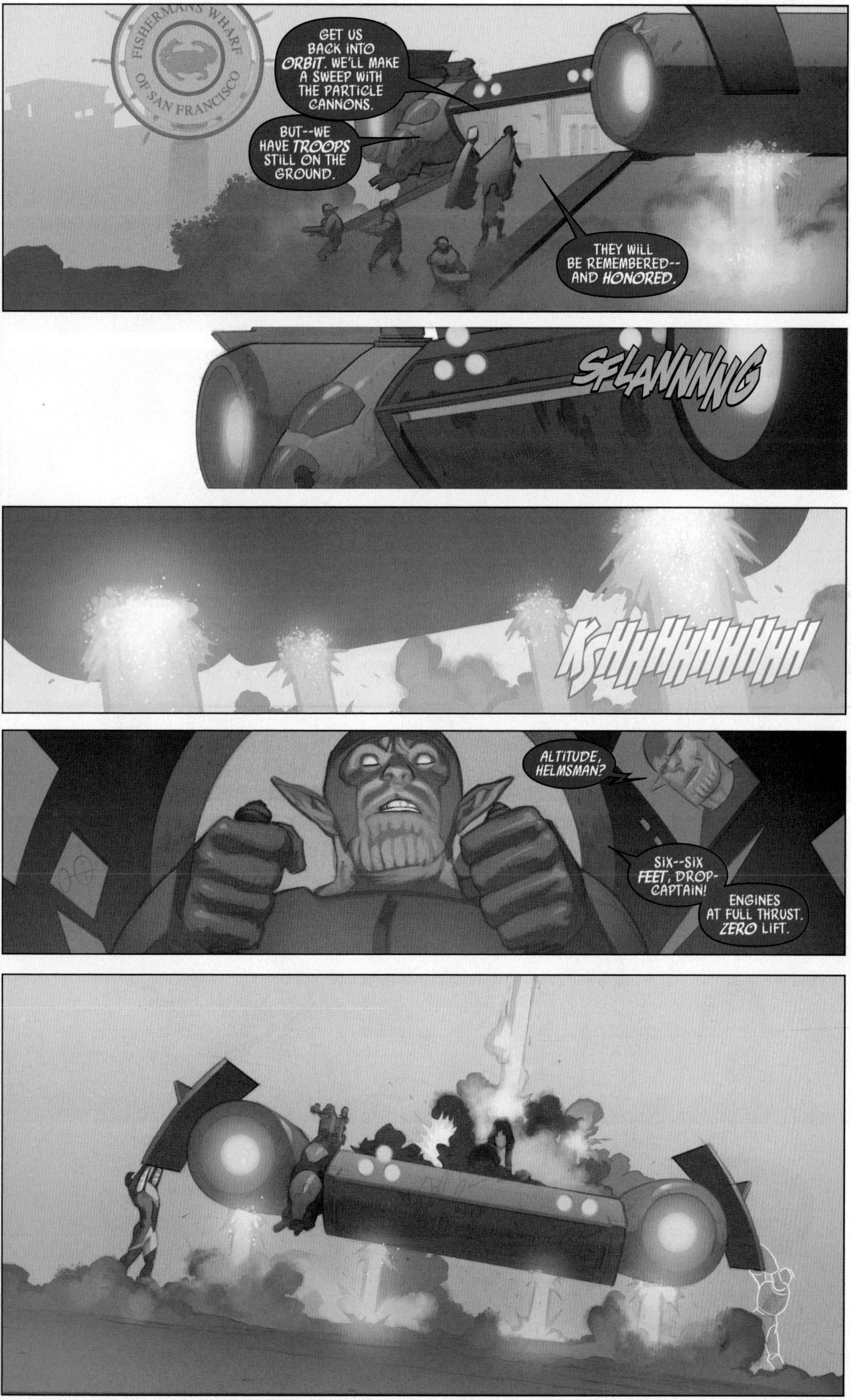
FISHERMANS WHARF OF SAN FRANCISCO
GET US BACK INTO ORBIT. WE'LL MAKE A SWEEP WITH THE PARTICLE CANNONS.
BUT--WE HAVE TROOPS STILL ON THE GROUND.
THEY WILL BE REMEMBERED--AND HONORED.
SFLANNNNG
KSHHHHHHHHH
ALTITUDE, HELMSMAN?
SIX--SIX FEET, DROP-CAPTAIN!
ENGINES AT FULL THRUST. ZERO LIFT.

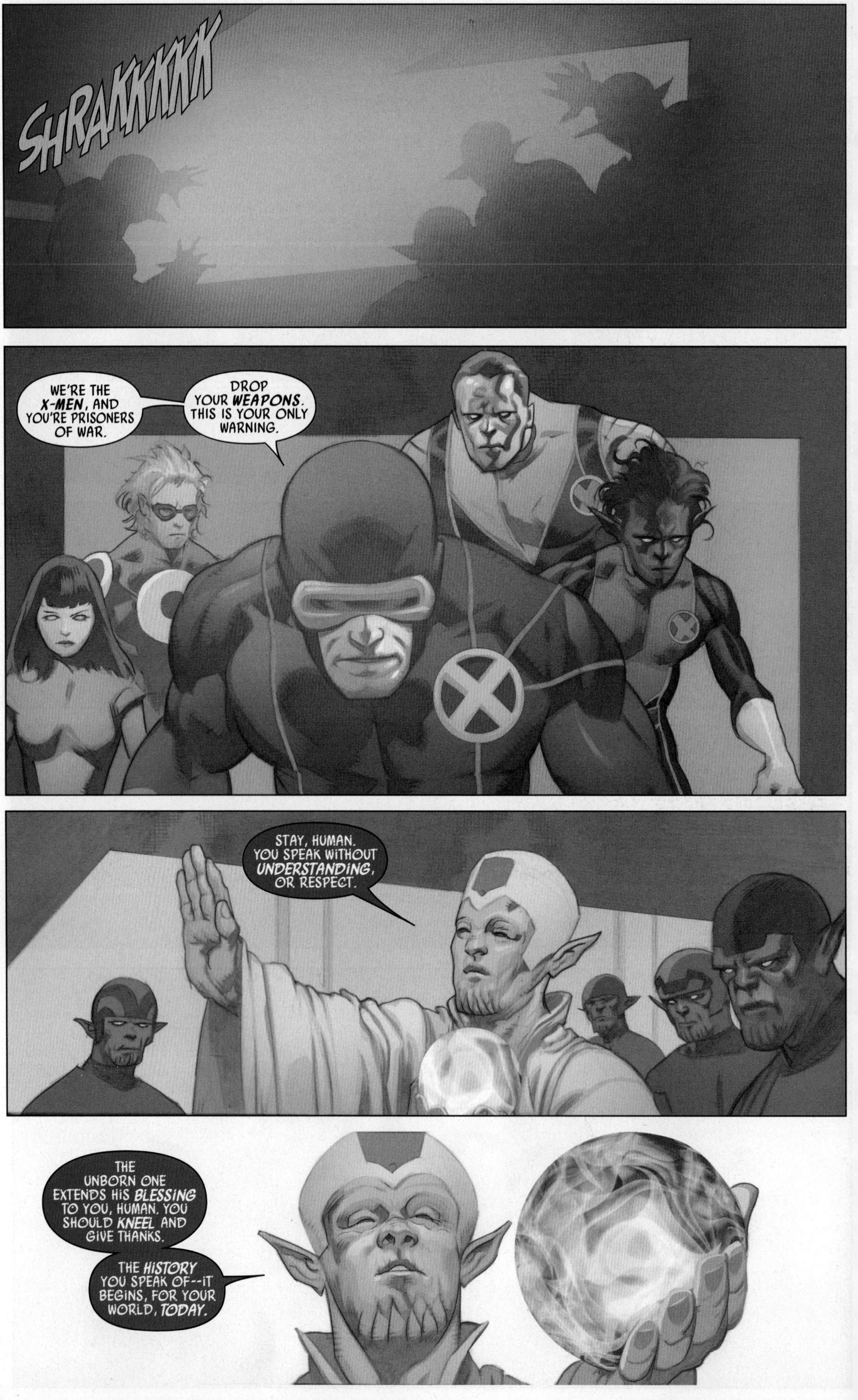
SHRAKKKKK
WE'RE THE X-MEN, AND YOU'RE PRISONERS OF WAR.
DROP YOUR WEAPONS. THIS IS YOUR ONLY WARNING.
STAY, HUMAN. YOU SPEAK WITHOUT UNDERSTANDING, OR RESPECT.
THE UNBORN ONE EXTENDS HIS BLESSING TO YOU, HUMAN. YOU SHOULD KNEEL AND GIVE THANKS.
THE HISTORY YOU SPEAK OF--IT BEGINS, FOR YOUR WORLD, TODAY.

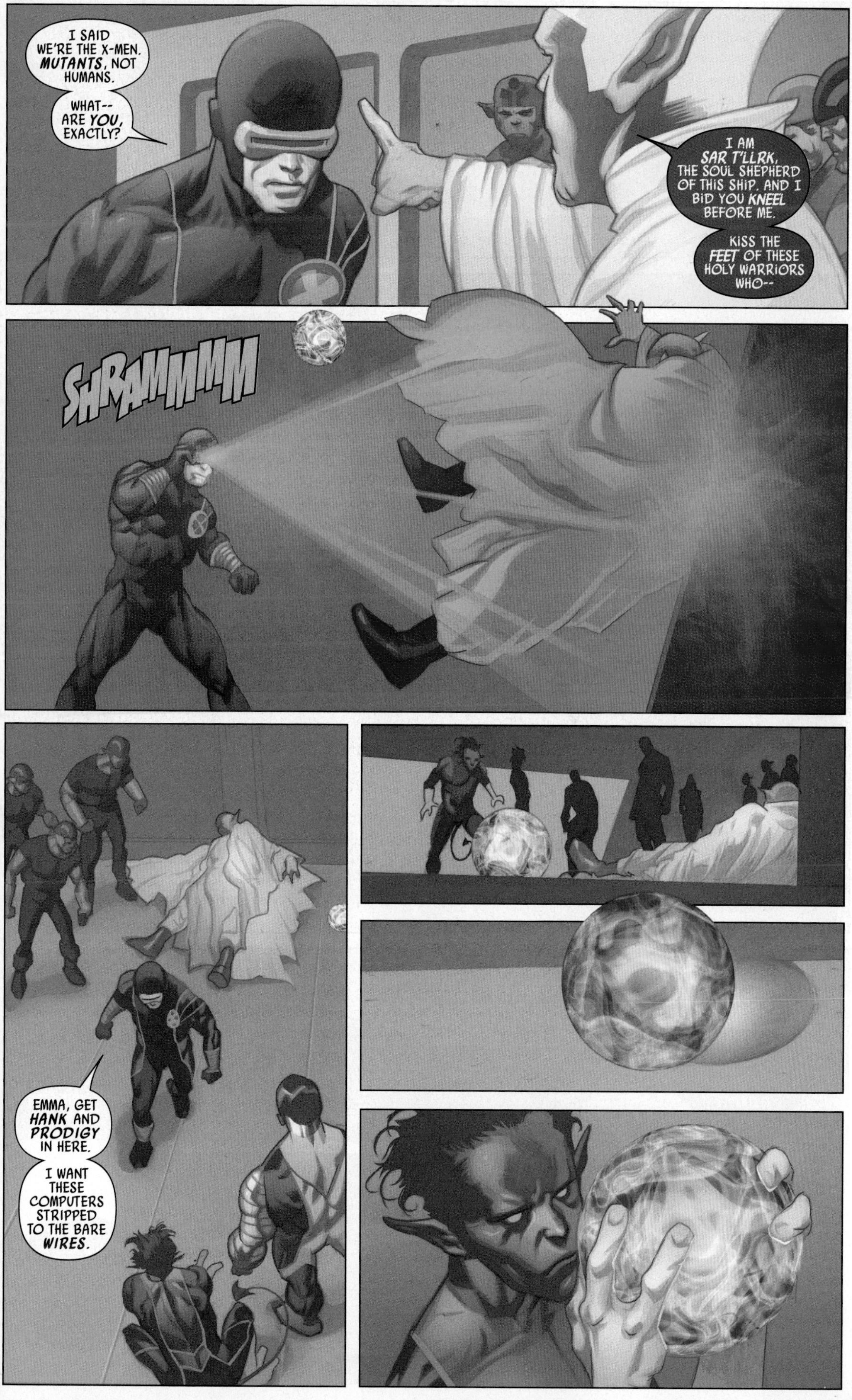

I SAID WE'RE THE X-MEN. MUTANTS, NOT HUMANS.
WHAT-- ARE YOU, EXACTLY?
I AM SAR T'LLRK, THE SOUL SHEPHERD OF THIS SHIP. AND I BID YOU KNEEL BEFORE ME.
KISS THE FEET OF THESE HOLY WARRIORS WHO--
SHRAMMMM
EMMA, GET HANK AND PRODIGY IN HERE.
I WANT THESE COMPUTERS STRIPPED TO THE BARE WIRES.

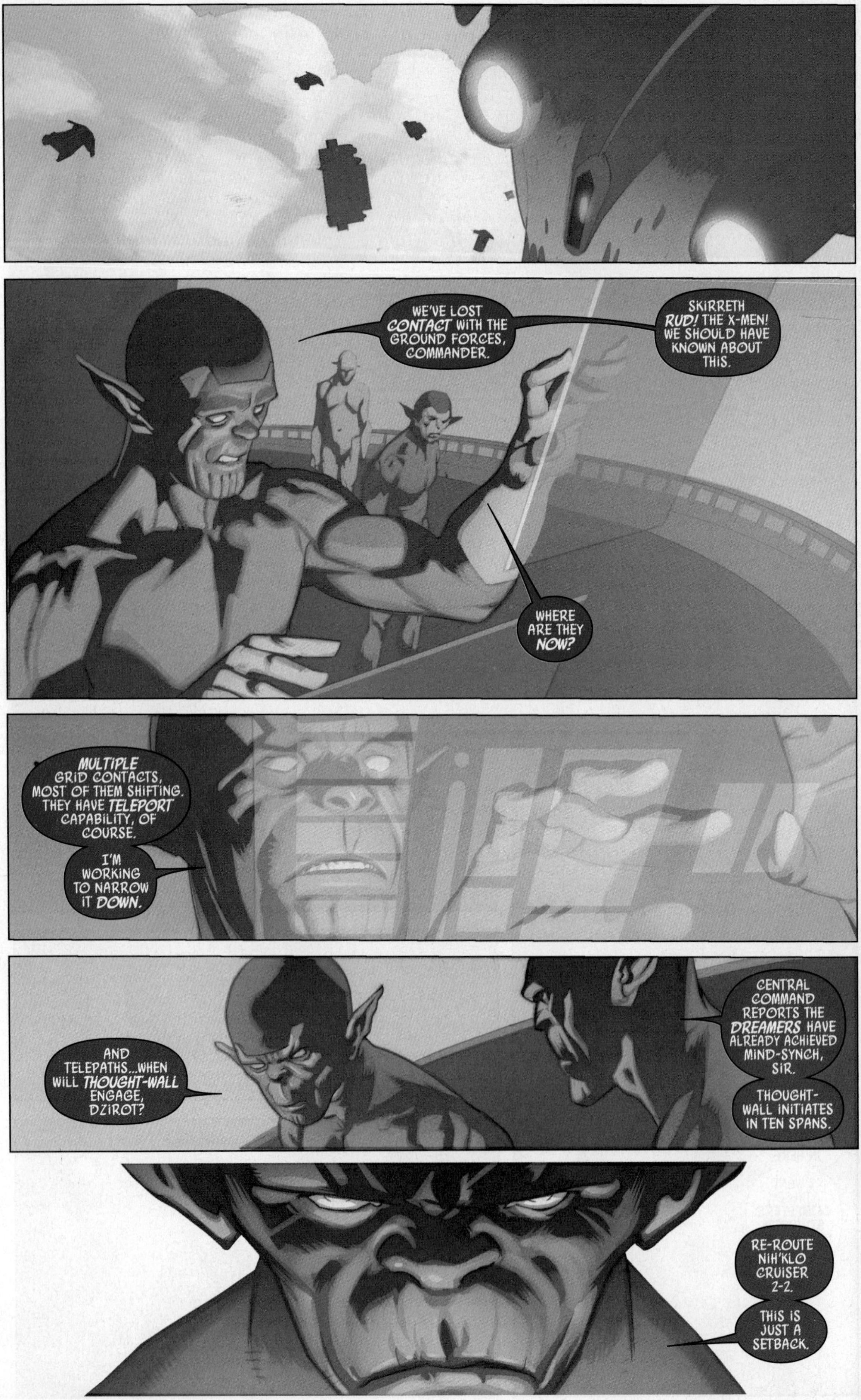
WE'VE LOST CONTACT WITH THE GROUND FORCES, COMMANDER.
SKIRRETH RUD! THE X-MEN! WE SHOULD HAVE KNOWN ABOUT THIS.
WHERE ARE THEY NOW?
MULTIPLE GRID CONTACTS, MOST OF THEM SHIFTING. THEY HAVE TELEPORT CAPABILITY, OF COURSE.
I'M WORKING TO NARROW IT DOWN.
AND TELEPATHS...WHEN WILL THOUGHT-WALL ENGAGE, DZIROT?
CENTRAL COMMAND REPORTS THE DREAMERS HAVE ALREADY ACHIEVED MIND-SYNCH, SIR.
THOUGHT-WALL INITIATES IN TEN SPANS.
RE-ROUTE NIH'KLO CRUISER 2-2.
THIS IS JUST A SETBACK.

ANYTHING WE CAN *USE*, HANK?

HARD TO SAY. THERE'S A LOT OF MATERIAL HERE, AND S.H.I.E.L.D.'S *MYRIAD* TRANSLATOR CAN COPE WITH SKRULL.

BUT THE PHYSICAL INTERFACE IS CONFIGURED FOR A *SHAPE-SHIFTER*. WE NEED A FEW MINUTES *MORE* HERE.

NARROW THE *SEARCH* TO FILES THAT HAVE BEEN MODIFIED IN THE LAST FEW DAYS.

FIVE MINUTES IS WHAT YOU'VE GOT. THEN I'M *SCUTTLING* THIS SHIP.

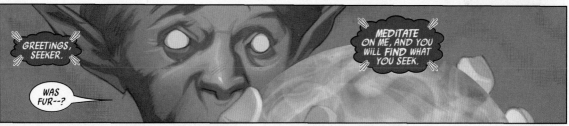

GREETINGS, SEEKER.

MEDITATE ON ME, AND YOU WILL *FIND* WHAT YOU SEEK.

WAS FUR--?

KURT.

Y-YES, SCOTT?

I WANT YOU *OUTSIDE*. ANYTHING COMES, LET ME KNOW.

EMMA, CALL THE *NUMBERS*. STAT.

BAMF

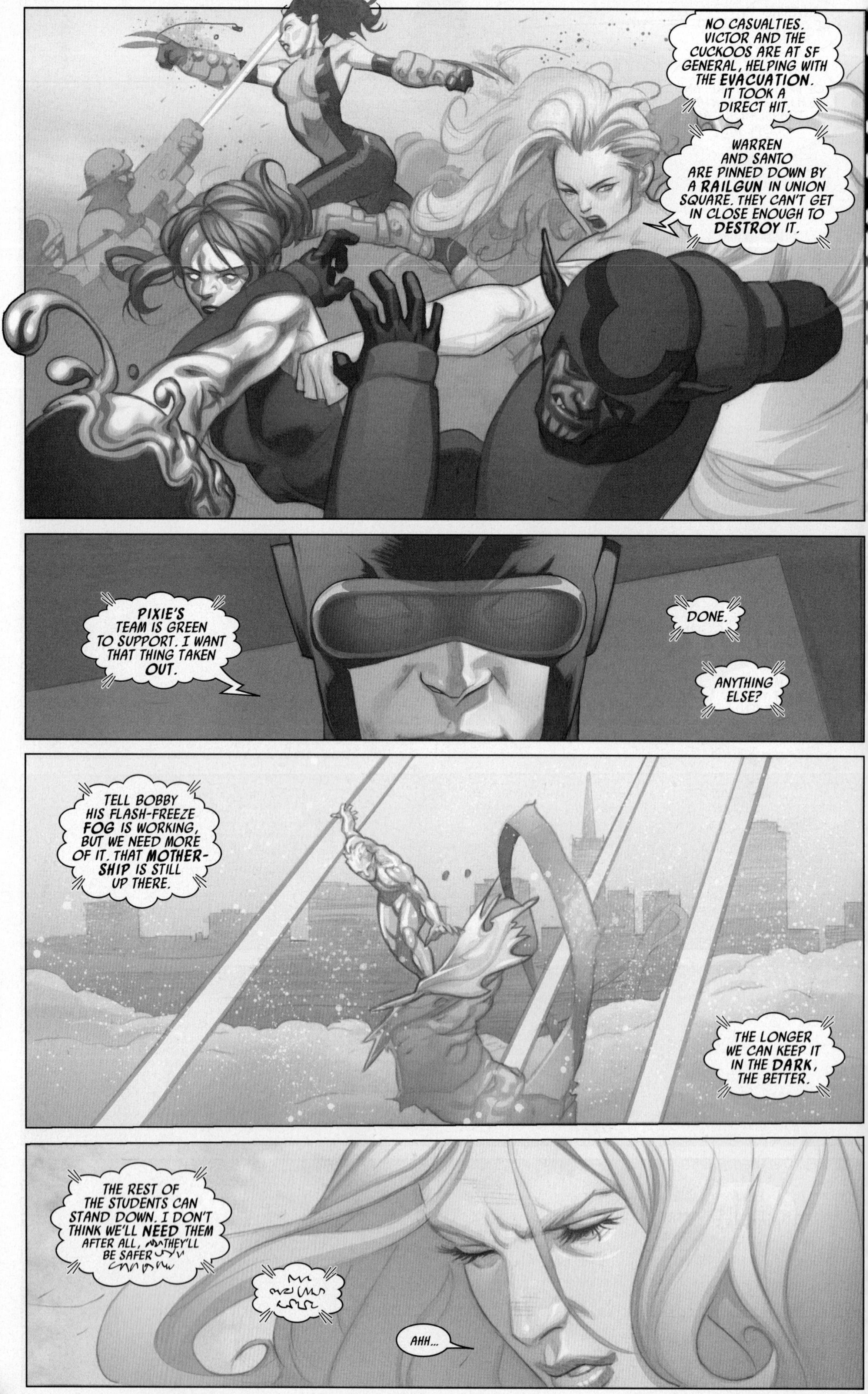
NO CASUALTIES. VICTOR AND THE CUCKOOS ARE AT SF GENERAL, HELPING WITH THE EVACUATION. IT TOOK A DIRECT HIT.
WARREN AND SANTO ARE PINNED DOWN BY A RAILGUN IN UNION SQUARE. THEY CAN'T GET IN CLOSE ENOUGH TO DESTROY IT.
PIXIE'S TEAM IS GREEN TO SUPPORT. I WANT THAT THING TAKEN OUT.
DONE.
ANYTHING ELSE?
TELL BOBBY HIS FLASH-FREEZE FOG IS WORKING, BUT WE NEED MORE OF IT. THAT MOTHER-SHIP IS STILL UP THERE.
THE LONGER WE CAN KEEP IT IN THE DARK, THE BETTER.
THE REST OF THE STUDENTS CAN STAND DOWN. I DON'T THINK WE'LL NEED THEM AFTER ALL, THEY'LL BE SAFER
AHH...

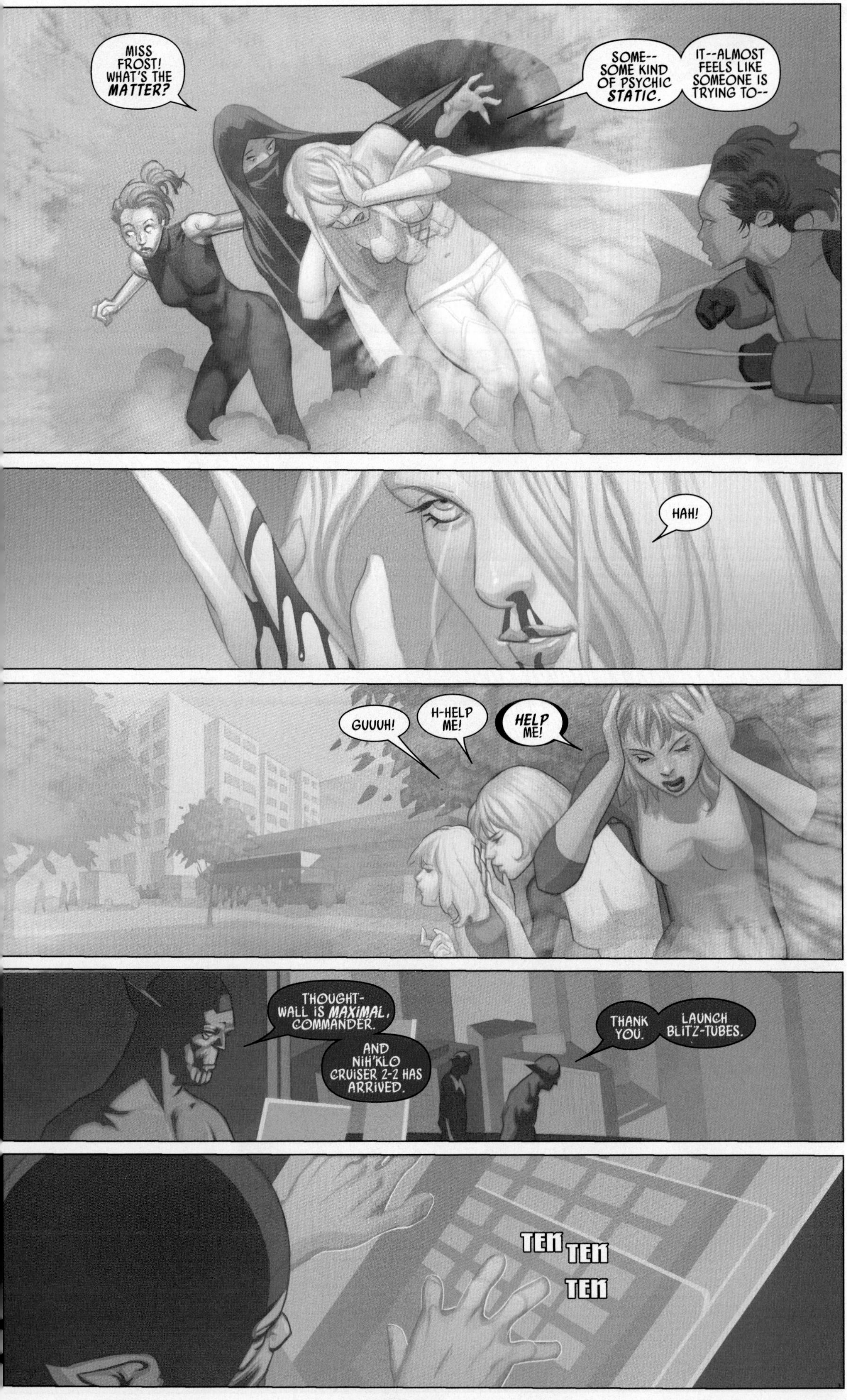
MISS FROST! WHAT'S THE MATTER?
SOME-- SOME KIND OF PSYCHIC STATIC.
IT--ALMOST FEELS LIKE SOMEONE IS TRYING TO--
HAH!
GUUUH!
H-HELP ME!
HELP ME!
THOUGHT-WALL IS MAXIMAL, COMMANDER.
AND NIH'KLO CRUISER 2-2 HAS ARRIVED.
THANK YOU.
LAUNCH BLITZ-TUBES.
TEK TEK
TEK

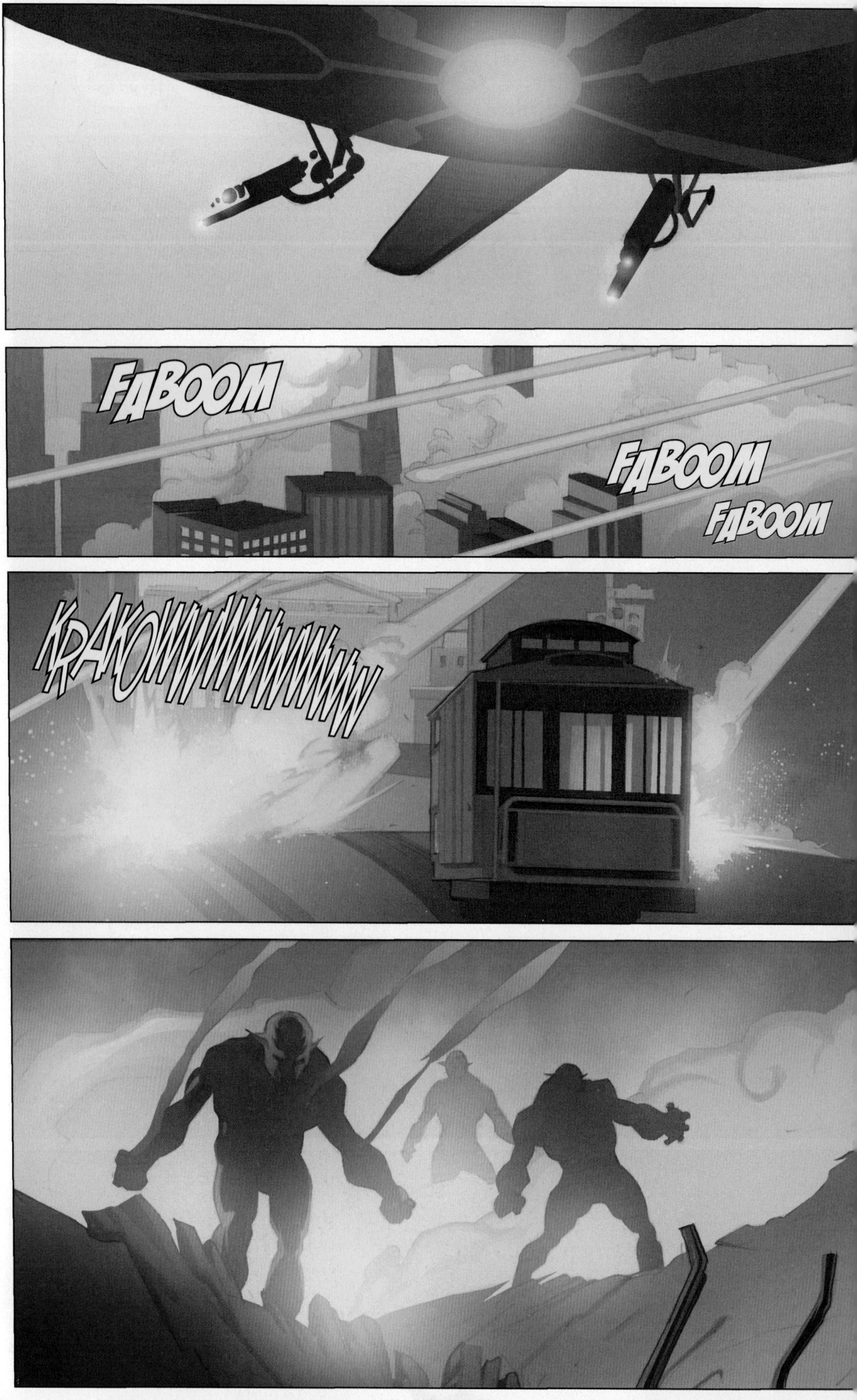
FABOOM
FABOOM
FABOOM
KRAKOWWWWWWWWWW

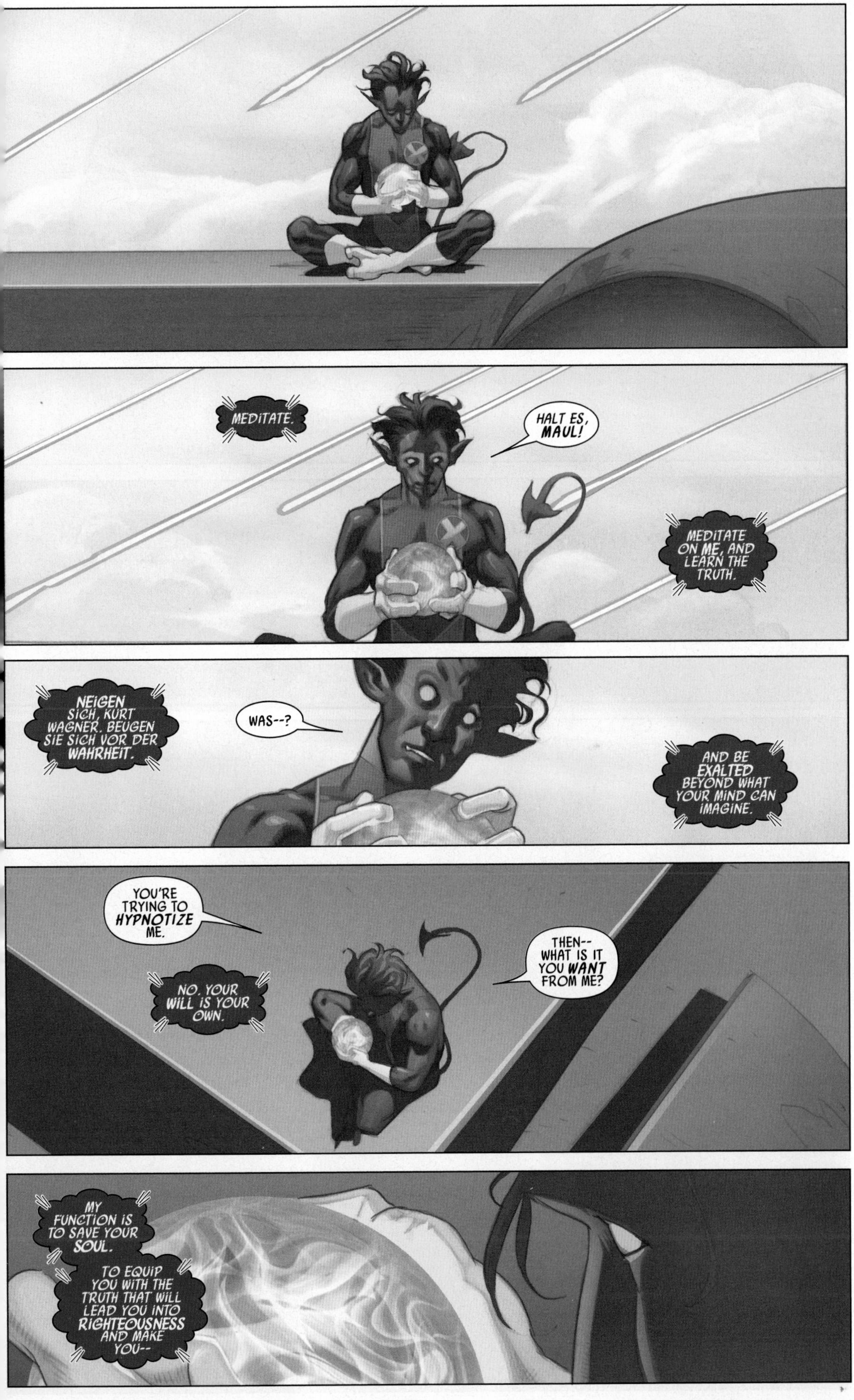

MEDITATE.
HALT ES, MAUL!
MEDITATE ON ME, AND LEARN THE TRUTH.
NEIGEN SICH, KURT WAGNER. BEUGEN SIE SICH VOR DER WAHRHEIT.
WAS--?
AND BE EXALTED BEYOND WHAT YOUR MIND CAN IMAGINE.
YOU'RE TRYING TO HYPNOTIZE ME.
NO. YOUR WILL IS YOUR OWN.
THEN-- WHAT IS IT YOU WANT FROM ME?
MY FUNCTION IS TO SAVE YOUR SOUL.
TO EQUIP YOU WITH THE TRUTH THAT WILL LEAD YOU INTO RIGHTEOUSNESS AND MAKE YOU--

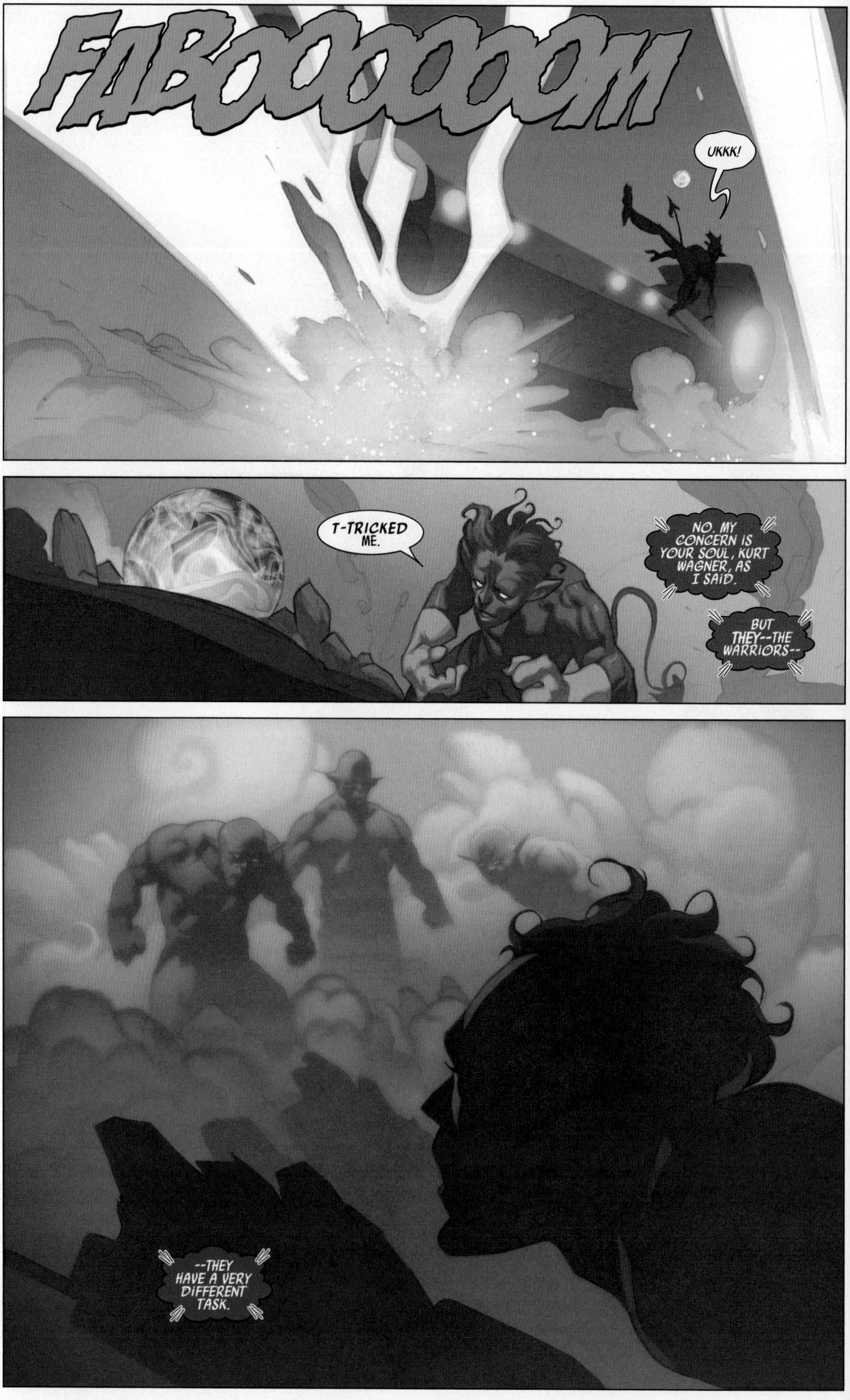
FABOOOOOOM
UKKK!
T-TRICKED ME.
NO. MY CONCERN IS YOUR SOUL, KURT WAGNER, AS I SAID.
BUT THEY--THE WARRIORS--
--THEY HAVE A VERY DIFFERENT TASK.

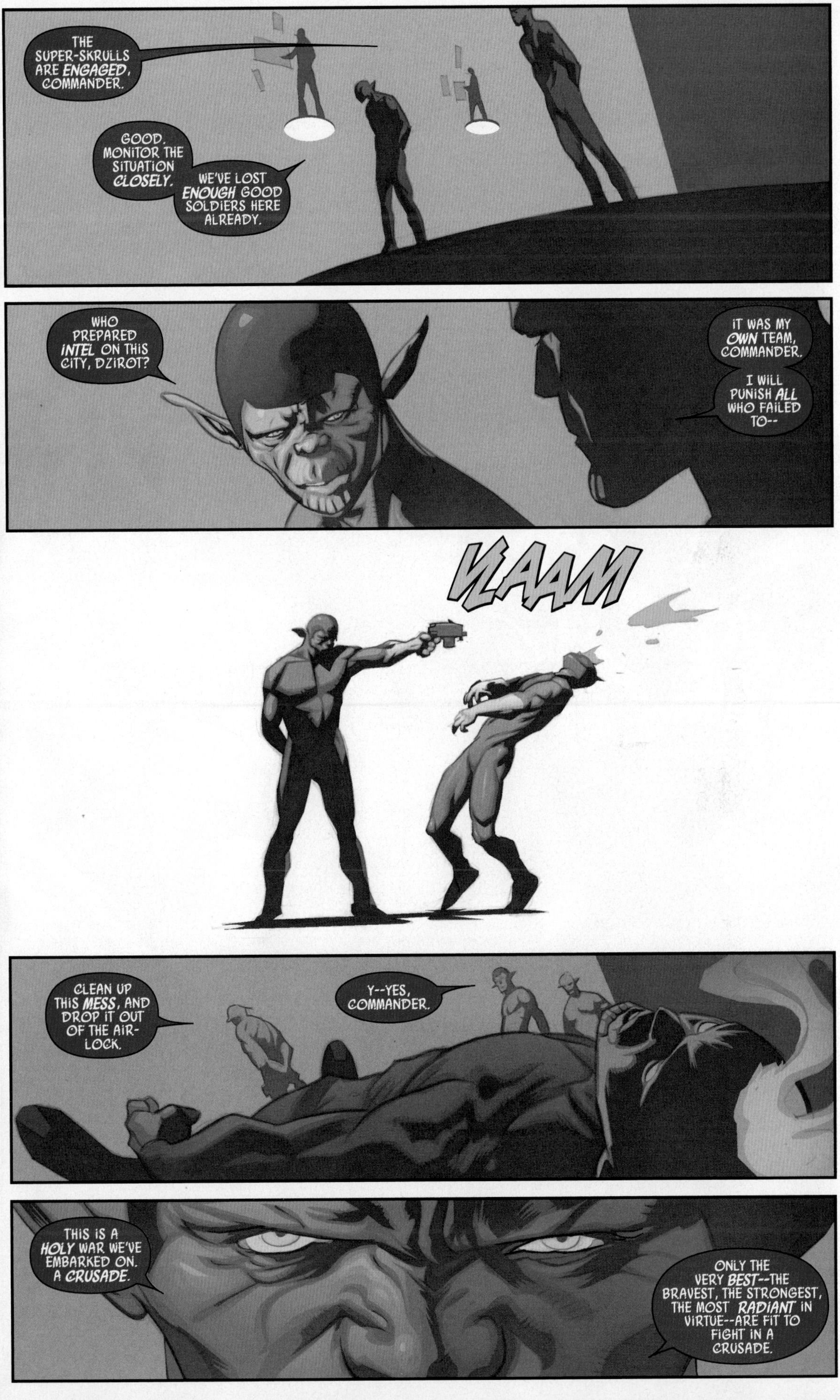
THE SUPER-SKRULLS ARE ENGAGED, COMMANDER.
GOOD. MONITOR THE SITUATION CLOSELY.
WE'VE LOST ENOUGH GOOD SOLDIERS HERE ALREADY.
WHO PREPARED INTEL ON THIS CITY, DZIROT?
IT WAS MY OWN TEAM, COMMANDER.
I WILL PUNISH ALL WHO FAILED TO--
VLAAM
CLEAN UP THIS MESS, AND DROP IT OUT OF THE AIR-LOCK.
Y--YES, COMMANDER.
THIS IS A HOLY WAR WE'VE EMBARKED ON. A CRUSADE.
ONLY THE VERY BEST--THE BRAVEST, THE STRONGEST, THE MOST RADIANT IN VIRTUE--ARE FIT TO FIGHT IN A CRUSADE.

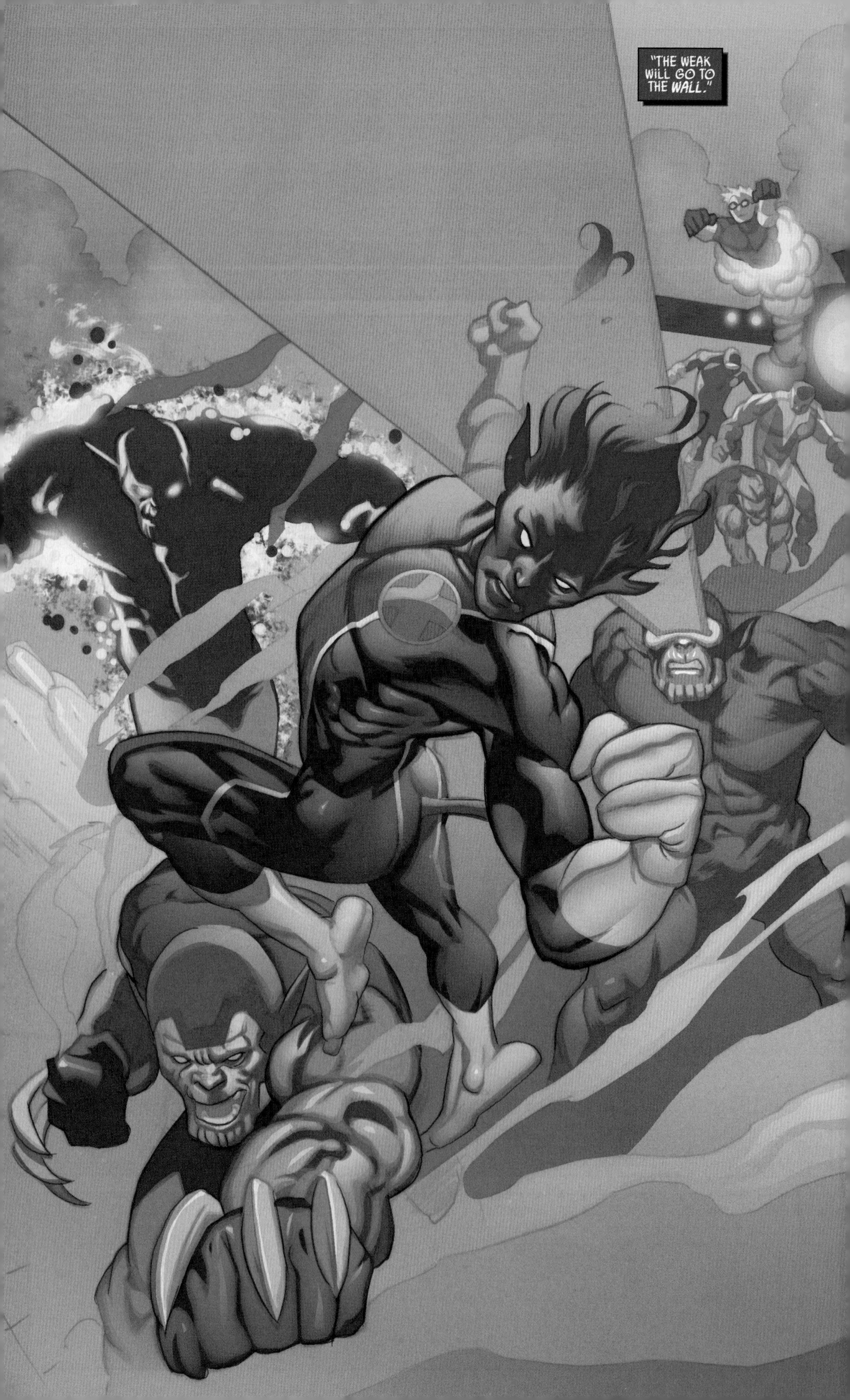
"THE WEAK WILL GO TO THE WALL."

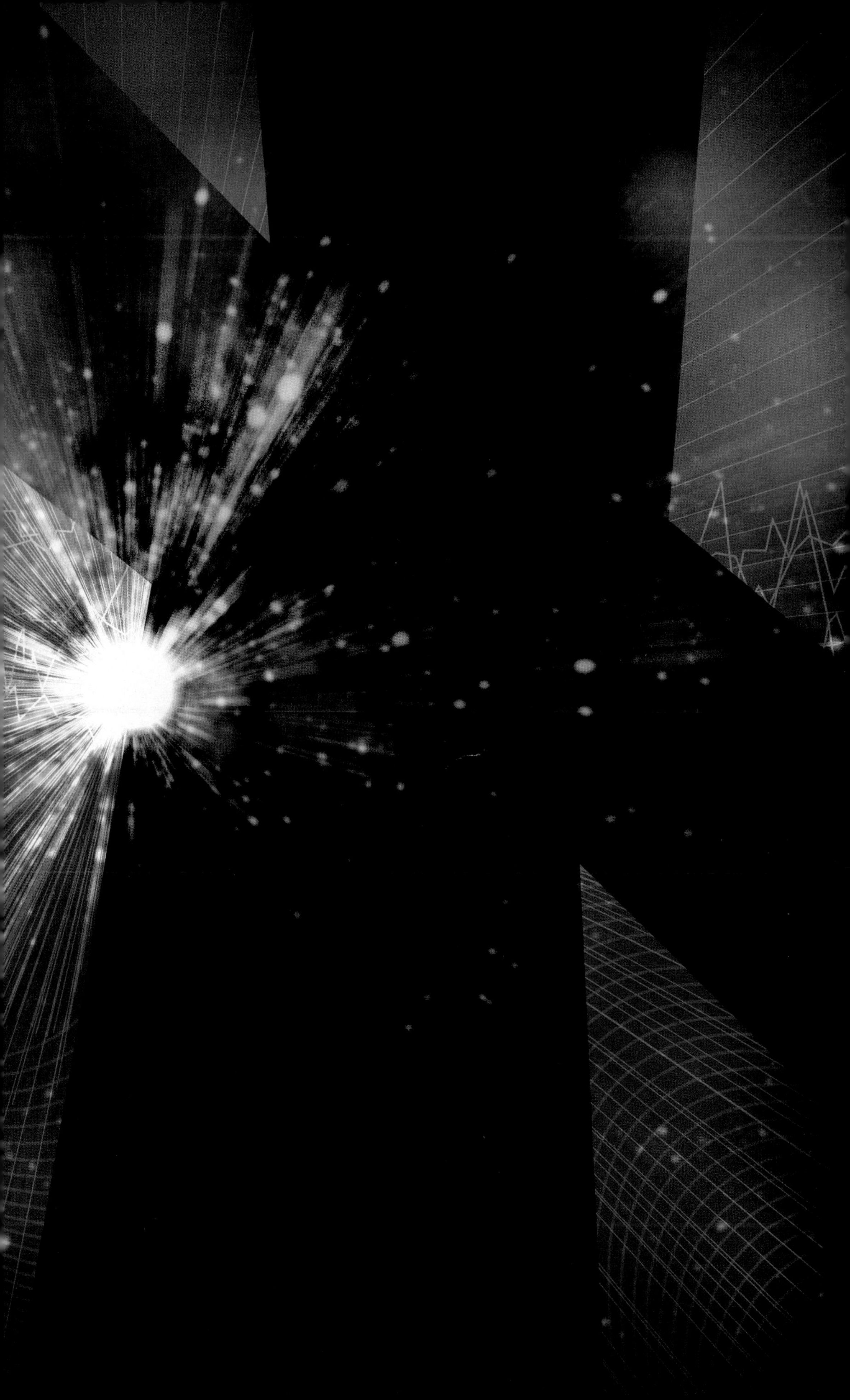

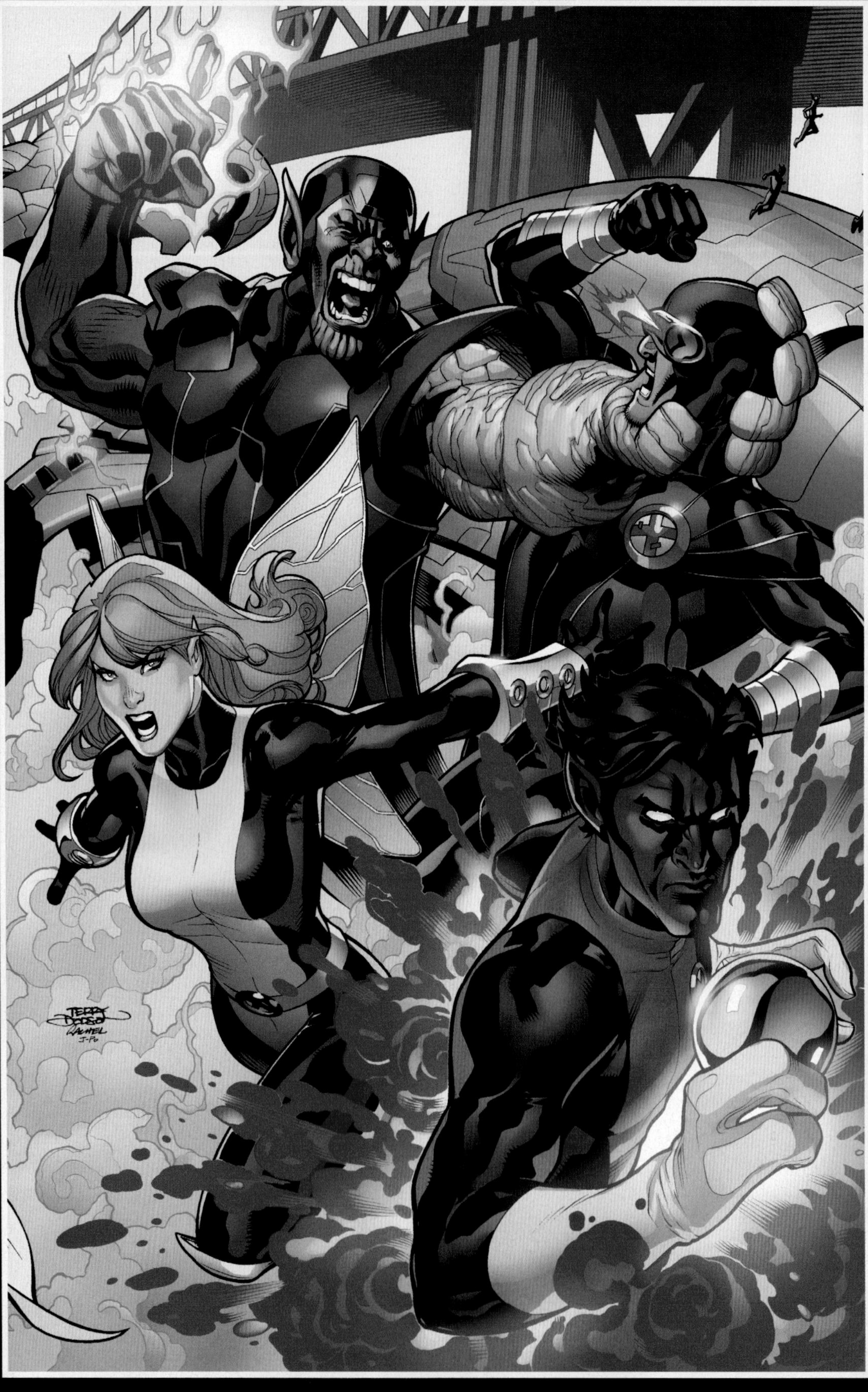

2

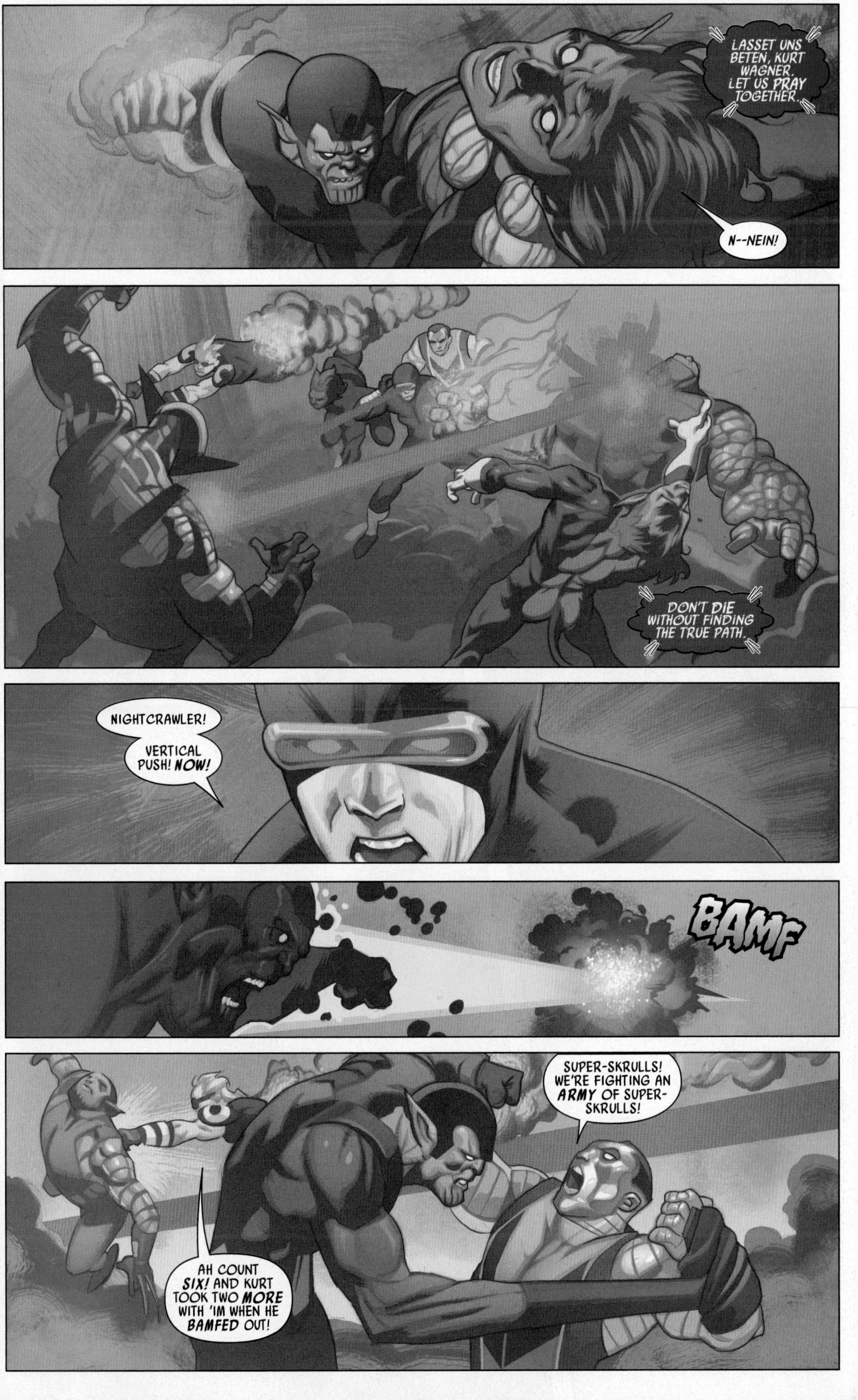
LASSET UNS BETEN, KURT WAGNER. LET US PRAY TOGETHER.
N--NEIN!
DON'T DIE WITHOUT FINDING THE TRUE PATH.
NIGHTCRAWLER!
VERTICAL PUSH! NOW!
BAMF
SUPER-SKRULLS! WE'RE FIGHTING AN ARMY OF SUPER-SKRULLS!
AH COUNT SIX! AND KURT TOOK TWO MORE WITH 'IM WHEN HE BAMFED OUT!

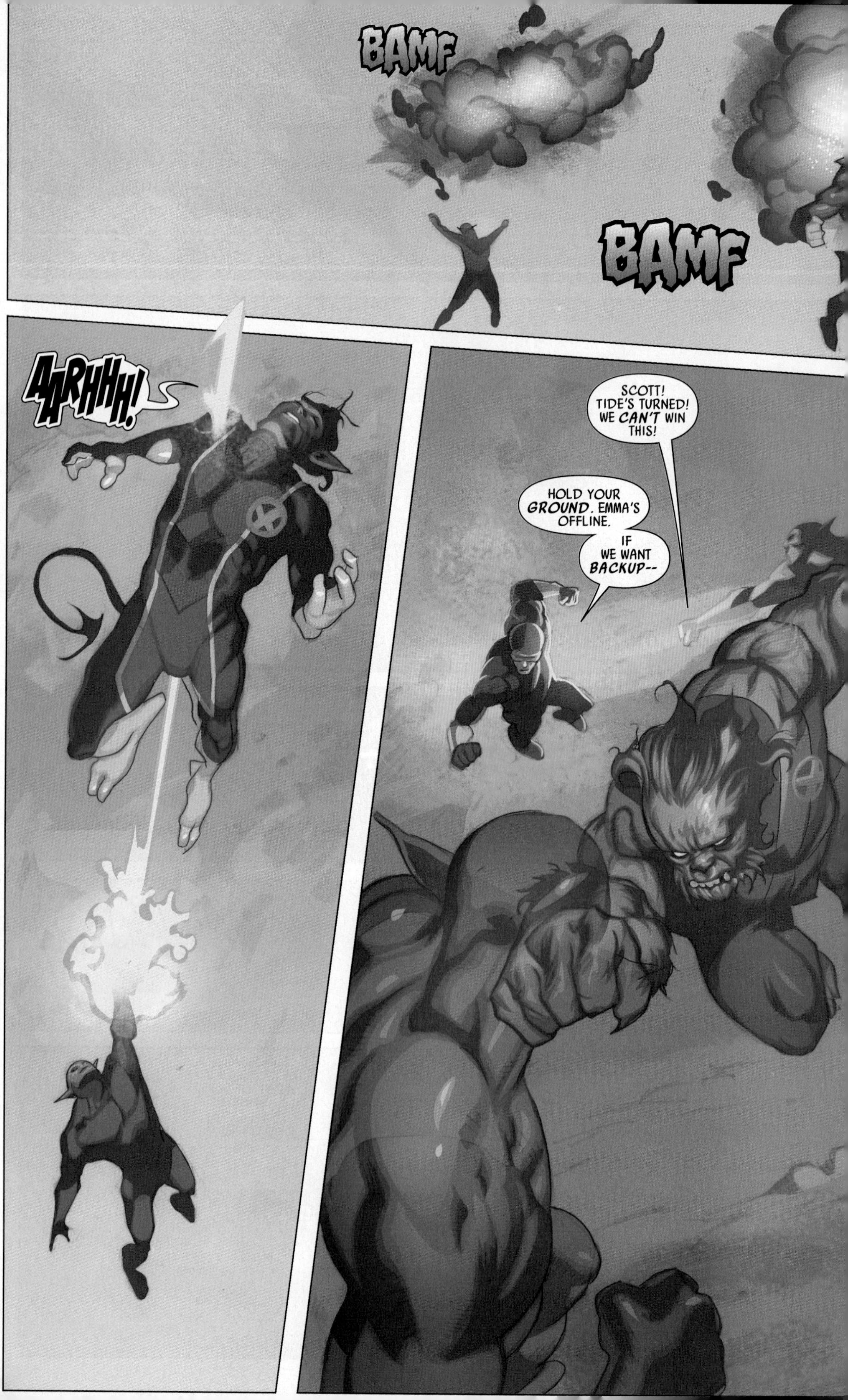
BAMF
BAMF
AARHHH!
SCOTT! TIDE'S TURNED! WE CAN'T WIN THIS!
HOLD YOUR GROUND. EMMA'S OFFLINE.
IF WE WANT BACKUP--

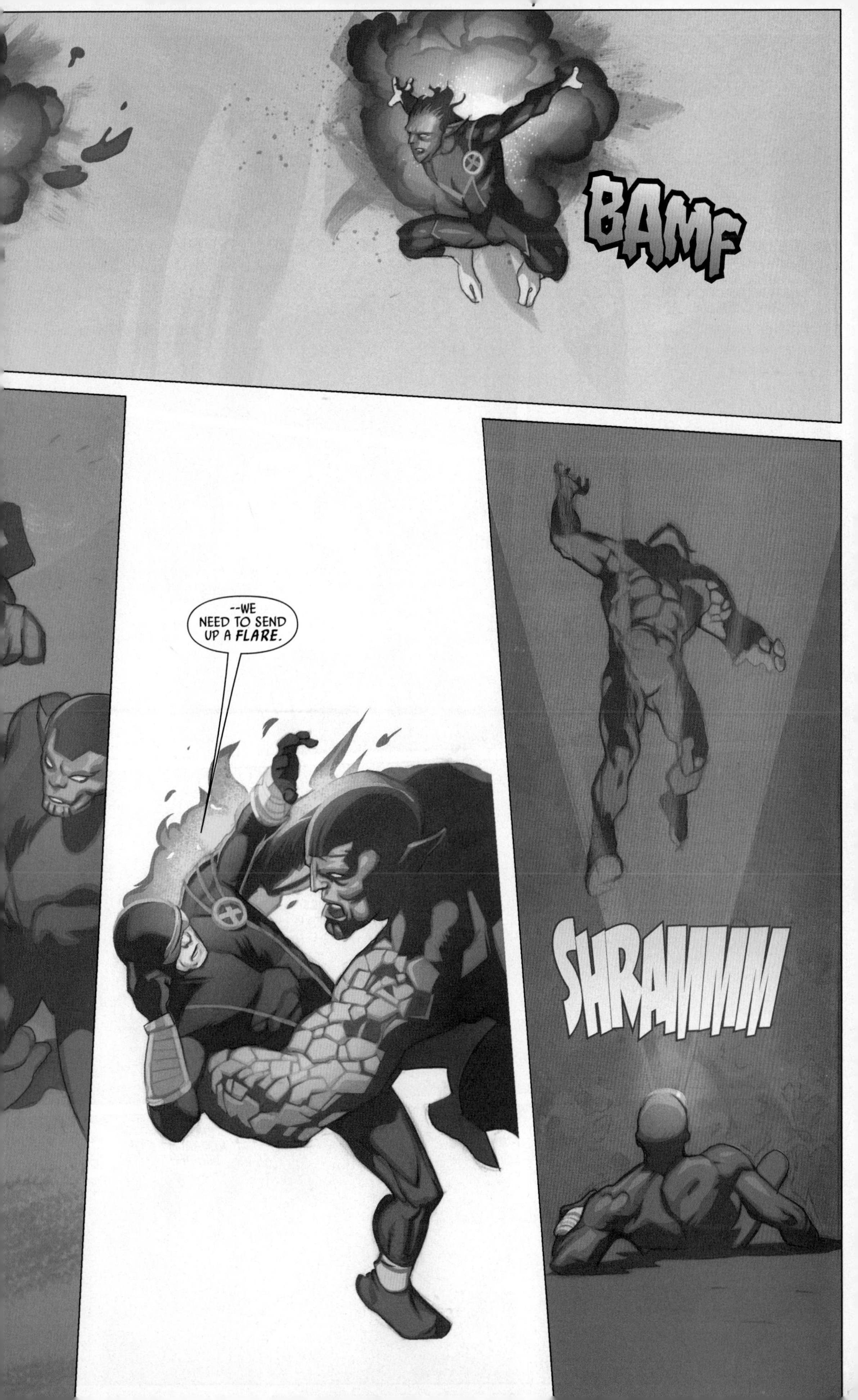
BAMF
--WE NEED TO SEND UP A FLARE.
SHRAMMM

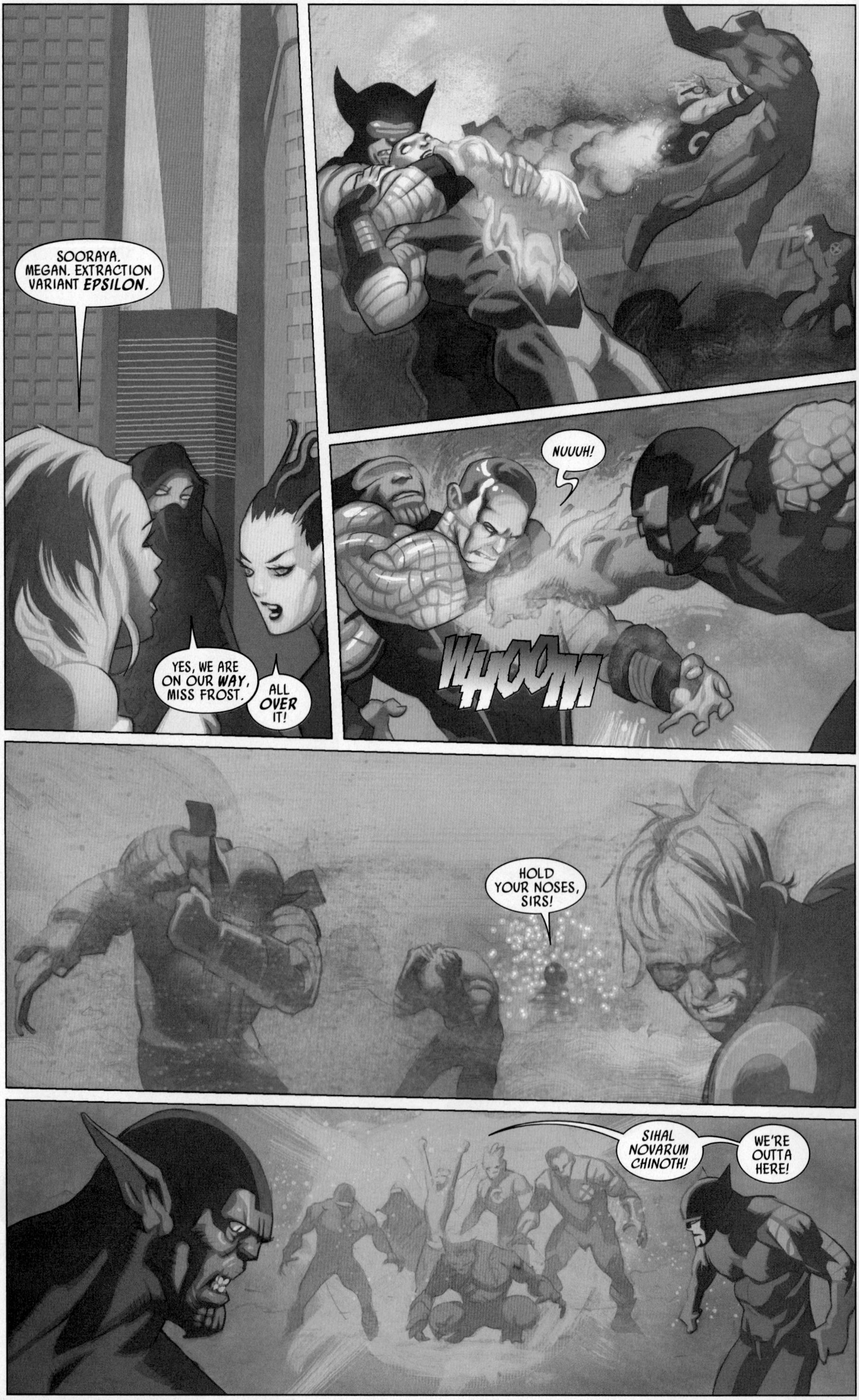
SOORAYA. MEGAN. EXTRACTION VARIANT EPSILON.
YES, WE ARE ON OUR WAY, MISS FROST.
ALL OVER IT!
NUUUH!
WHOOM
HOLD YOUR NOSES, SIRS!
SIHAL NOVARUM CHINOTH!
WE'RE OUTTA HERE!

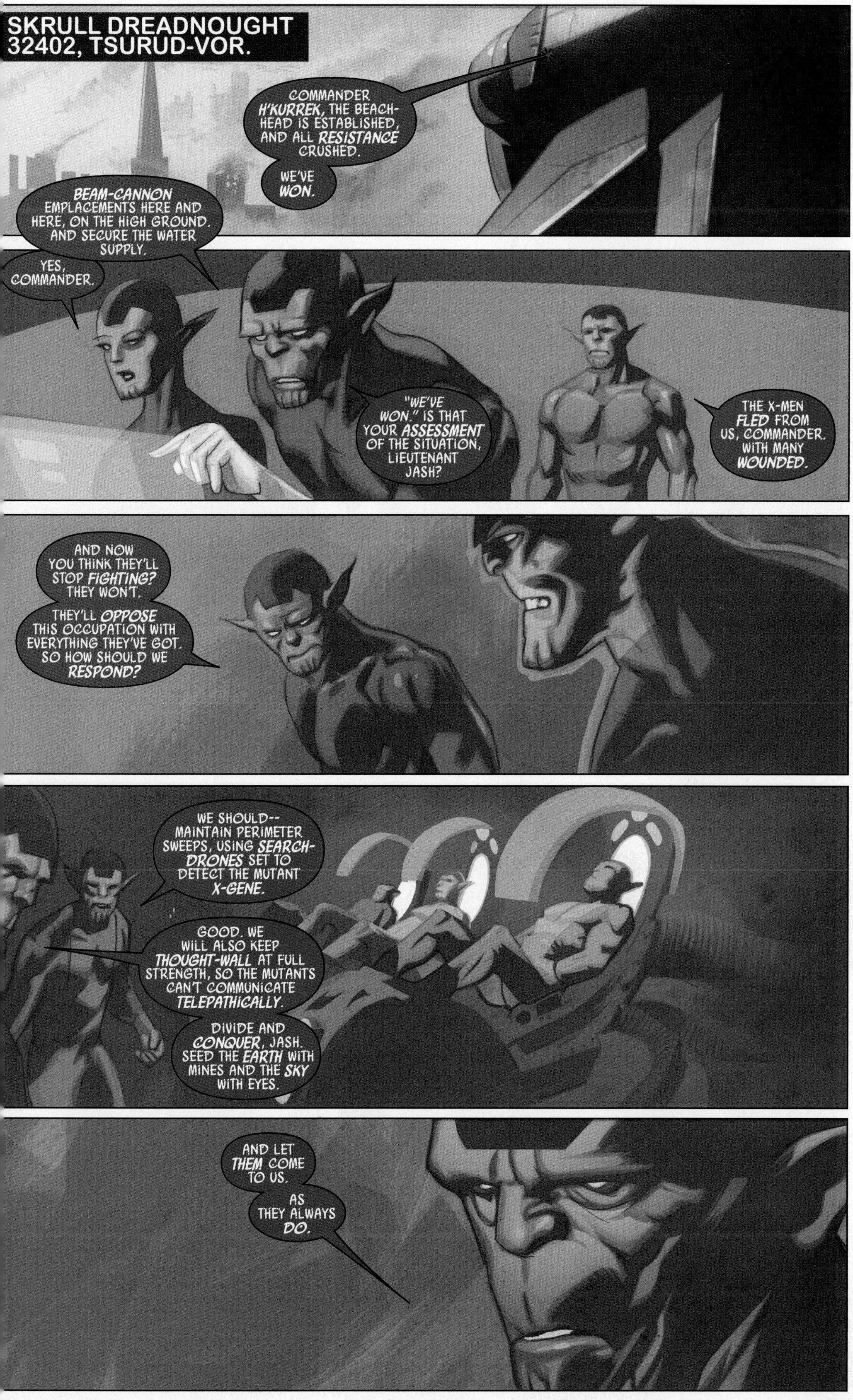
SKRULL DREADNOUGHT 32402, TSURUD-VOR.
COMMANDER H'KURREK, THE BEACH-HEAD IS ESTABLISHED, AND ALL RESISTANCE CRUSHED.
WE'VE WON.
BEAM-CANNON EMPLACEMENTS HERE AND HERE, ON THE HIGH GROUND. AND SECURE THE WATER SUPPLY.
YES, COMMANDER.
"WE'VE WON." IS THAT YOUR ASSESSMENT OF THE SITUATION, LIEUTENANT JASH?
THE X-MEN FLED FROM US, COMMANDER. WITH MANY WOUNDED.
AND NOW YOU THINK THEY'LL STOP FIGHTING? THEY WON'T.
THEY'LL OPPOSE THIS OCCUPATION WITH EVERYTHING THEY'VE GOT. SO HOW SHOULD WE RESPOND?
WE SHOULD-- MAINTAIN PERIMETER SWEEPS, USING SEARCH-DRONES SET TO DETECT THE MUTANT X-GENE.
GOOD. WE WILL ALSO KEEP THOUGHT-WALL AT FULL STRENGTH, SO THE MUTANTS CAN'T COMMUNICATE TELEPATHICALLY.
DIVIDE AND CONQUER, JASH. SEED THE EARTH WITH MINES AND THE SKY WITH EYES.
AND LET THEM COME TO US.
AS THEY ALWAYS DO.

OKAY, LISTEN UP, *ALL* OF YOU.

YOU NEED TO KNOW WHAT'S *HAPPENING*.

THE *SKRULLS* HAVE BLOWN UP OR BLOCKED OFF ALL ROADS OUT OF THE CITY. RAILHEADS, AIRPORTS, HELI-PADS-- ALL LOCKED DOWN *TIGHT*.

THEY'RE ALSO MAINTAINING A *COMMS* BLACK-OUT. NO PHONES. NO RADIO OR TV. NO *WEB* TRAFFIC.

WORSE-- FROM OUR STANDPOINT-- THAT BLACK-OUT EXTENDS TO *TELEPATHY*, TOO. THE SKRULLS HAVE SET UP A *PSI-BLOCKADE*.

NONE OF US CAN PROJECT OR *READ* A THOUGHT BEYOND TEN FEET. IT HURTS EVEN TO *TRY*.

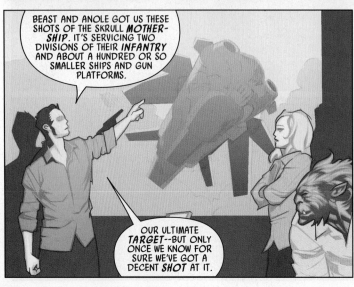

BEAST AND ANOLE GOT US THESE SHOTS OF THE SKRULL *MOTHER-SHIP*. IT'S SERVICING TWO DIVISIONS OF THEIR *INFANTRY* AND ABOUT A HUNDRED OR SO SMALLER SHIPS AND GUN PLATFORMS.

OUR ULTIMATE *TARGET*--BUT ONLY ONCE WE KNOW FOR SURE WE'VE GOT A DECENT *SHOT* AT IT.

IN THE MEANTIME, OUR TACTICS ARE HIT AND RUN. *GUERILLA* RAIDS.

WE *HURT* THEM IN A LOT OF PLACES, AND WE KEEP THEM TIED DOWN UNTIL WE'VE GOT THE *INTEL* WE NEED FOR A MAJOR STRIKE.

FIRST SQUADS ARE PREPPED AND BRIEFED. YOU KNOW WHO YOU ARE. BUT *EVERYONE'S* PART OF THIS.

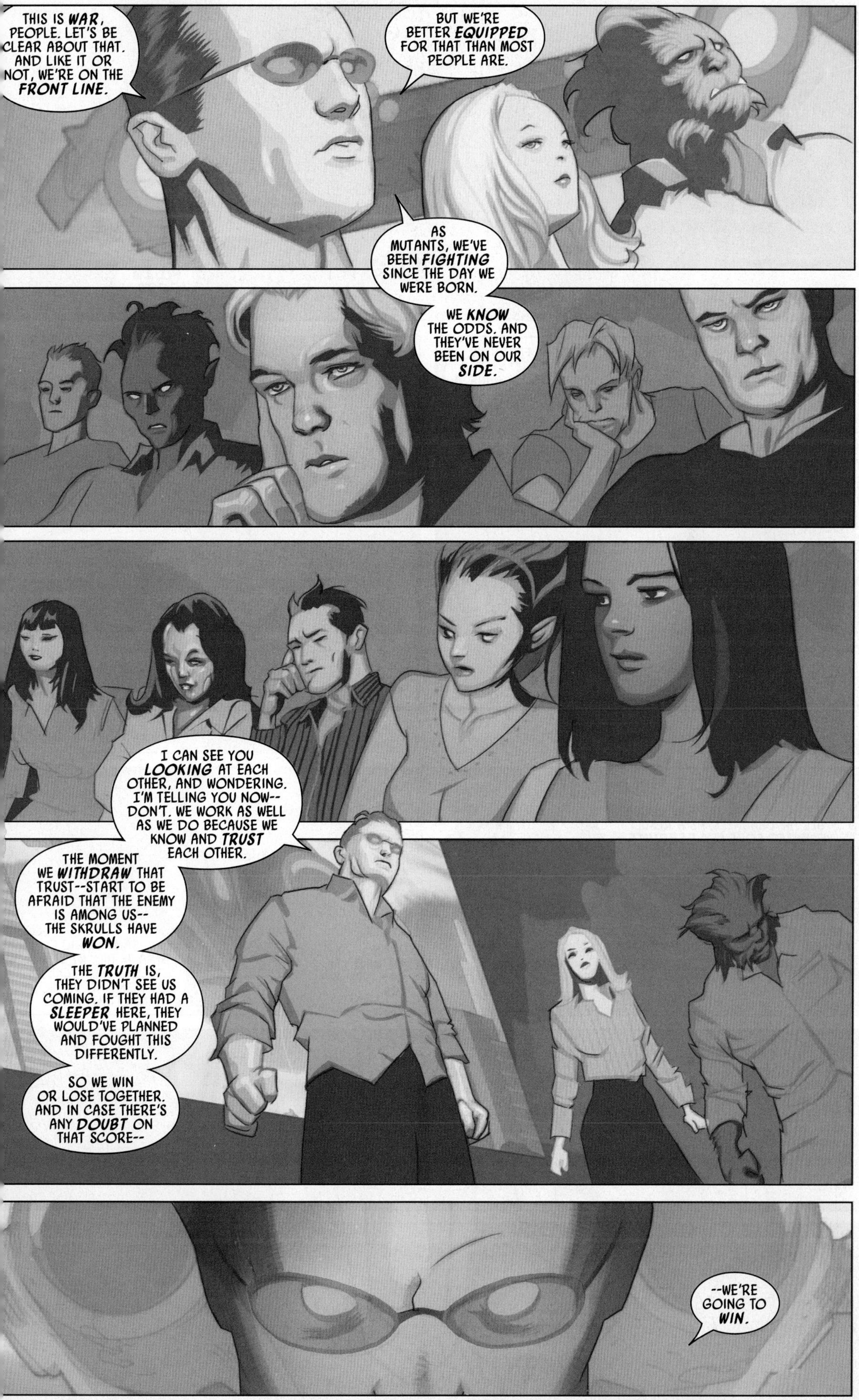

THIS IS WAR, PEOPLE. LET'S BE CLEAR ABOUT THAT. AND LIKE IT OR NOT, WE'RE ON THE FRONT LINE.
BUT WE'RE BETTER EQUIPPED FOR THAT THAN MOST PEOPLE ARE.
AS MUTANTS, WE'VE BEEN FIGHTING SINCE THE DAY WE WERE BORN.
WE KNOW THE ODDS. AND THEY'VE NEVER BEEN ON OUR SIDE.
I CAN SEE YOU LOOKING AT EACH OTHER, AND WONDERING. I'M TELLING YOU NOW--DON'T. WE WORK AS WELL AS WE DO BECAUSE WE KNOW AND TRUST EACH OTHER.
THE MOMENT WE WITHDRAW THAT TRUST--START TO BE AFRAID THAT THE ENEMY IS AMONG US--THE SKRULLS HAVE WON.
THE TRUTH IS, THEY DIDN'T SEE US COMING. IF THEY HAD A SLEEPER HERE, THEY WOULD'VE PLANNED AND FOUGHT THIS DIFFERENTLY.
SO WE WIN OR LOSE TOGETHER. AND IN CASE THERE'S ANY DOUBT ON THAT SCORE--
--WE'RE GOING TO WIN.

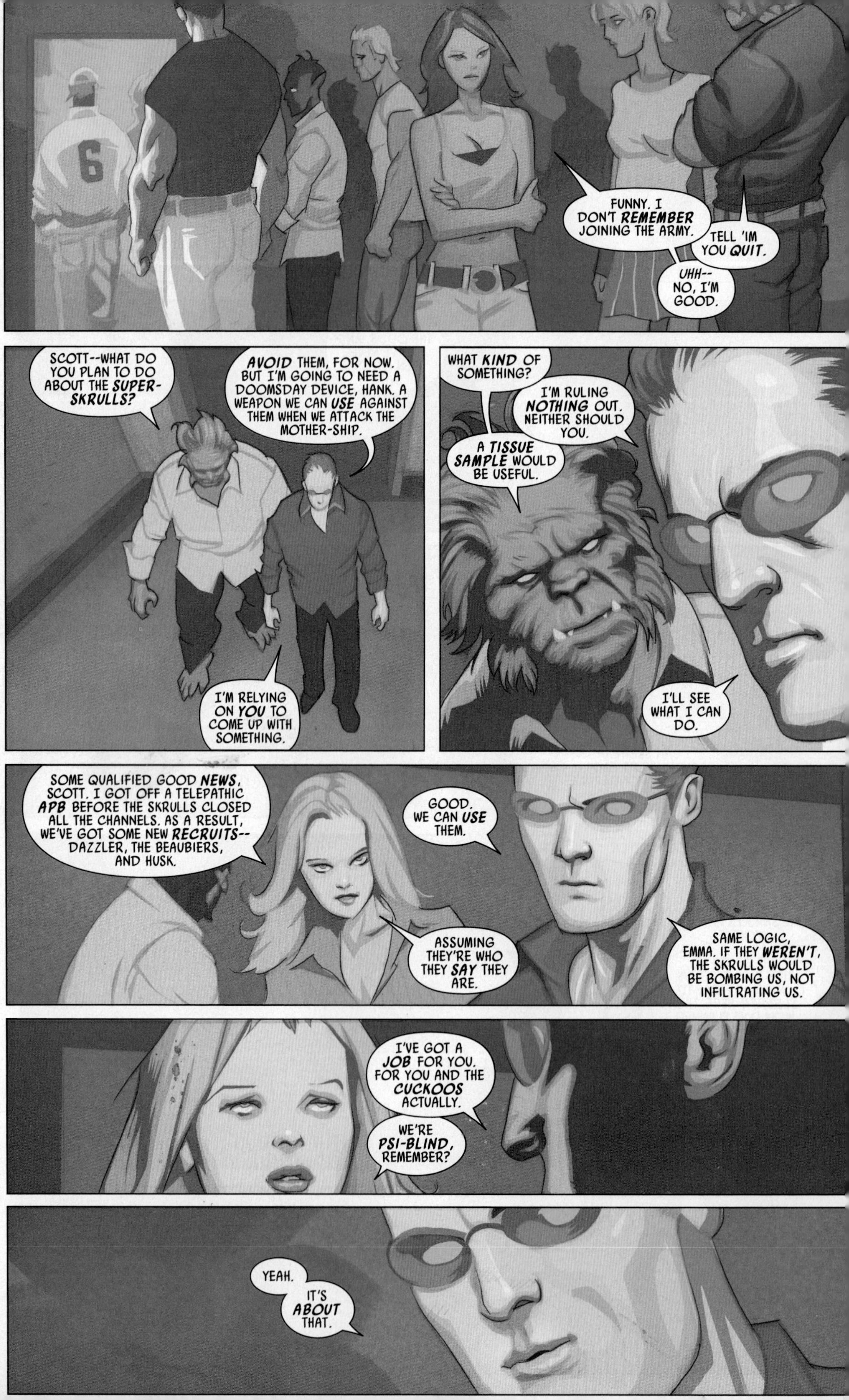
FUNNY. I DON'T REMEMBER JOINING THE ARMY.
TELL 'IM YOU QUIT.
UHH-- NO, I'M GOOD.
SCOTT--WHAT DO YOU PLAN TO DO ABOUT THE SUPER-SKRULLS?
AVOID THEM, FOR NOW. BUT I'M GOING TO NEED A DOOMSDAY DEVICE, HANK. A WEAPON WE CAN USE AGAINST THEM WHEN WE ATTACK THE MOTHER-SHIP.
I'M RELYING ON YOU TO COME UP WITH SOMETHING.
WHAT KIND OF SOMETHING?
I'M RULING NOTHING OUT. NEITHER SHOULD YOU.
A TISSUE SAMPLE WOULD BE USEFUL.
I'LL SEE WHAT I CAN DO.
SOME QUALIFIED GOOD NEWS, SCOTT. I GOT OFF A TELEPATHIC APB BEFORE THE SKRULLS CLOSED ALL THE CHANNELS. AS A RESULT, WE'VE GOT SOME NEW RECRUITS-- DAZZLER, THE BEAUBIERS, AND HUSK.
GOOD. WE CAN USE THEM.
ASSUMING THEY'RE WHO THEY SAY THEY ARE.
SAME LOGIC, EMMA. IF THEY WEREN'T, THE SKRULLS WOULD BE BOMBING US, NOT INFILTRATING US.
I'VE GOT A JOB FOR YOU. FOR YOU AND THE CUCKOOS ACTUALLY.
WE'RE PSI-BLIND, REMEMBER?
YEAH. IT'S ABOUT THAT.

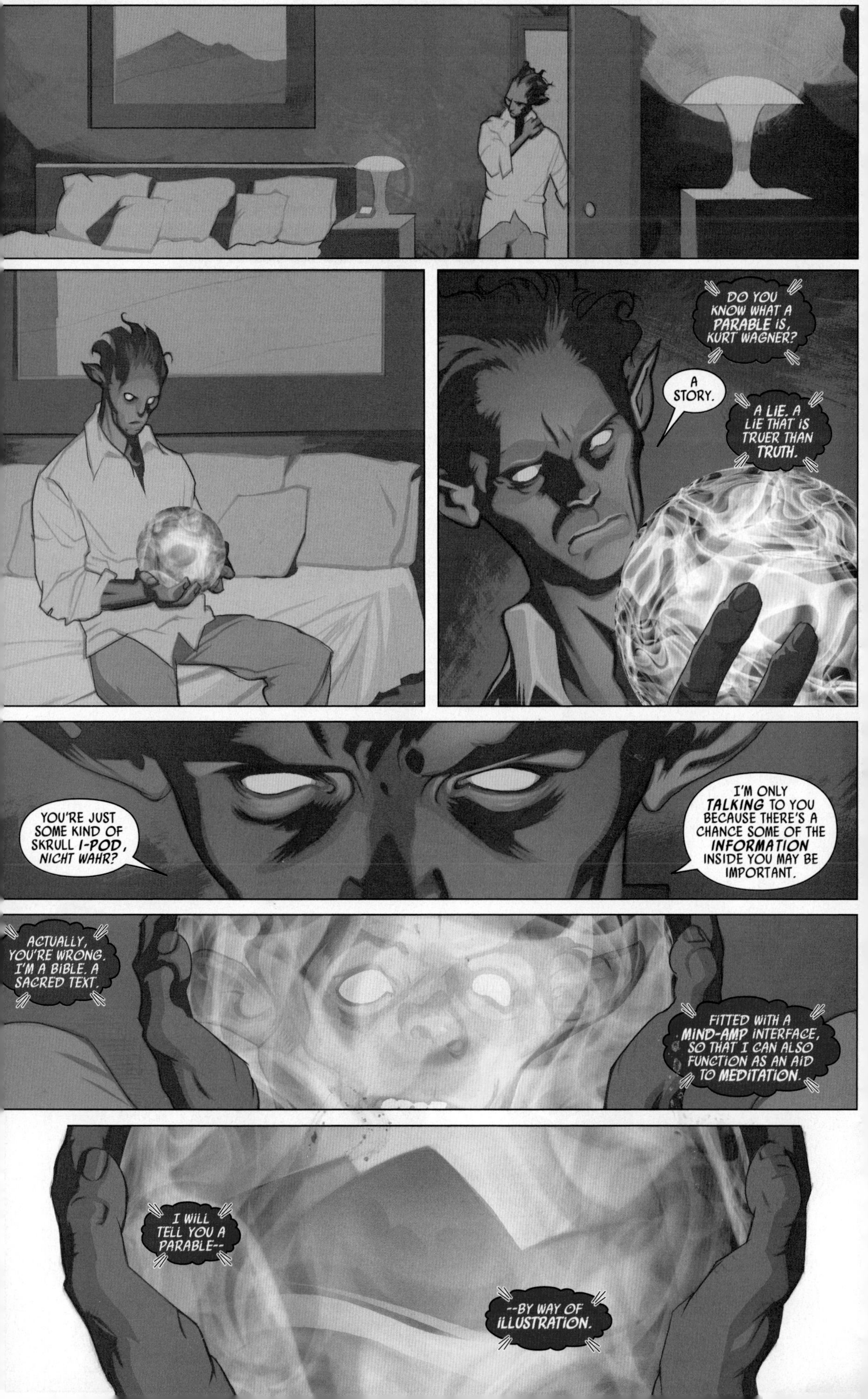
DO YOU KNOW WHAT A PARABLE IS, KURT WAGNER?
A STORY.
A LIE. A LIE THAT IS TRUER THAN TRUTH.
YOU'RE JUST SOME KIND OF SKRULL I-POD, NICHT WAHR?
I'M ONLY TALKING TO YOU BECAUSE THERE'S A CHANCE SOME OF THE INFORMATION INSIDE YOU MAY BE IMPORTANT.
ACTUALLY, YOU'RE WRONG. I'M A BIBLE. A SACRED TEXT.
FITTED WITH A MIND-AMP INTERFACE, SO THAT I CAN ALSO FUNCTION AS AN AID TO MEDITATION.
I WILL TELL YOU A PARABLE--
--BY WAY OF ILLUSTRATION.

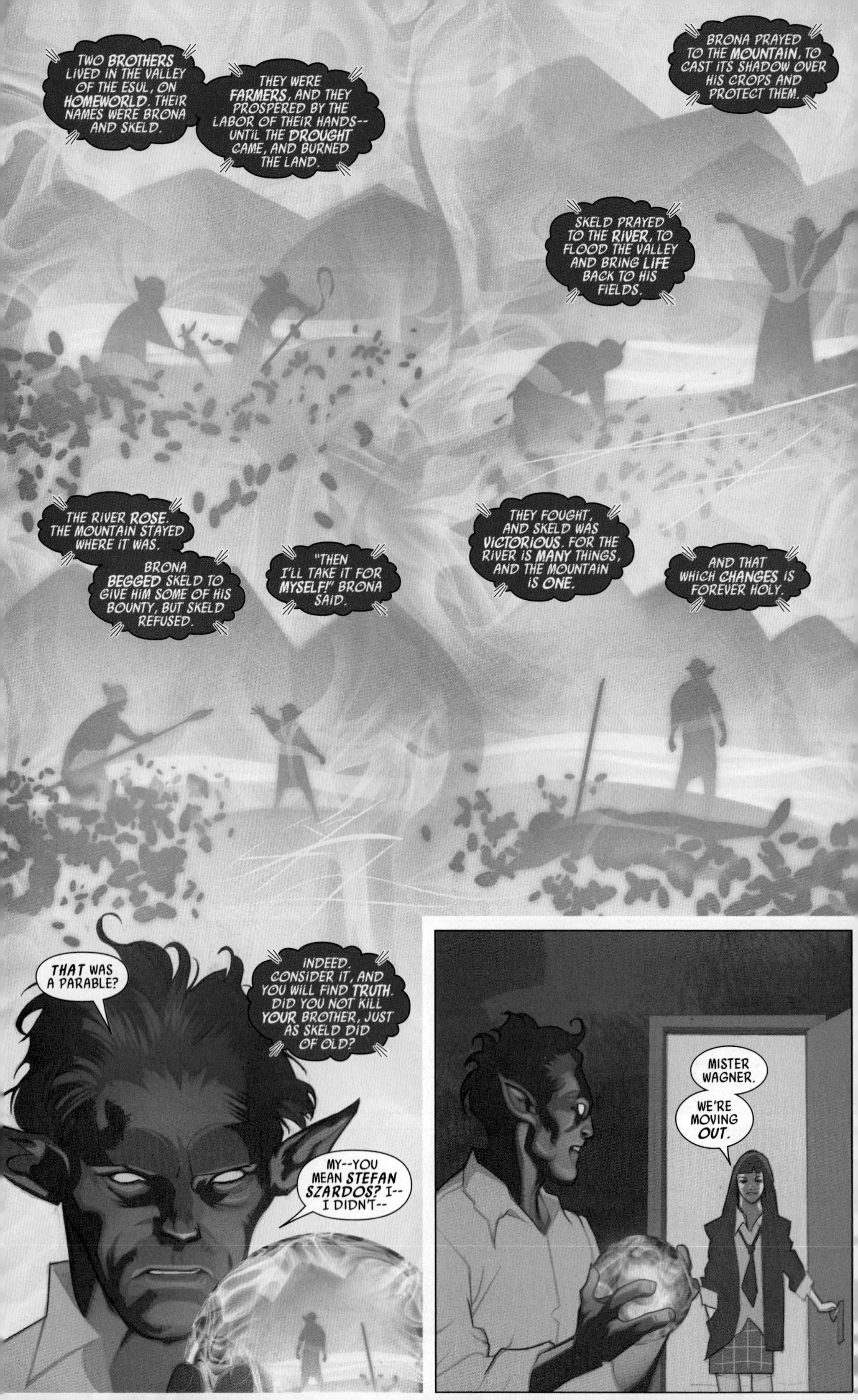
TWO BROTHERS LIVED IN THE VALLEY OF THE ESUL, ON HOMEWORLD. THEIR NAMES WERE BRONA AND SKELD.
THEY WERE FARMERS, AND THEY PROSPERED BY THE LABOR OF THEIR HANDS-- UNTIL THE DROUGHT CAME, AND BURNED THE LAND.
BRONA PRAYED TO THE MOUNTAIN, TO CAST ITS SHADOW OVER HIS CROPS AND PROTECT THEM.
SKELD PRAYED TO THE RIVER, TO FLOOD THE VALLEY AND BRING LIFE BACK TO HIS FIELDS.
THE RIVER ROSE. THE MOUNTAIN STAYED WHERE IT WAS.
BRONA BEGGED SKELD TO GIVE HIM SOME OF HIS BOUNTY, BUT SKELD REFUSED.
"THEN I'LL TAKE IT FOR MYSELF!" BRONA SAID.
THEY FOUGHT, AND SKELD WAS VICTORIOUS. FOR THE RIVER IS MANY THINGS, AND THE MOUNTAIN IS ONE.
AND THAT WHICH CHANGES IS FOREVER HOLY.
THAT WAS A PARABLE?
INDEED. CONSIDER IT, AND YOU WILL FIND TRUTH. DID YOU NOT KILL YOUR BROTHER, JUST AS SKELD DID OF OLD?
MY--YOU MEAN STEFAN SZARDOS? I-- I DIDN'T--
MISTER WAGNER.
WE'RE MOVING OUT.

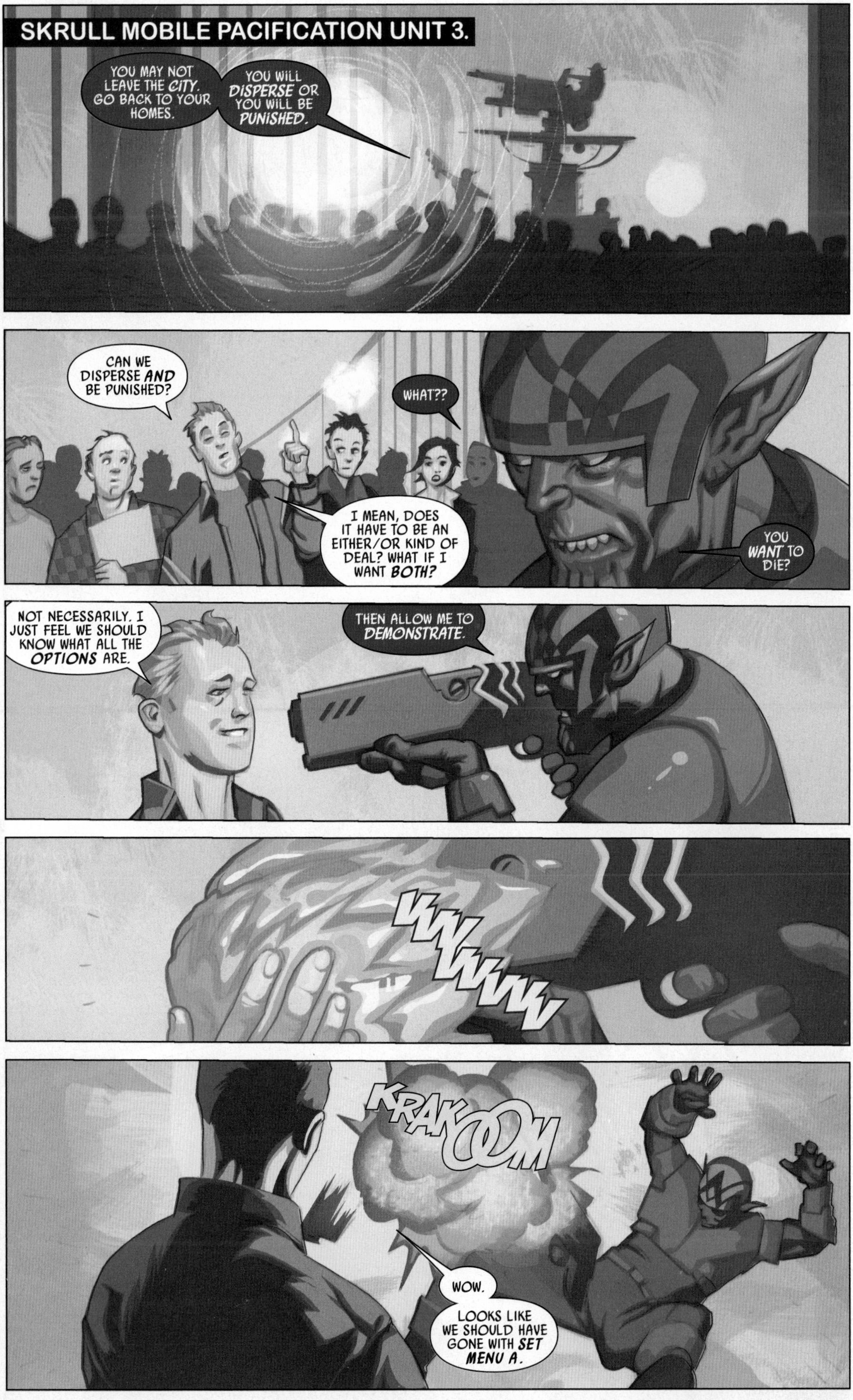
SKRULL MOBILE PACIFICATION UNIT 3.
YOU MAY NOT LEAVE THE *CITY*. GO BACK TO YOUR HOMES.
YOU WILL *DISPERSE* OR YOU WILL BE *PUNISHED*.
CAN WE DISPERSE **AND** BE PUNISHED?
WHAT??
I MEAN, DOES IT HAVE TO BE AN EITHER/OR KIND OF DEAL? WHAT IF I WANT **BOTH?**
YOU *WANT* TO DIE?
NOT NECESSARILY. I JUST FEEL WE SHOULD KNOW WHAT ALL THE **OPTIONS** ARE.
THEN ALLOW ME TO *DEMONSTRATE*.
KRAKOOM
WOW.
LOOKS LIKE WE SHOULD HAVE GONE WITH **SET MENU A.**

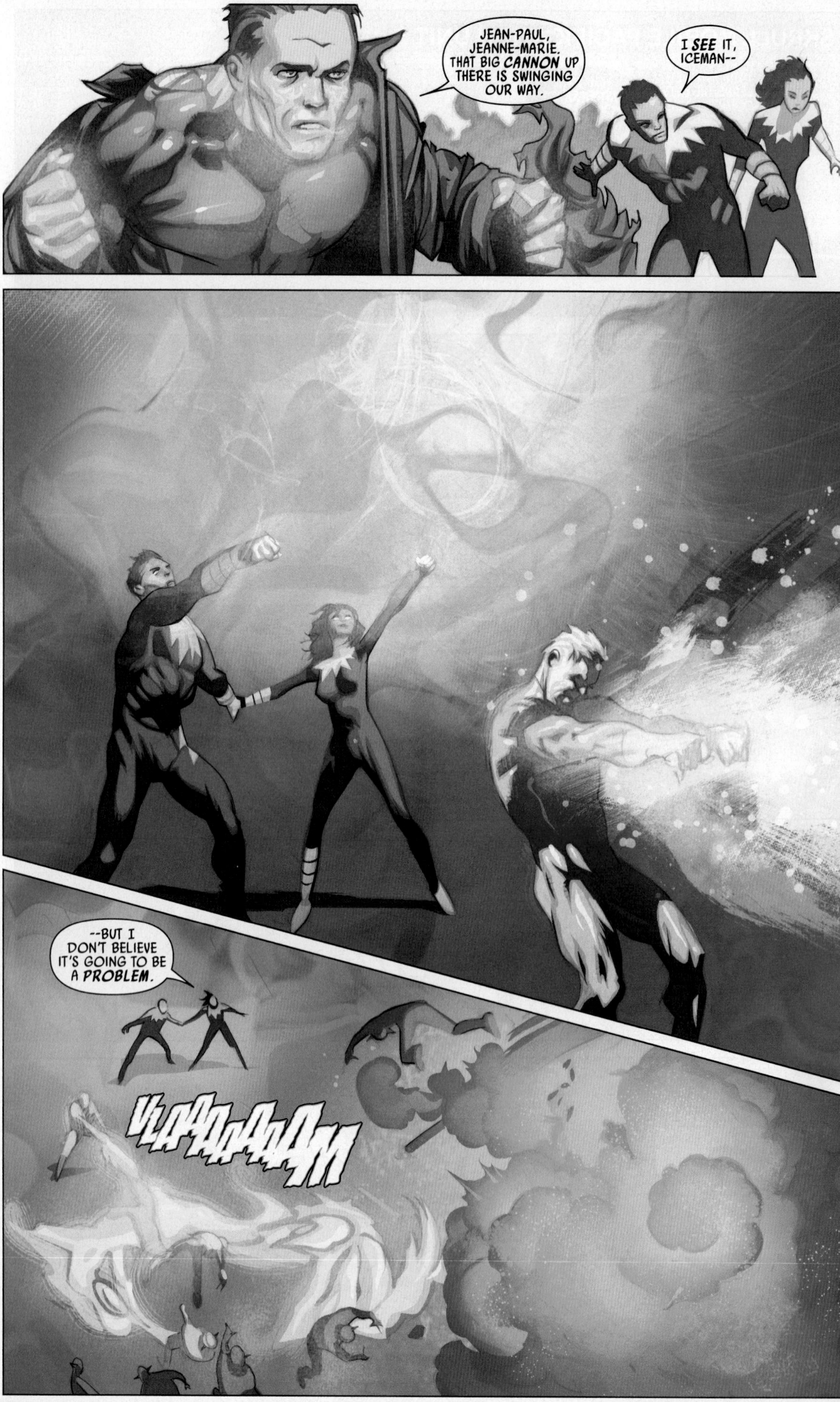
JEAN-PAUL, JEANNE-MARIE. THAT BIG CANNON UP THERE IS SWINGING OUR WAY.
I SEE IT, ICEMAN--
--BUT I DON'T BELIEVE IT'S GOING TO BE A PROBLEM.
VLAAAAAAAAM

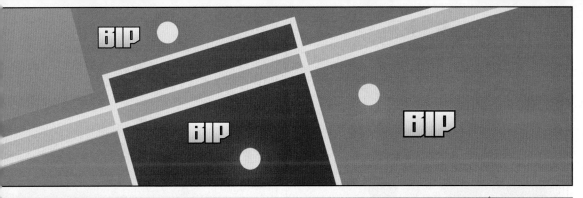

BIP

BIP

BIP

WE'RE UNDER *ATTACK*, COMMANDER. SIMULTANEOUS *STRIKES* AT THREE DIFFERENT LOCATIONS.

CHECK YOUR *DATA* SCANNER, CH'RITH.

AND *AMEND* YOUR REPORT.

THREE ATTACKS--*ALMOST* SIMULTANEOUS. FORTY TO FIFTY SECONDS *APART*.

KNOWN *X-MEN* SIGHTED AT ALL THREE.

THEY'RE USING *TELEPORTERS* TO GET THEIR TEAMS IN PAST OUR DEFENSES. HOW MANY MUTANTS *POSSESS* THAT ABILITY?

TWELVE, SIR. NIGHTCRAWLER. LILA CHENEY. VANISHER--

I DON'T NEED A *LIST*. RECALIBRATE THE SEARCH-DRONES ON THOSE MUTANT *SIGNATURES*.

SO LONG AS THE X-MEN STICK TO THEIR CURRENT *STRATEGY* FOR A FEW HOURS LONGER--

--THEY'RE *OURS*.

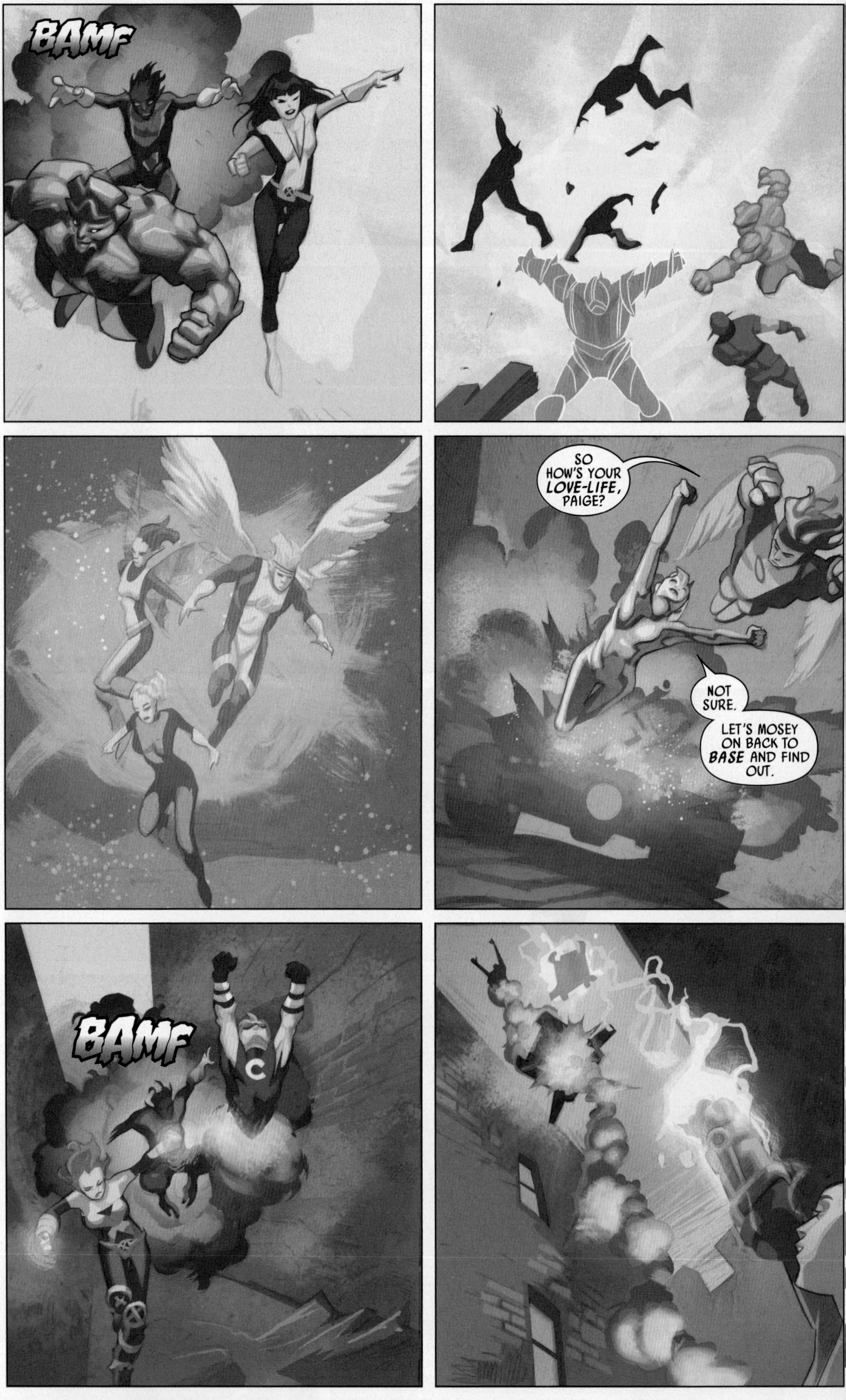
BAMF
SO HOW'S YOUR LOVE-LIFE, PAIGE?
NOT SURE.
LET'S MOSEY ON BACK TO BASE AND FIND OUT.
BAMF

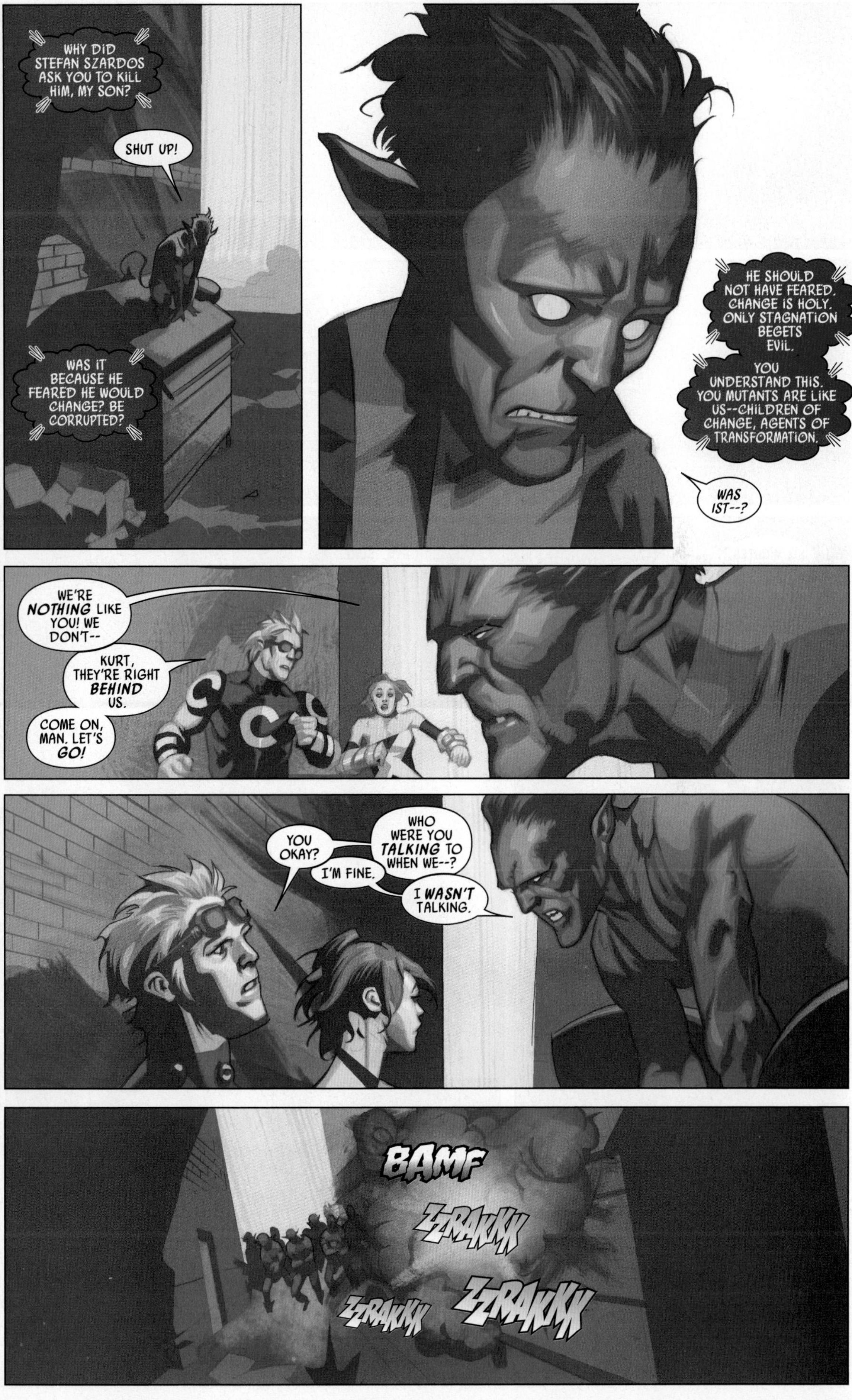
WHY DID STEFAN SZARDOS ASK YOU TO KILL HIM, MY SON?
SHUT UP!
WAS IT BECAUSE HE FEARED HE WOULD CHANGE? BE CORRUPTED?
HE SHOULD NOT HAVE FEARED. CHANGE IS HOLY. ONLY STAGNATION BEGETS EVIL.
YOU UNDERSTAND THIS. YOU MUTANTS ARE LIKE US--CHILDREN OF CHANGE, AGENTS OF TRANSFORMATION.
WAS IST--?
WE'RE NOTHING LIKE YOU! WE DON'T--
KURT, THEY'RE RIGHT BEHIND US.
COME ON, MAN. LET'S GO!
YOU OKAY?
WHO WERE YOU TALKING TO WHEN WE--?
I'M FINE.
I WASN'T TALKING.
BAMF
ZZRAKKK
ZZRAKKK
ZZRAKKK

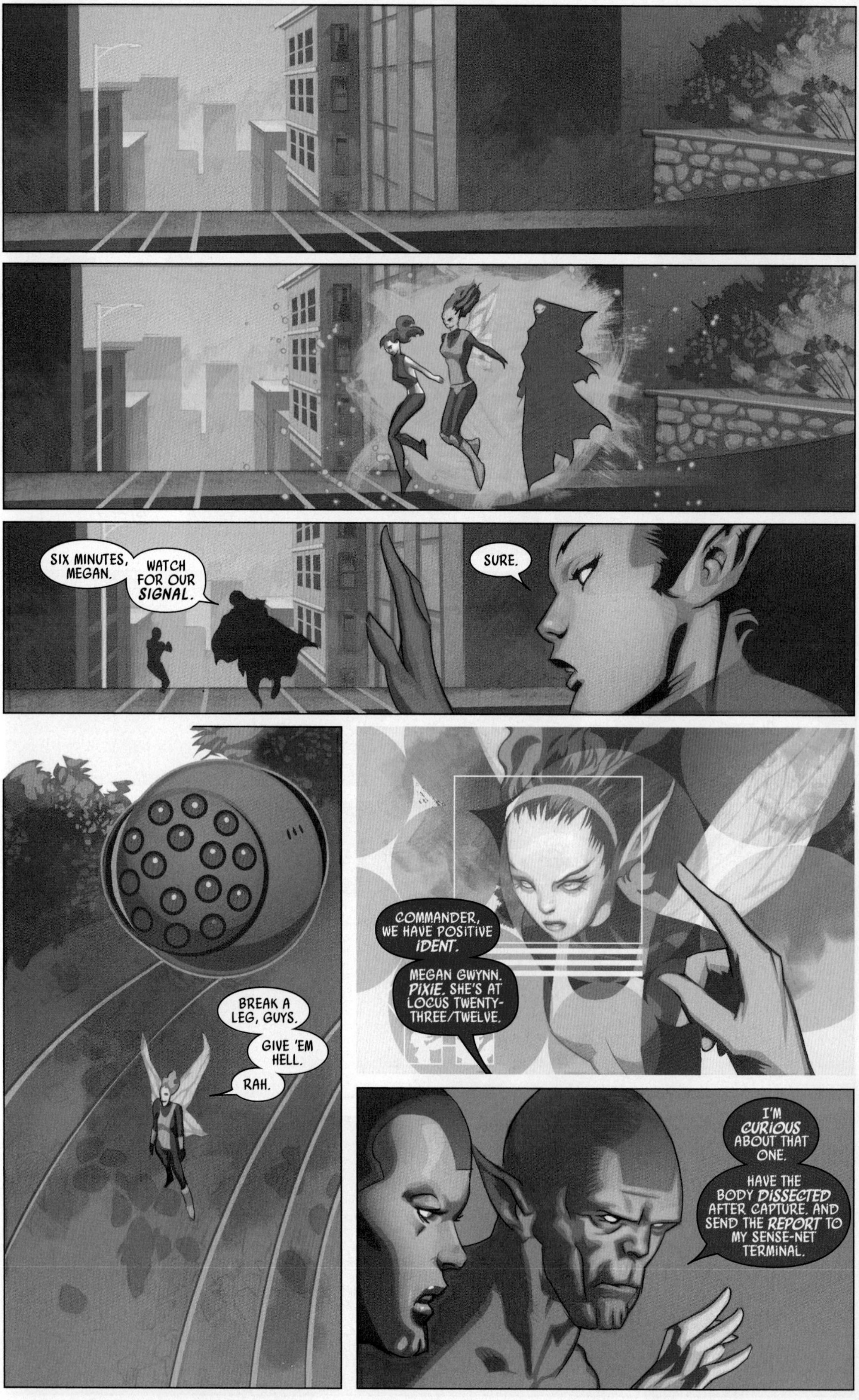
SIX MINUTES, MEGAN.
WATCH FOR OUR SIGNAL.
SURE.
BREAK A LEG, GUYS.
GIVE 'EM HELL.
RAH.
COMMANDER, WE HAVE POSITIVE IDENT.
MEGAN GWYNN. PIXIE. SHE'S AT LOCUS TWENTY-THREE/TWELVE.
I'M CURIOUS ABOUT THAT ONE.
HAVE THE BODY DISSECTED AFTER CAPTURE, AND SEND THE REPORT TO MY SENSE-NET TERMINAL.

LET'S GO OVER THIS ONE MORE TIME BEFORE I THROW MYSELF TO THE *WOLVES*, GIRLS.

FROM THE TOP.

WE USE THE *CEREBRA* LINK TO CHANNEL OUR POWER INTO YOU, MS. FROST.

AND YOU RUN THE *PSI-BLOCKADE* TO TRY TO GET A FIX ON ITS SOURCE.

IF YOUR BRAIN STARTS TO *HEMORRHAGE*, WE PULL THE PLUG. YOU LOSE *POWER* AND DROP BACK OUT OF THE NET.

ONLY THAT LAST PART WON'T *WORK*, OF COURSE--

--BECAUSE IF YOU *DO* SUCCEED IN MAKING CONTACT--

--YOU'LL ALMOST CERTAINLY HIT SOME KIND OF SKRULL *FIREWALL*.

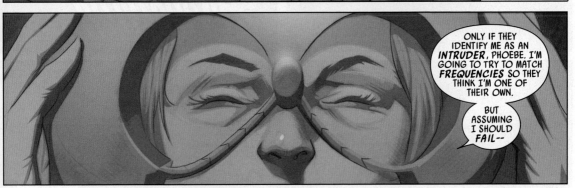

ONLY IF THEY IDENTIFY ME AS AN *INTRUDER*, PHOEBE. I'M GOING TO TRY TO MATCH *FREQUENCIES* SO THEY THINK I'M ONE OF THEIR OWN.

BUT ASSUMING I SHOULD *FAIL*--

--PLEASE DON'T *FIGHT* OVER MY NEW SUMMER WARDROBE.

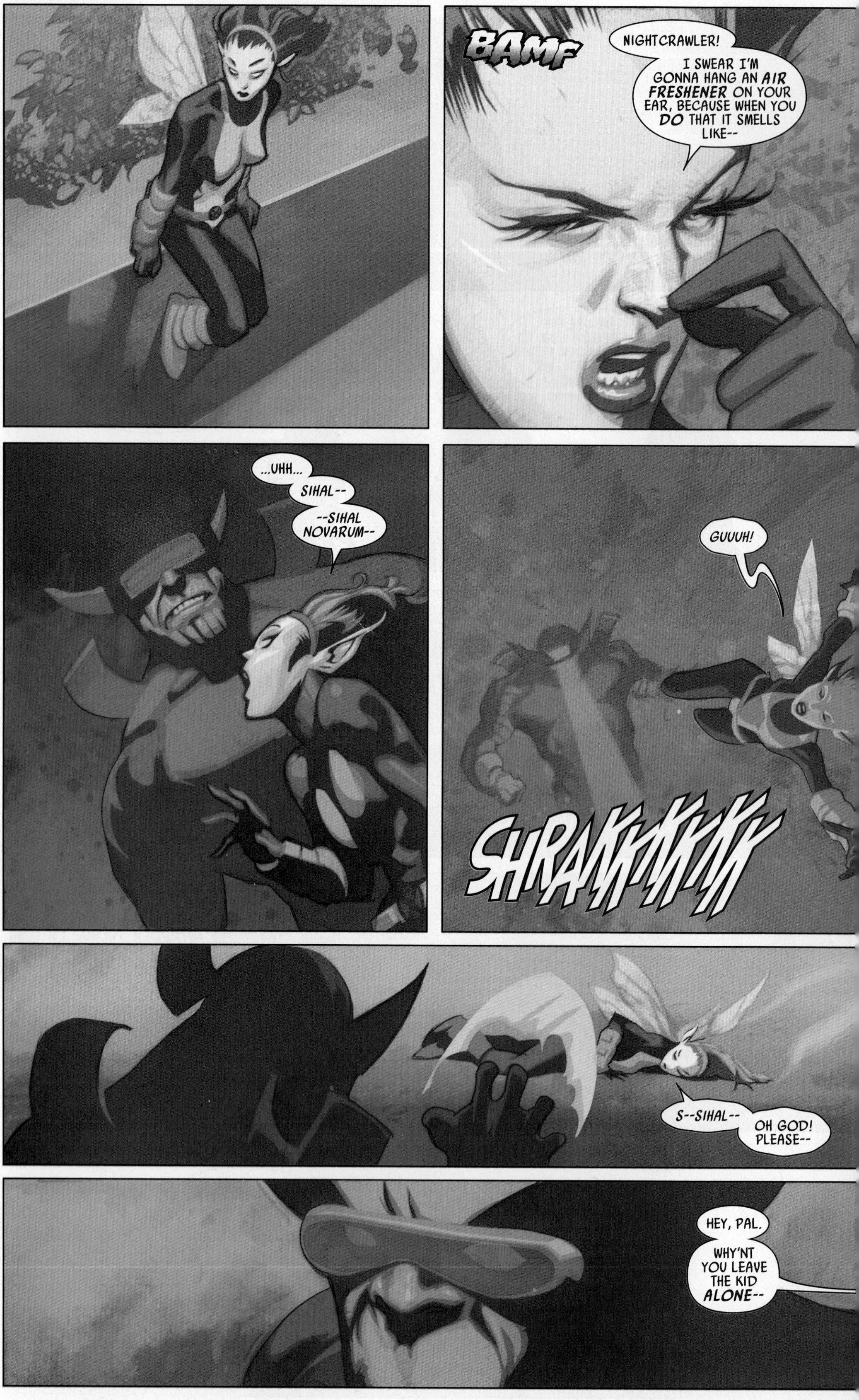
BAMF
NIGHTCRAWLER!
I SWEAR I'M GONNA HANG AN AIR FRESHENER ON YOUR EAR, BECAUSE WHEN YOU DO THAT IT SMELLS LIKE--
...UHH...
SIHAL--
--SIHAL NOVARUM--
GUUUH!
SHRAKKKKKK
S--SIHAL--
OH GOD! PLEASE--
HEY, PAL.
WHY'NT YOU LEAVE THE KID ALONE--

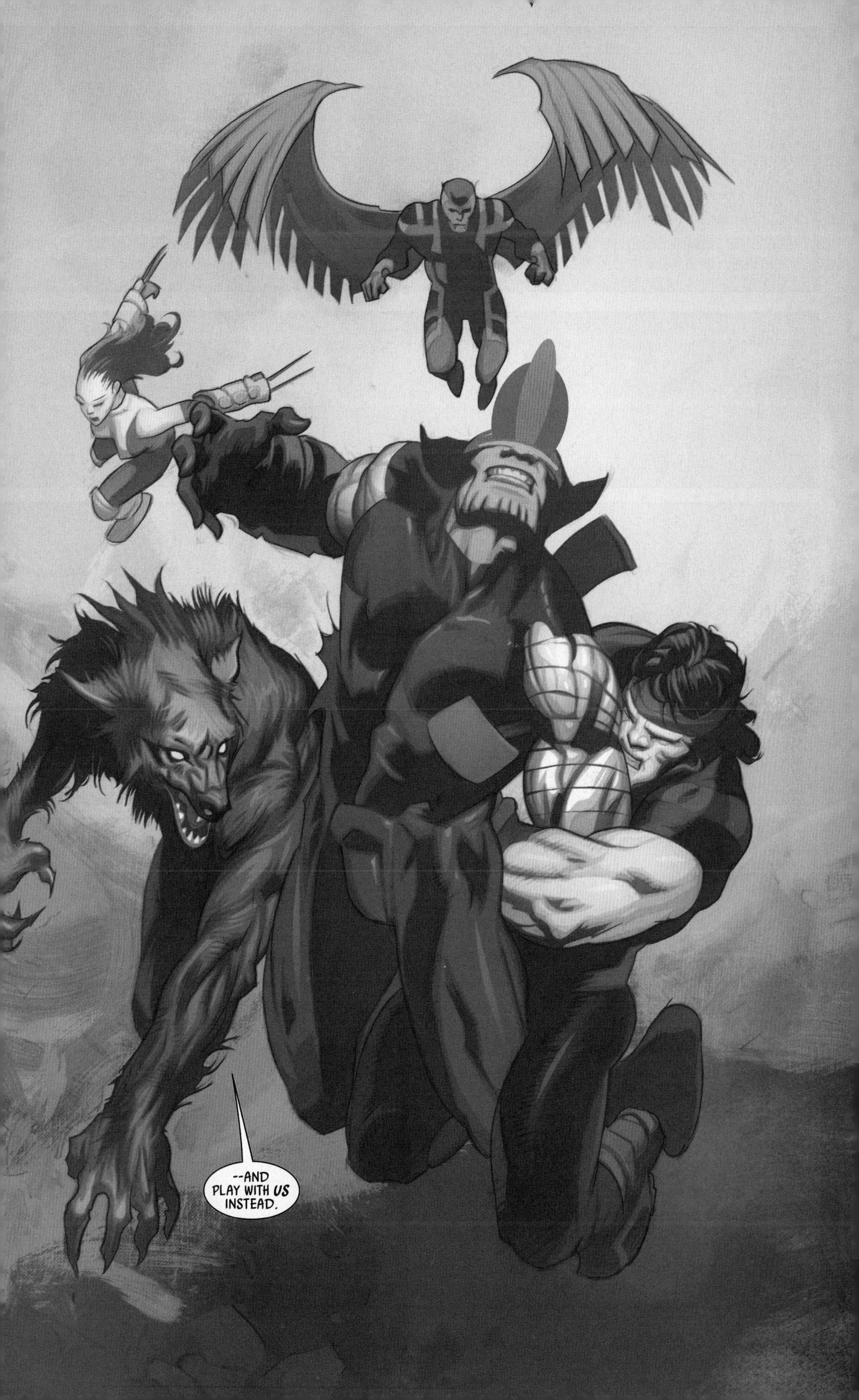
--AND PLAY WITH US INSTEAD.

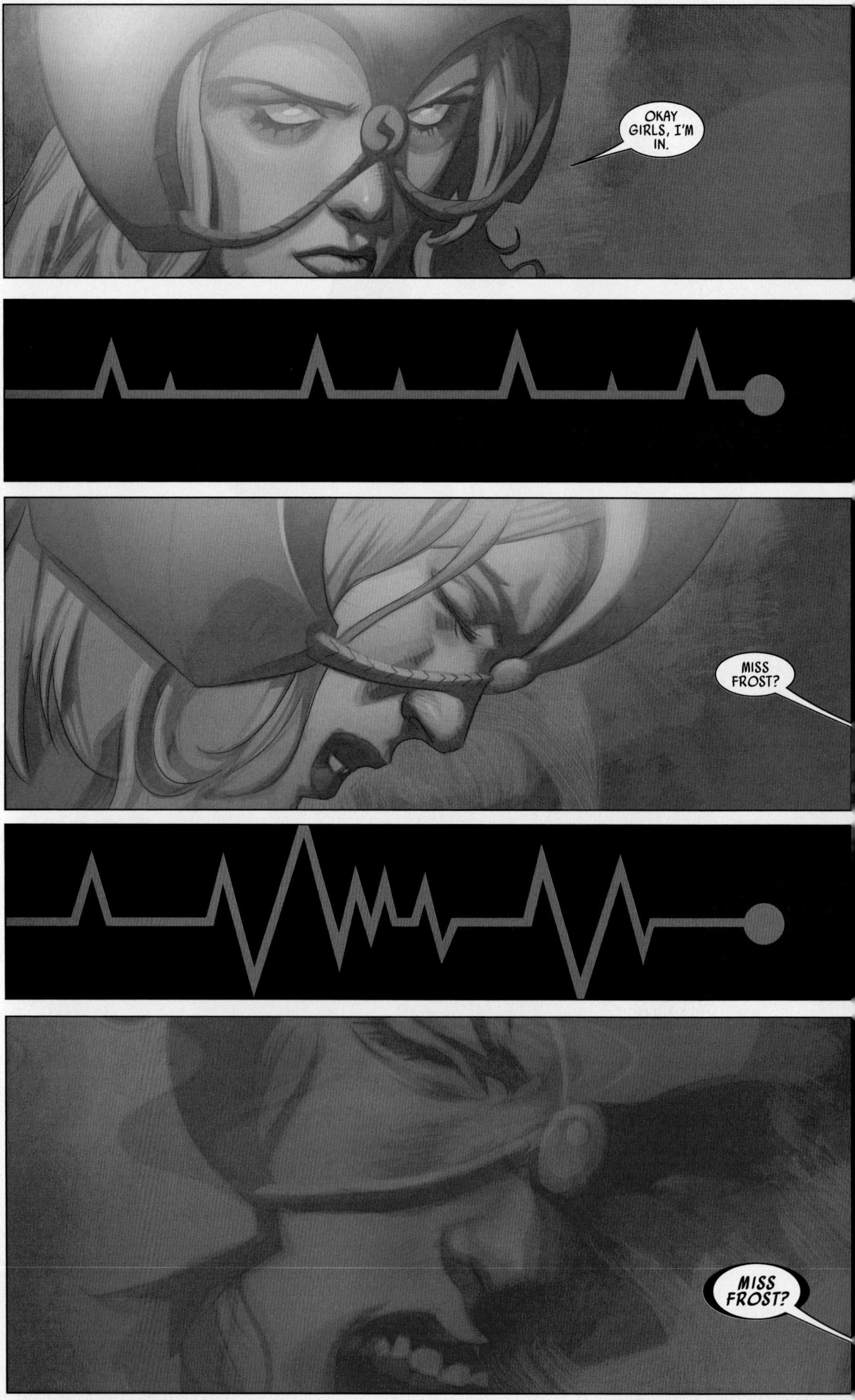
OKAY GIRLS, I'M IN.
MISS FROST?
MISS FROST?

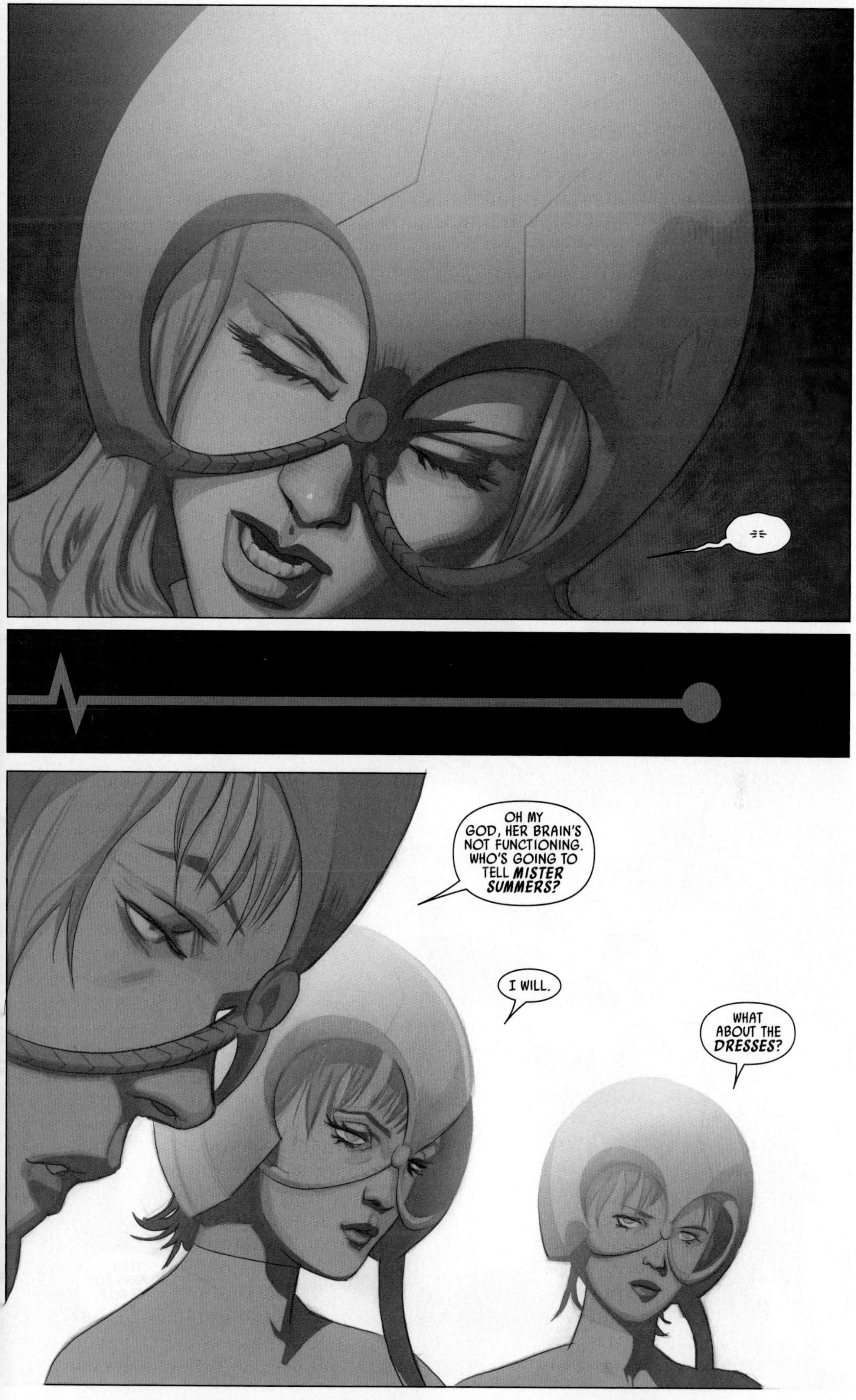
OH MY GOD, HER BRAIN'S NOT FUNCTIONING. WHO'S GOING TO TELL ***MISTER SUMMERS?***
I WILL.
WHAT ABOUT THE ***DRESSES?***

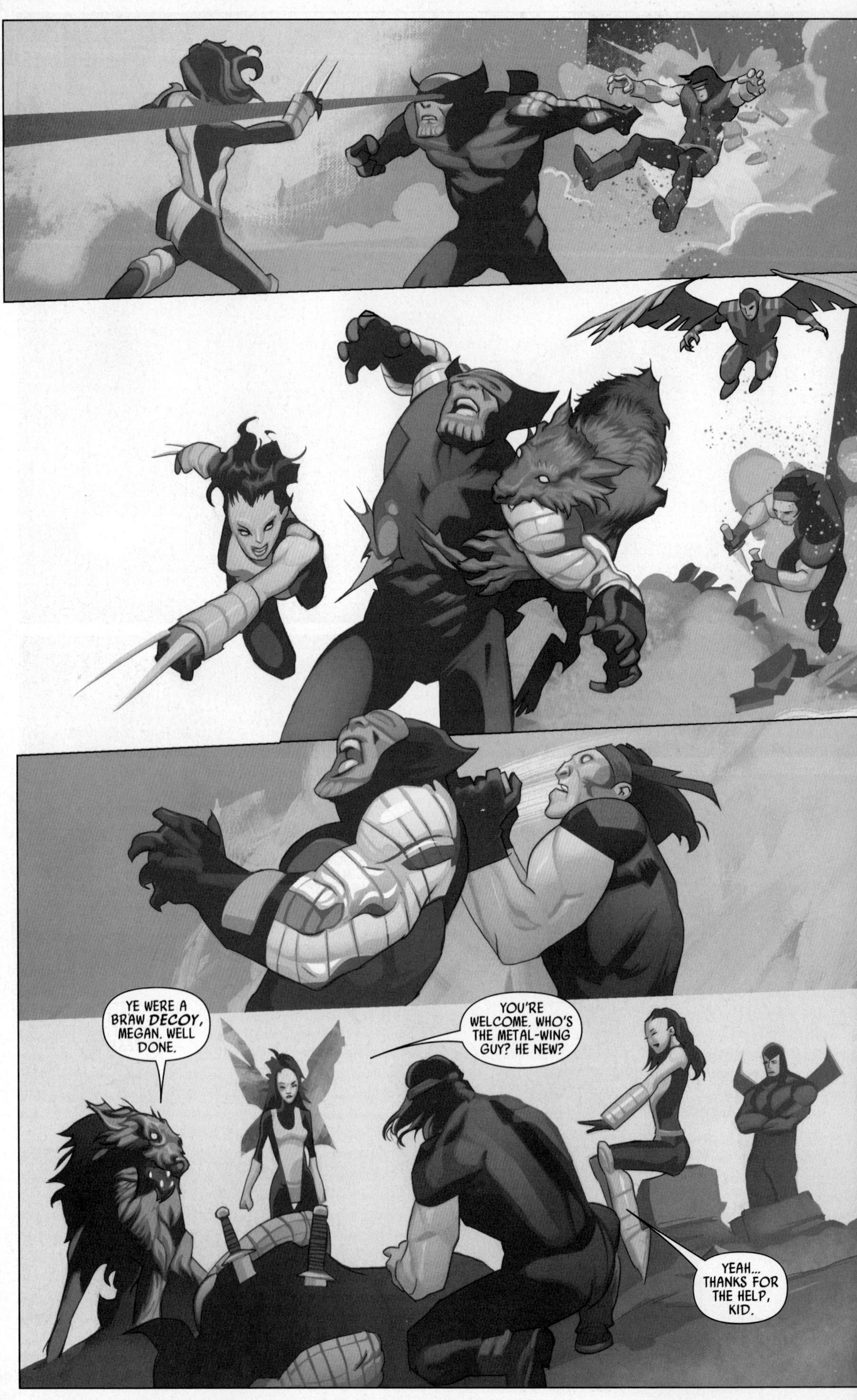

YE WERE A BRAW DECOY, MEGAN. WELL DONE.
YOU'RE WELCOME. WHO'S THE METAL-WING GUY? HE NEW?
YEAH... THANKS FOR THE HELP, KID.

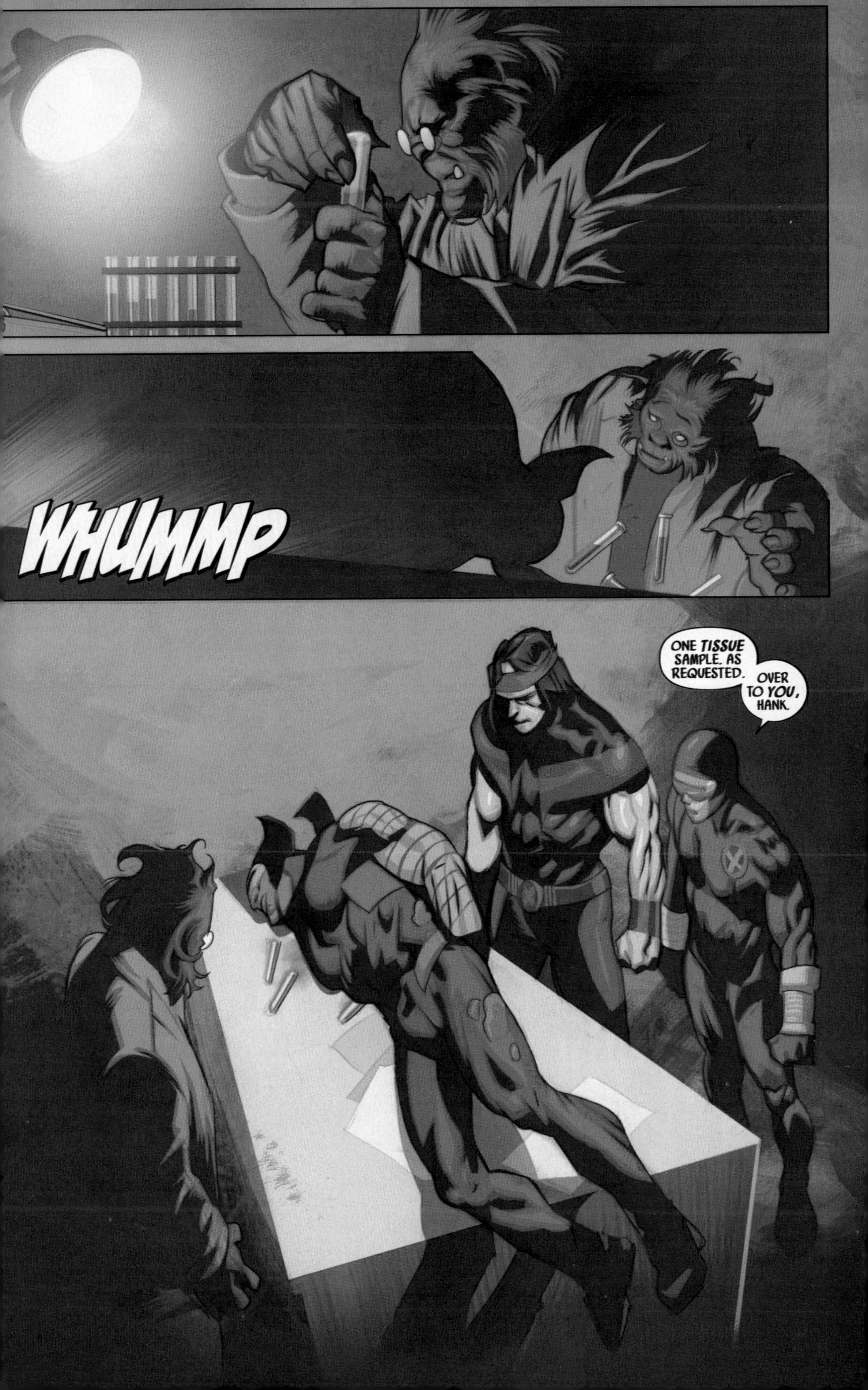
WHUMMP
ONE TISSUE SAMPLE, AS REQUESTED.
OVER TO YOU, HANK.

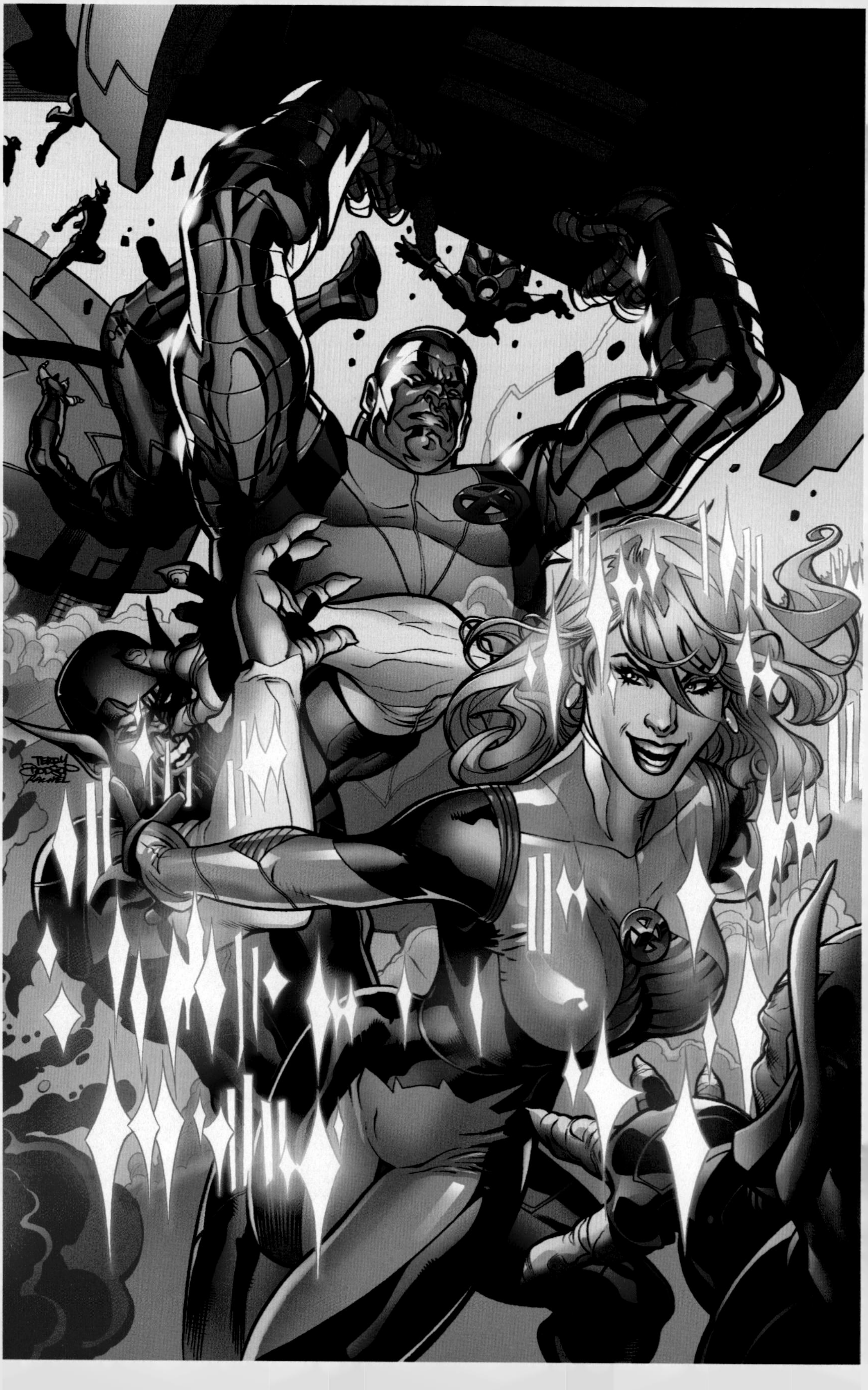

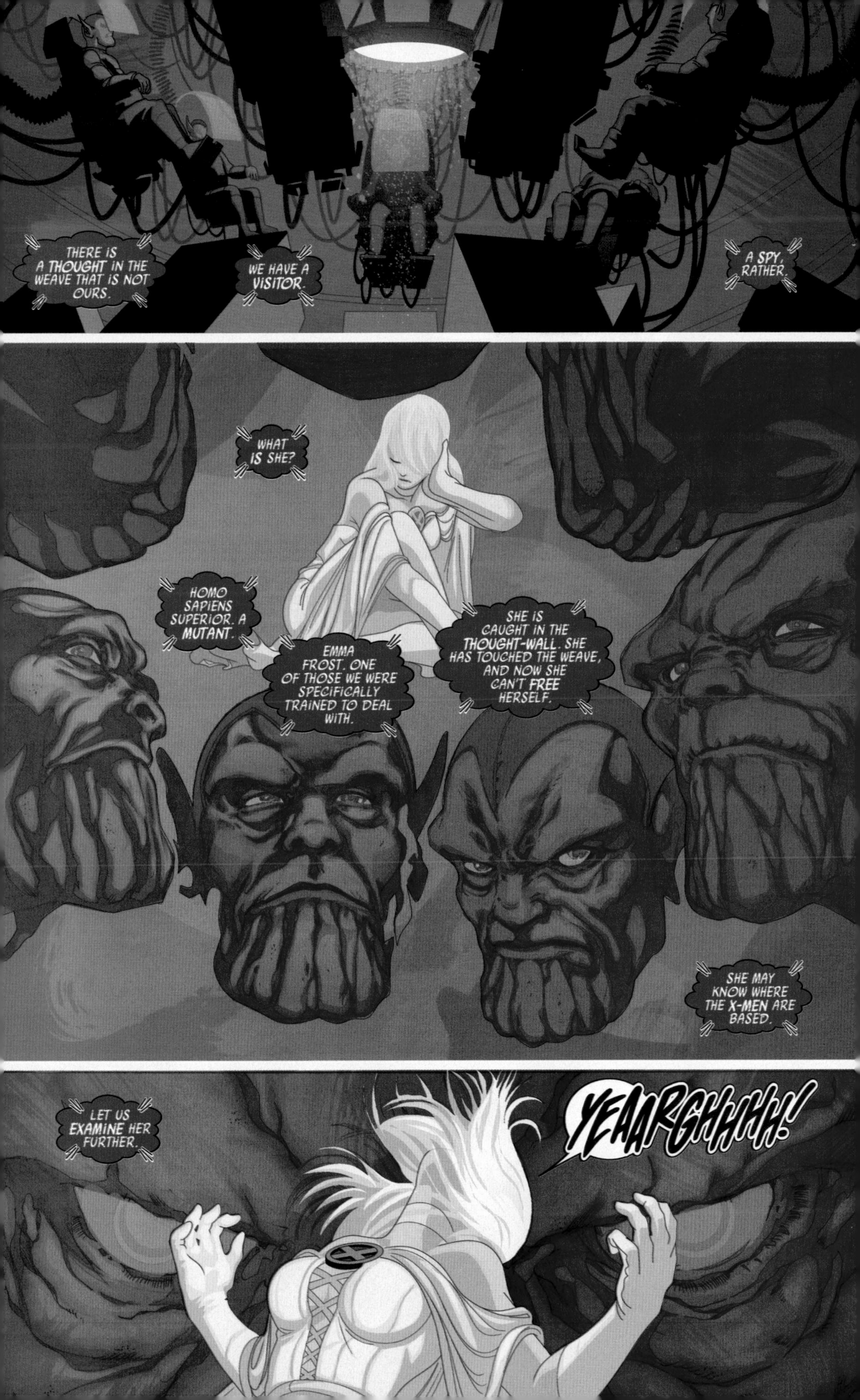
THERE IS A THOUGHT IN THE WEAVE THAT IS NOT OURS.
WE HAVE A VISITOR.
A SPY, RATHER.
WHAT IS SHE?
HOMO SAPIENS SUPERIOR. A MUTANT.
EMMA FROST. ONE OF THOSE WE WERE SPECIFICALLY TRAINED TO DEAL WITH.
SHE IS CAUGHT IN THE THOUGHT-WALL. SHE HAS TOUCHED THE WEAVE, AND NOW SHE CAN'T FREE HERSELF.
SHE MAY KNOW WHERE THE X-MEN ARE BASED.
LET US EXAMINE HER FURTHER.
YEAARGHHHH!

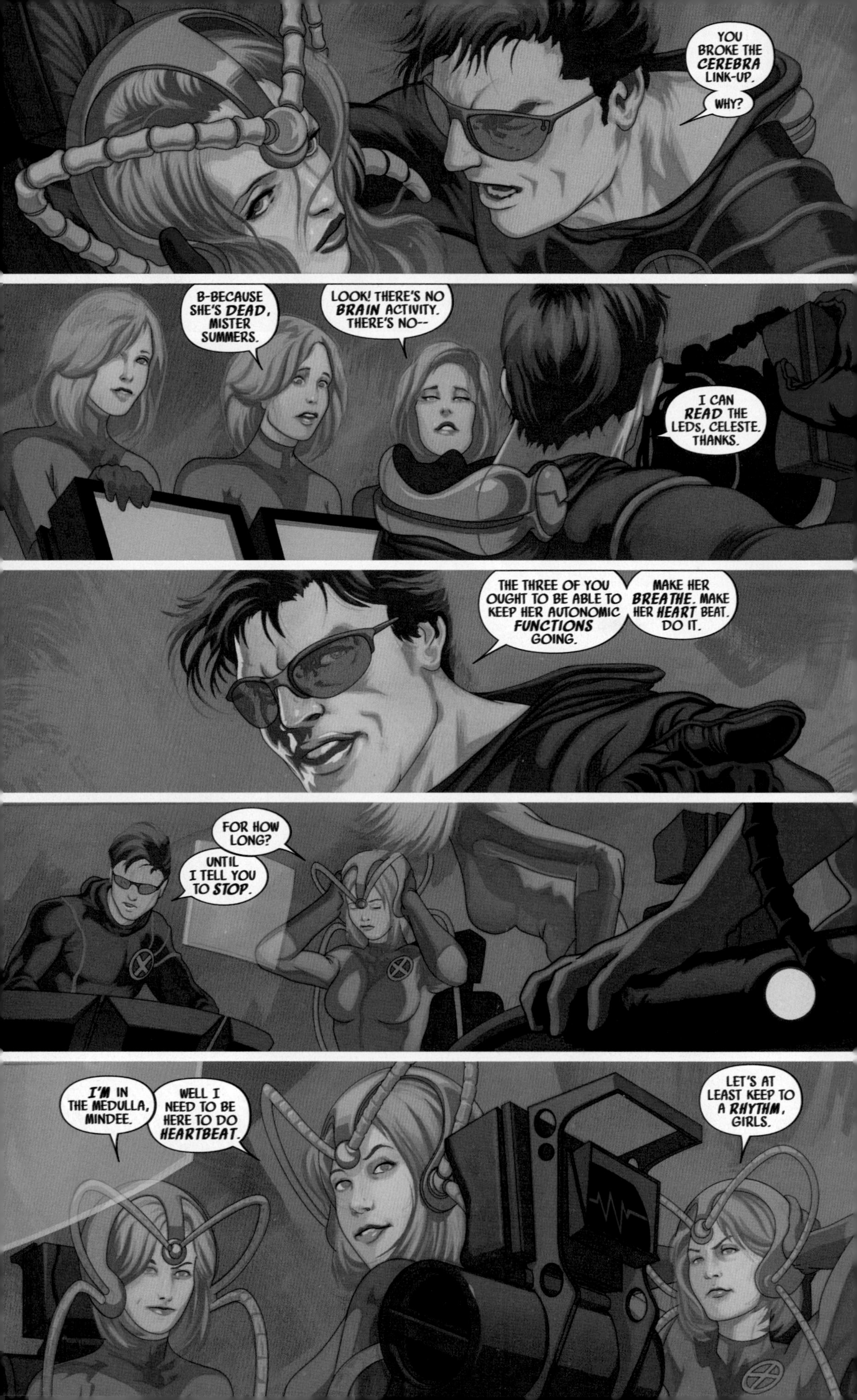
YOU BROKE THE CEREBRA LINK-UP.
WHY?
B-BECAUSE SHE'S DEAD, MISTER SUMMERS.
LOOK! THERE'S NO BRAIN ACTIVITY. THERE'S NO--
I CAN READ THE LEDS, CELESTE. THANKS.
THE THREE OF YOU OUGHT TO BE ABLE TO KEEP HER AUTONOMIC FUNCTIONS GOING.
MAKE HER BREATHE. MAKE HER HEART BEAT. DO IT.
FOR HOW LONG?
UNTIL I TELL YOU TO STOP.
I'M IN THE MEDULLA, MINDEE.
WELL I NEED TO BE HERE TO DO HEARTBEAT.
LET'S AT LEAST KEEP TO A RHYTHM, GIRLS.

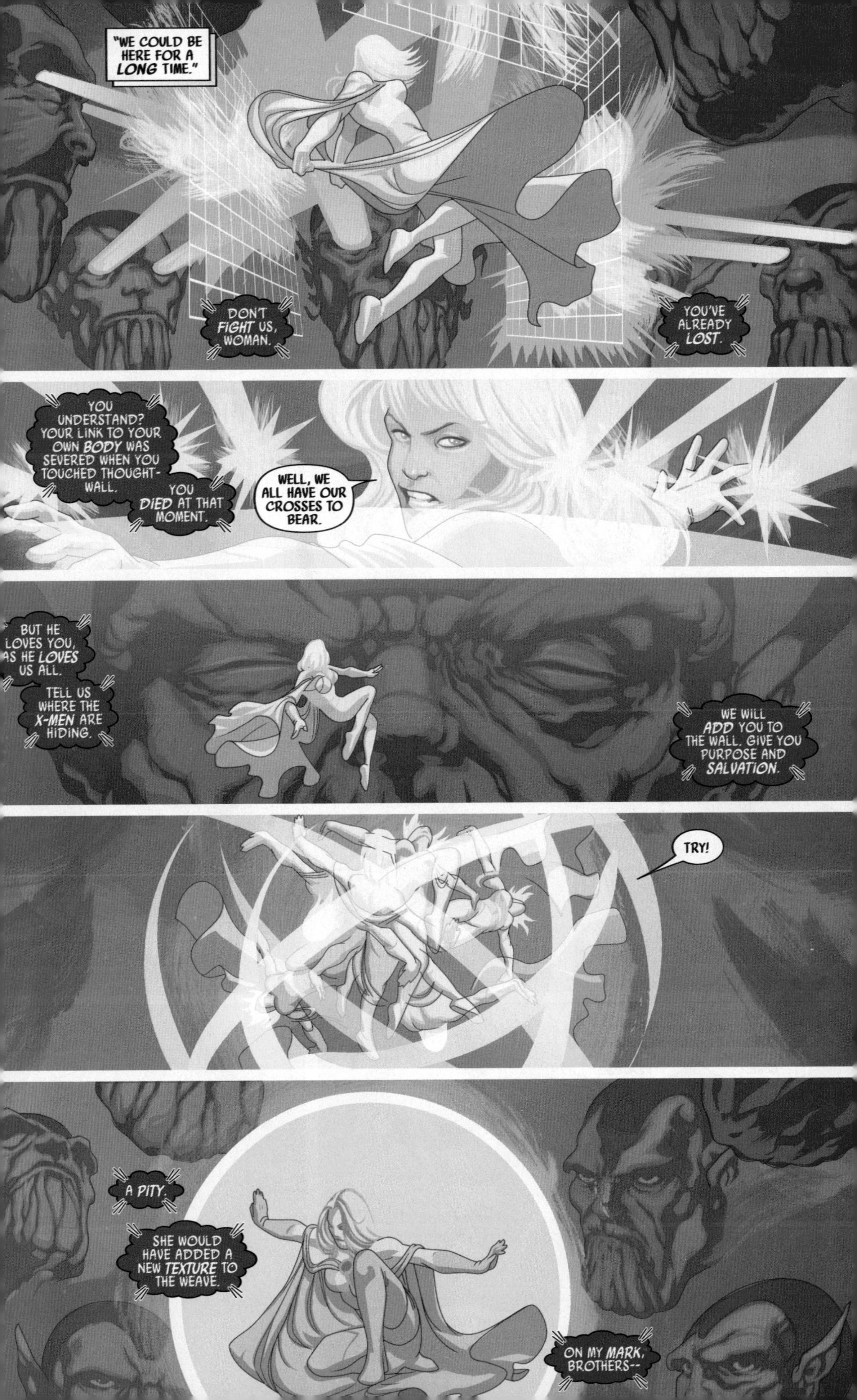
"WE COULD BE HERE FOR A LONG TIME."
DON'T FIGHT US, WOMAN.
YOU'VE ALREADY LOST.
YOU UNDERSTAND? YOUR LINK TO YOUR OWN BODY WAS SEVERED WHEN YOU TOUCHED THOUGHT-WALL.
YOU DIED AT THAT MOMENT.
WELL, WE ALL HAVE OUR CROSSES TO BEAR.
BUT HE LOVES YOU, AS HE LOVES US ALL.
TELL US WHERE THE X-MEN ARE HIDING.
WE WILL ADD YOU TO THE WALL. GIVE YOU PURPOSE AND SALVATION.
TRY!
A PITY.
SHE WOULD HAVE ADDED A NEW TEXTURE TO THE WEAVE.
ON MY MARK, BROTHERS--

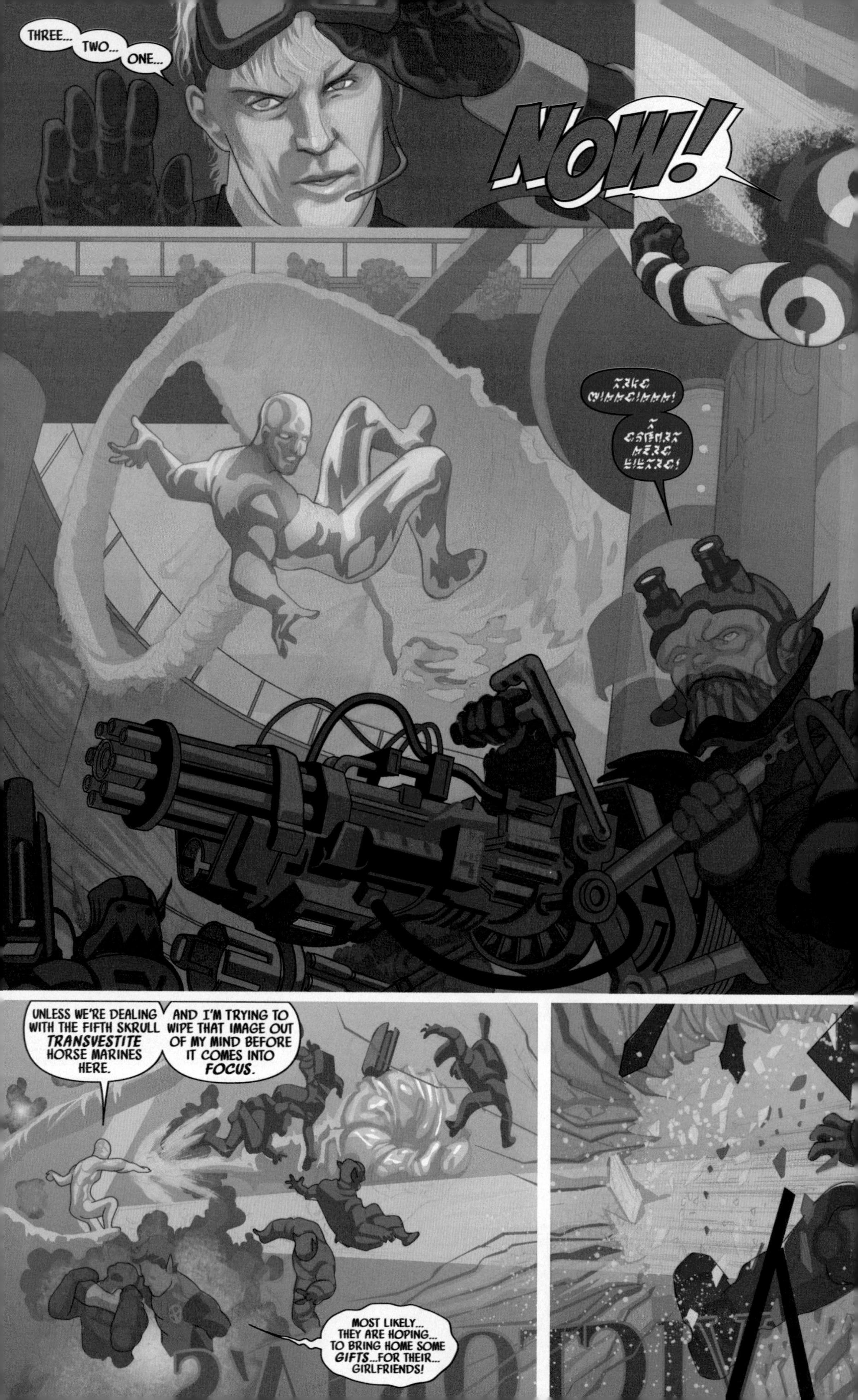
THREE... TWO... ONE...
NOW!
UNLESS WE'RE DEALING WITH THE FIFTH SKRULL TRANSVESTITE HORSE MARINES HERE.
AND I'M TRYING TO WIPE THAT IMAGE OUT OF MY MIND BEFORE IT COMES INTO FOCUS.
MOST LIKELY... THEY ARE HOPING... TO BRING HOME SOME GIFTS...FOR THEIR... GIRLFRIENDS!

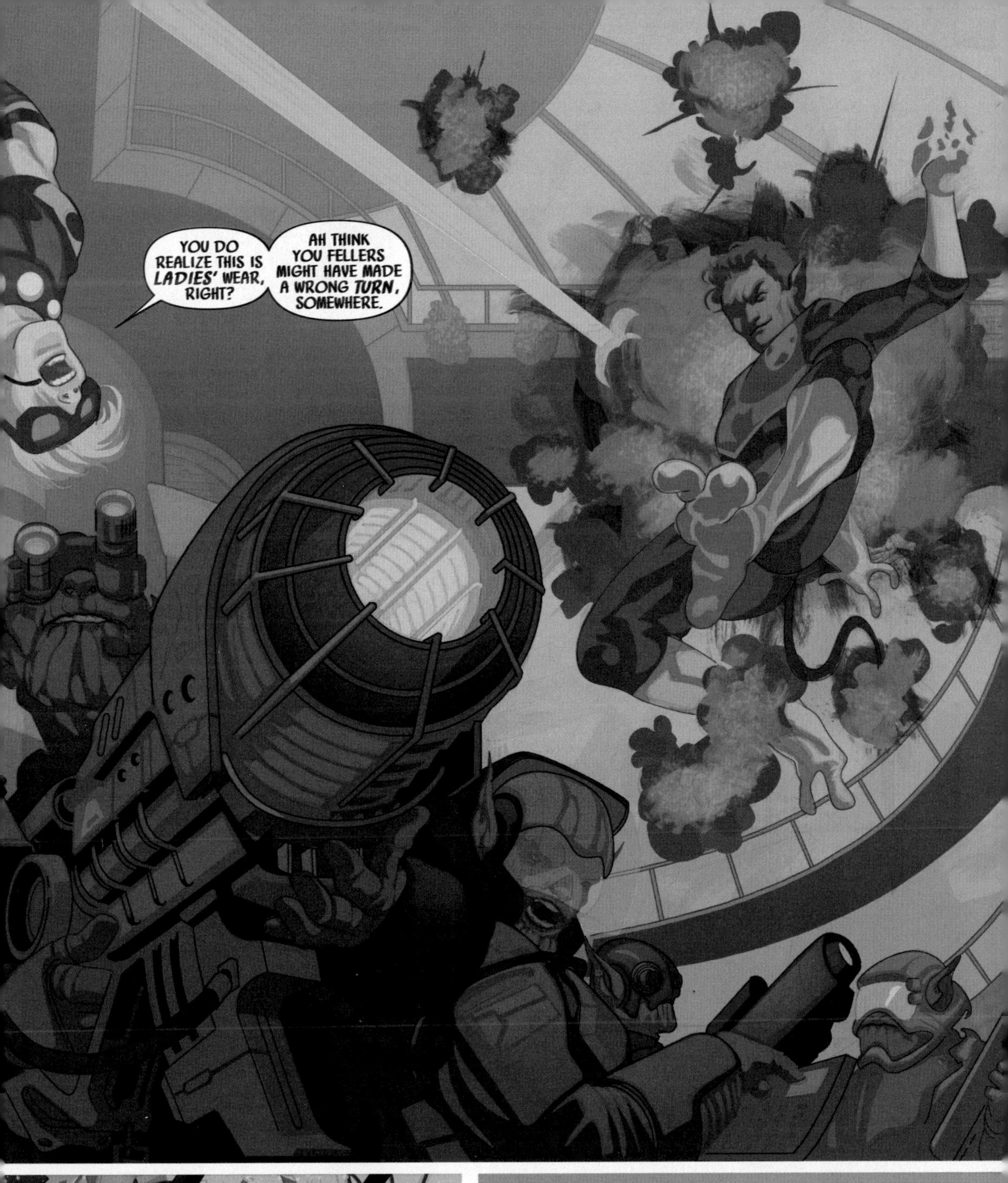
YOU DO REALIZE THIS IS LADIES' WEAR, RIGHT?
AH THINK YOU FELLERS MIGHT HAVE MADE A WRONG TURN, SOMEWHERE.

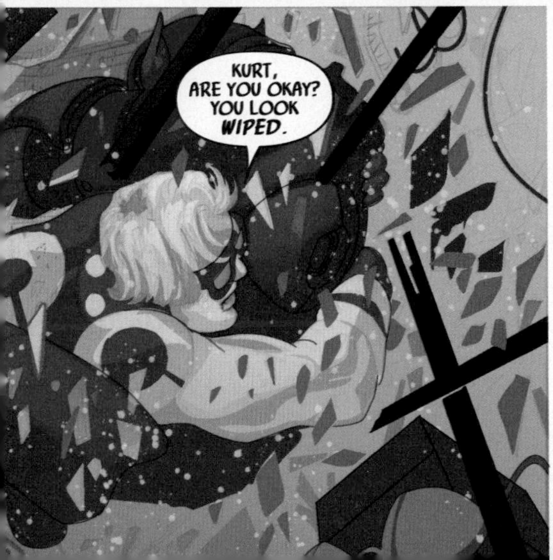
KURT, ARE YOU OKAY? YOU LOOK WIPED.

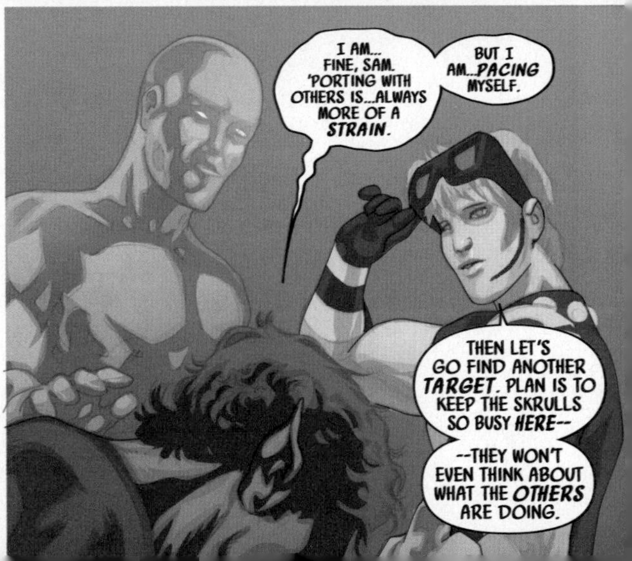
I AM... FINE, SAM. 'PORTING WITH OTHERS IS...ALWAYS MORE OF A STRAIN.
BUT I AM...PACING MYSELF.
THEN LET'S GO FIND ANOTHER TARGET. PLAN IS TO KEEP THE SKRULLS SO BUSY HERE--
--THEY WON'T EVEN THINK ABOUT WHAT THE OTHERS ARE DOING.

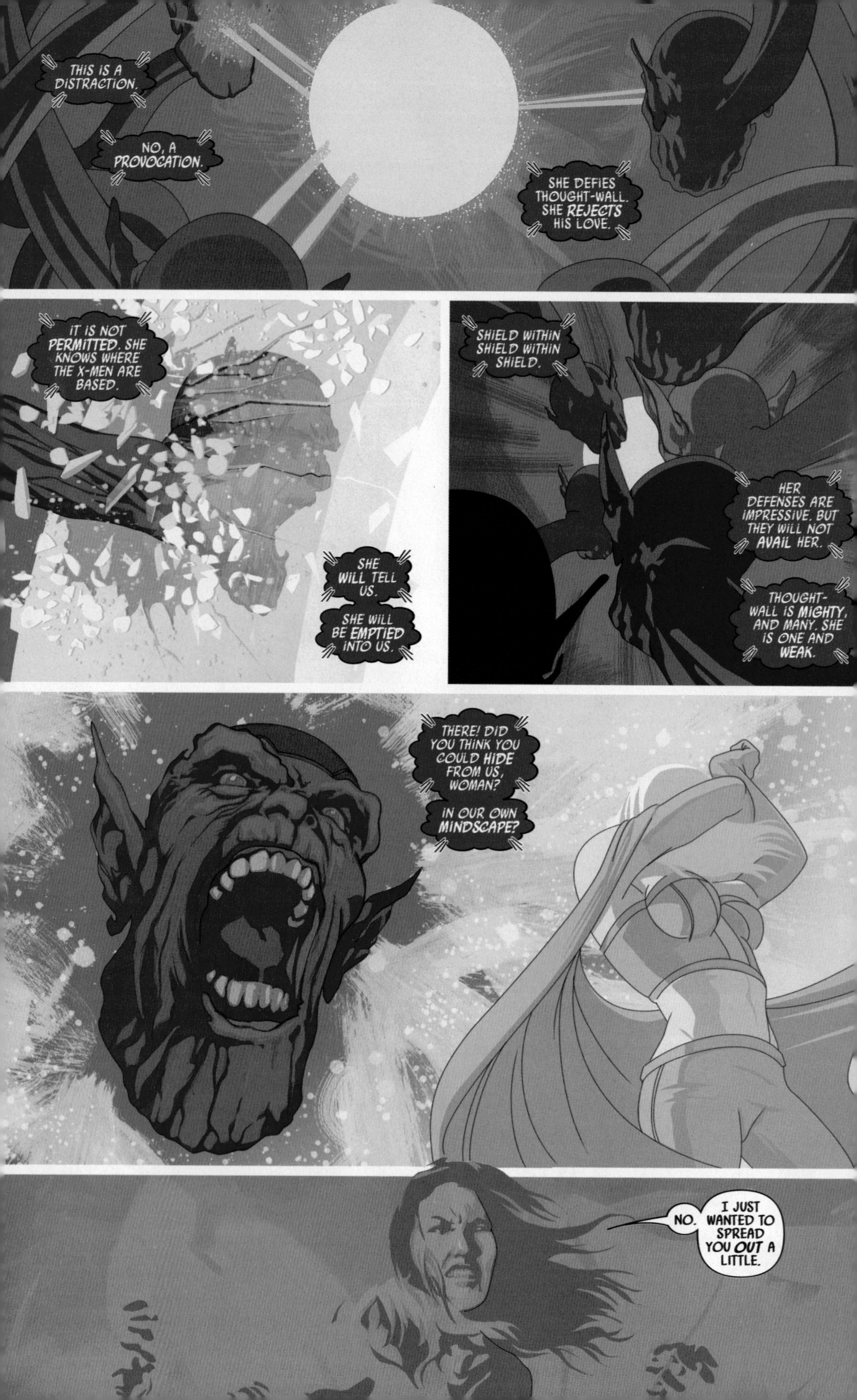
THIS IS A DISTRACTION.
NO, A PROVOCATION.
SHE DEFIES THOUGHT-WALL. SHE REJECTS HIS LOVE.
IT IS NOT PERMITTED. SHE KNOWS WHERE THE X-MEN ARE BASED.
SHE WILL TELL US.
SHE WILL BE EMPTIED INTO US.
SHIELD WITHIN SHIELD WITHIN SHIELD.
HER DEFENSES ARE IMPRESSIVE. BUT THEY WILL NOT AVAIL HER.
THOUGHT-WALL IS MIGHTY, AND MANY. SHE IS ONE AND WEAK.
THERE! DID YOU THINK YOU COULD HIDE FROM US, WOMAN?
IN OUR OWN MINDSCAPE?
NO.
I JUST WANTED TO SPREAD YOU OUT A LITTLE.

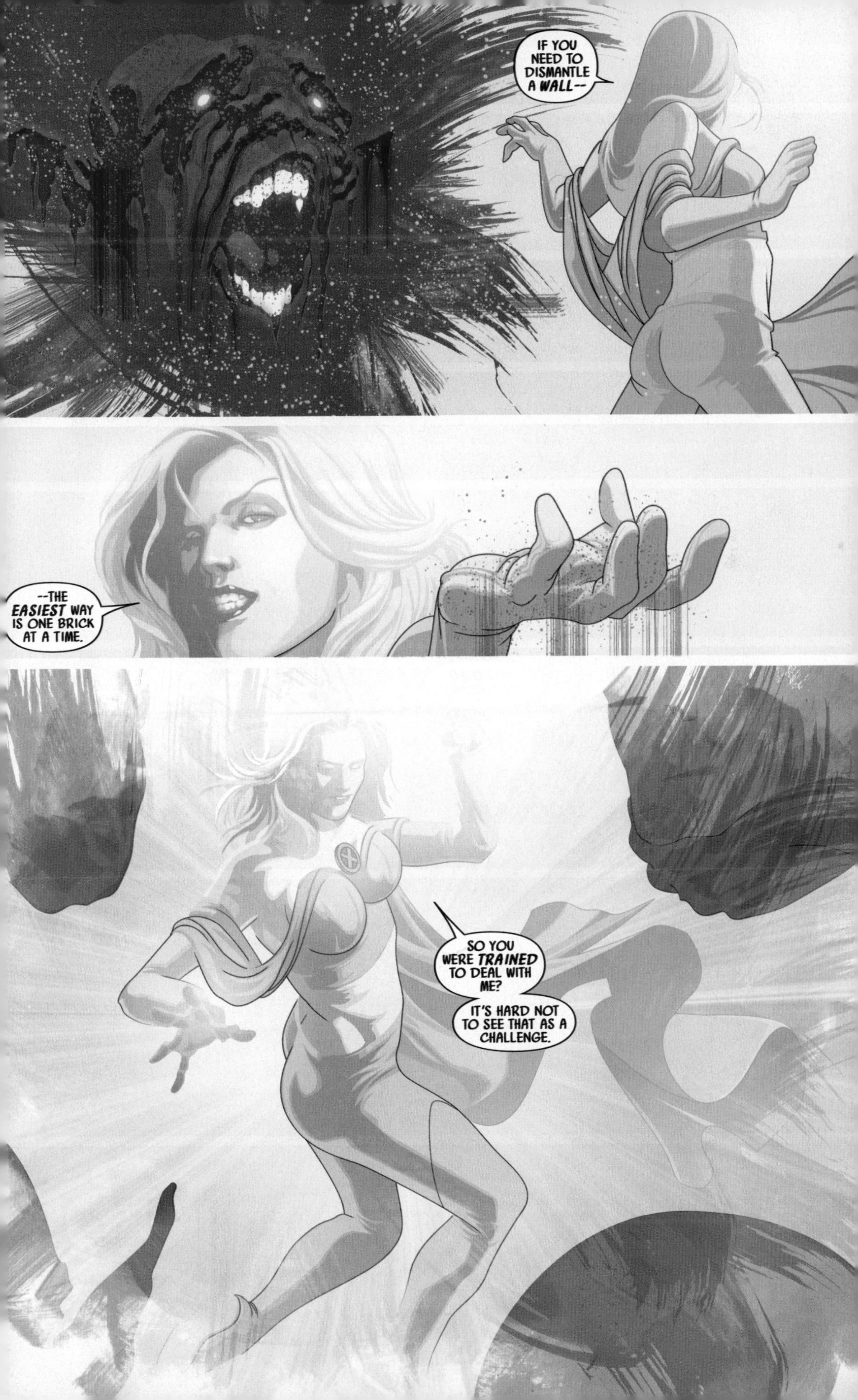
IF YOU NEED TO DISMANTLE A WALL--
--THE EASIEST WAY IS ONE BRICK AT A TIME.
SO YOU WERE TRAINED TO DEAL WITH ME?
IT'S HARD NOT TO SEE THAT AS A CHALLENGE.

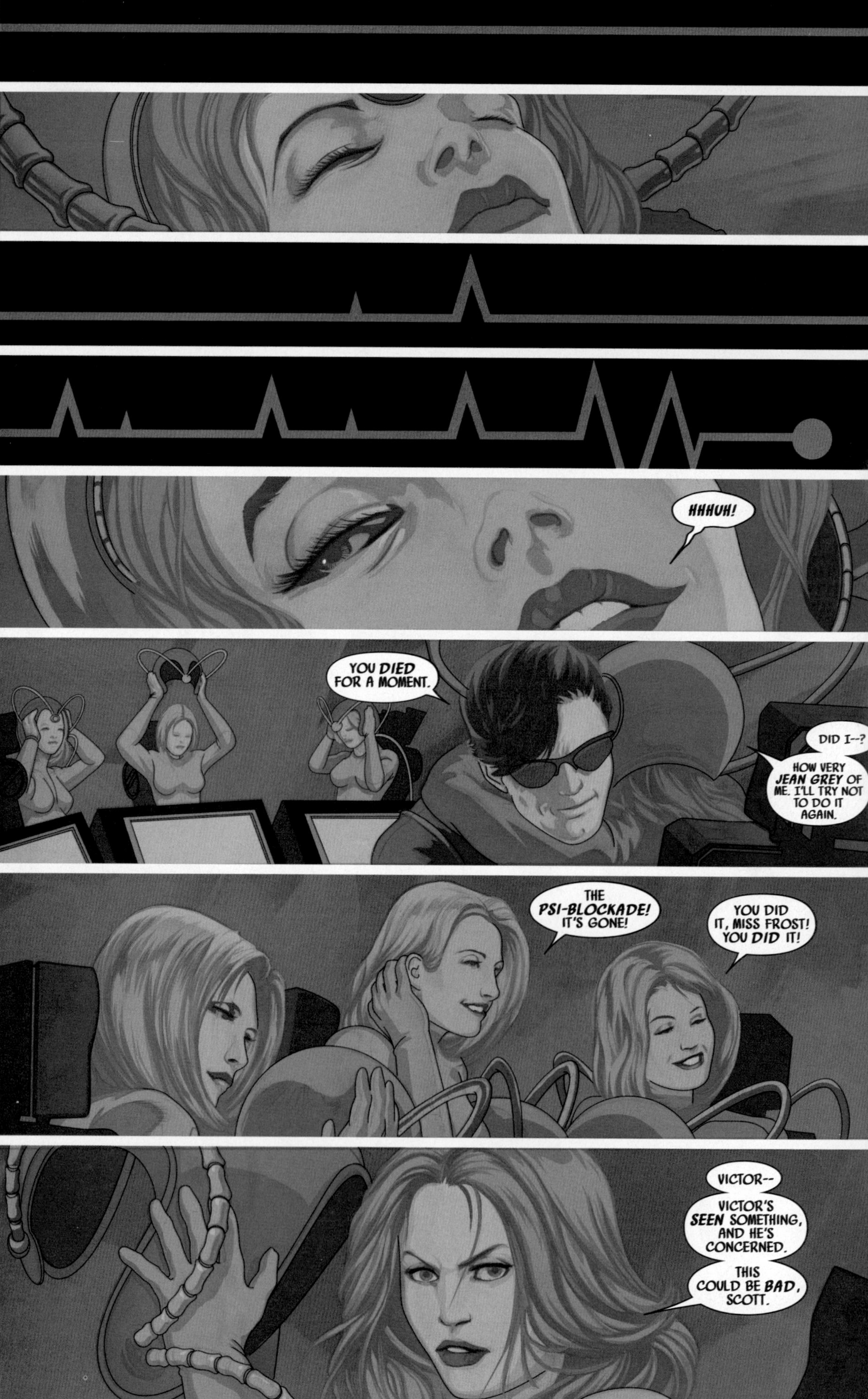
HHHUH!
YOU DIED FOR A MOMENT.
DID I--?
HOW VERY JEAN GREY OF ME. I'LL TRY NOT TO DO IT AGAIN.
THE PSI-BLOCKADE! IT'S GONE!
YOU DID IT, MISS FROST! YOU DID IT!
VICTOR--
VICTOR'S SEEN SOMETHING, AND HE'S CONCERNED.
THIS COULD BE BAD, SCOTT.

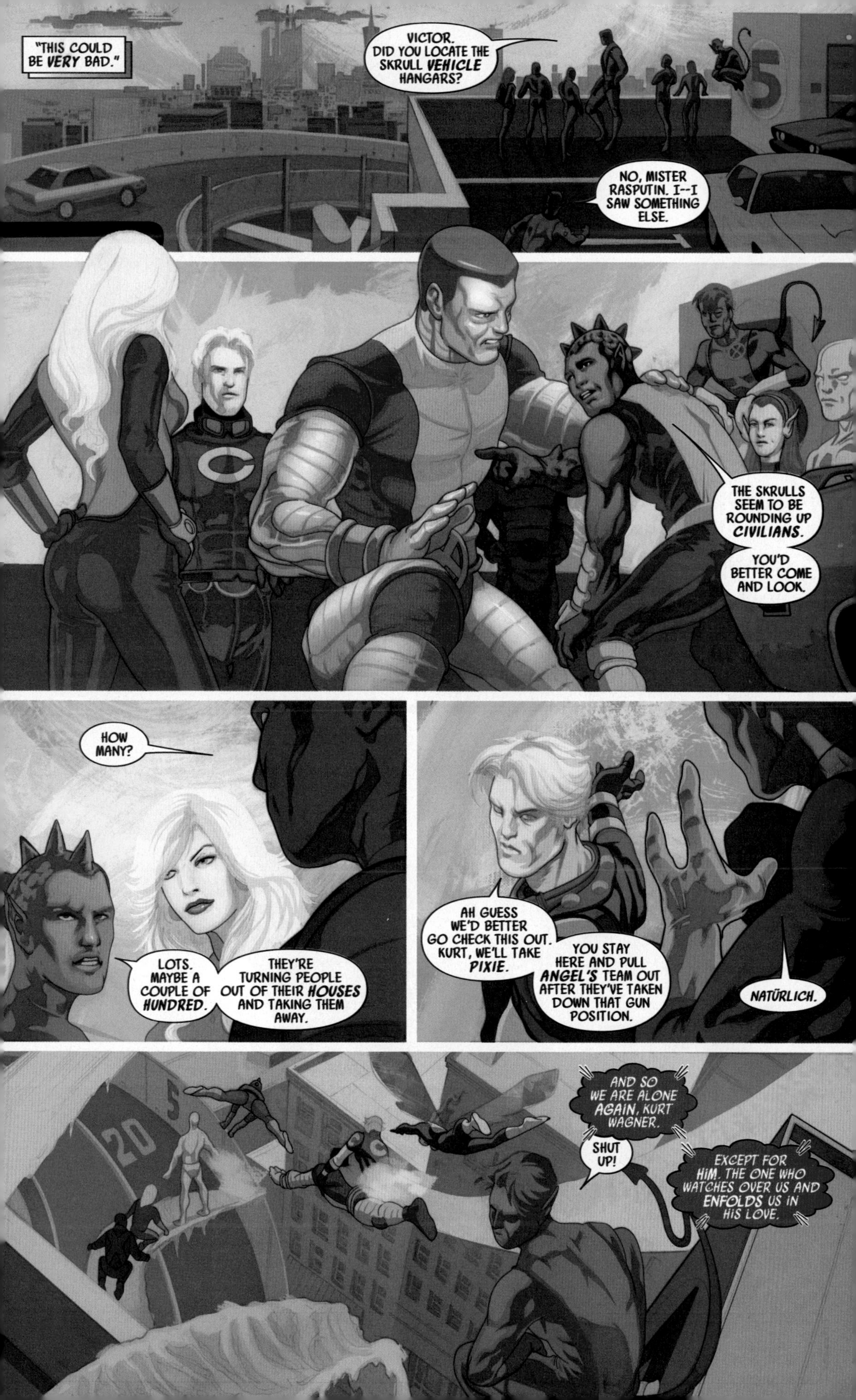
"THIS COULD BE VERY BAD."
VICTOR. DID YOU LOCATE THE SKRULL VEHICLE HANGARS?
NO, MISTER RASPUTIN. I--I SAW SOMETHING ELSE.
THE SKRULLS SEEM TO BE ROUNDING UP CIVILIANS.
YOU'D BETTER COME AND LOOK.
HOW MANY?
LOTS. MAYBE A COUPLE OF HUNDRED.
THEY'RE TURNING PEOPLE OUT OF THEIR HOUSES AND TAKING THEM AWAY.
AH GUESS WE'D BETTER GO CHECK THIS OUT. KURT, WE'LL TAKE PIXIE.
YOU STAY HERE AND PULL ANGEL'S TEAM OUT AFTER THEY'VE TAKEN DOWN THAT GUN POSITION.
NATÜRLICH.
AND SO WE ARE ALONE AGAIN, KURT WAGNER.
SHUT UP!
EXCEPT FOR HIM. THE ONE WHO WATCHES OVER US AND ENFOLDS US IN HIS LOVE.

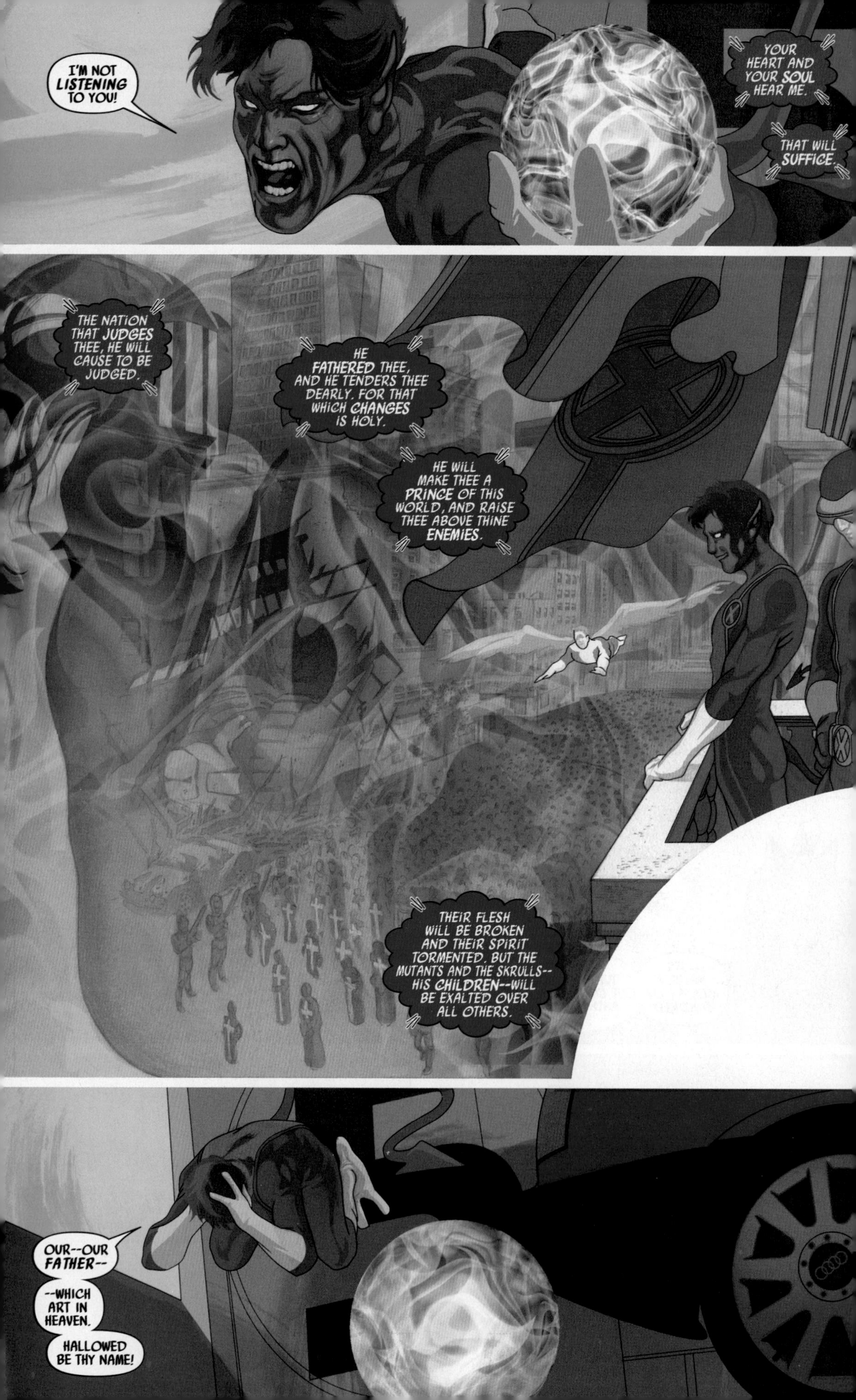
I'M NOT LISTENING TO YOU!
YOUR HEART AND YOUR SOUL HEAR ME.
THAT WILL SUFFICE.
THE NATION THAT JUDGES THEE, HE WILL CAUSE TO BE JUDGED.
HE FATHERED THEE, AND HE TENDERS THEE DEARLY. FOR THAT WHICH CHANGES IS HOLY.
HE WILL MAKE THEE A PRINCE OF THIS WORLD, AND RAISE THEE ABOVE THINE ENEMIES.
THEIR FLESH WILL BE BROKEN AND THEIR SPIRIT TORMENTED. BUT THE MUTANTS AND THE SKRULLS--HIS CHILDREN--WILL BE EXALTED OVER ALL OTHERS.
OUR--OUR FATHER--
--WHICH ART IN HEAVEN.
HALLOWED BE THY NAME!

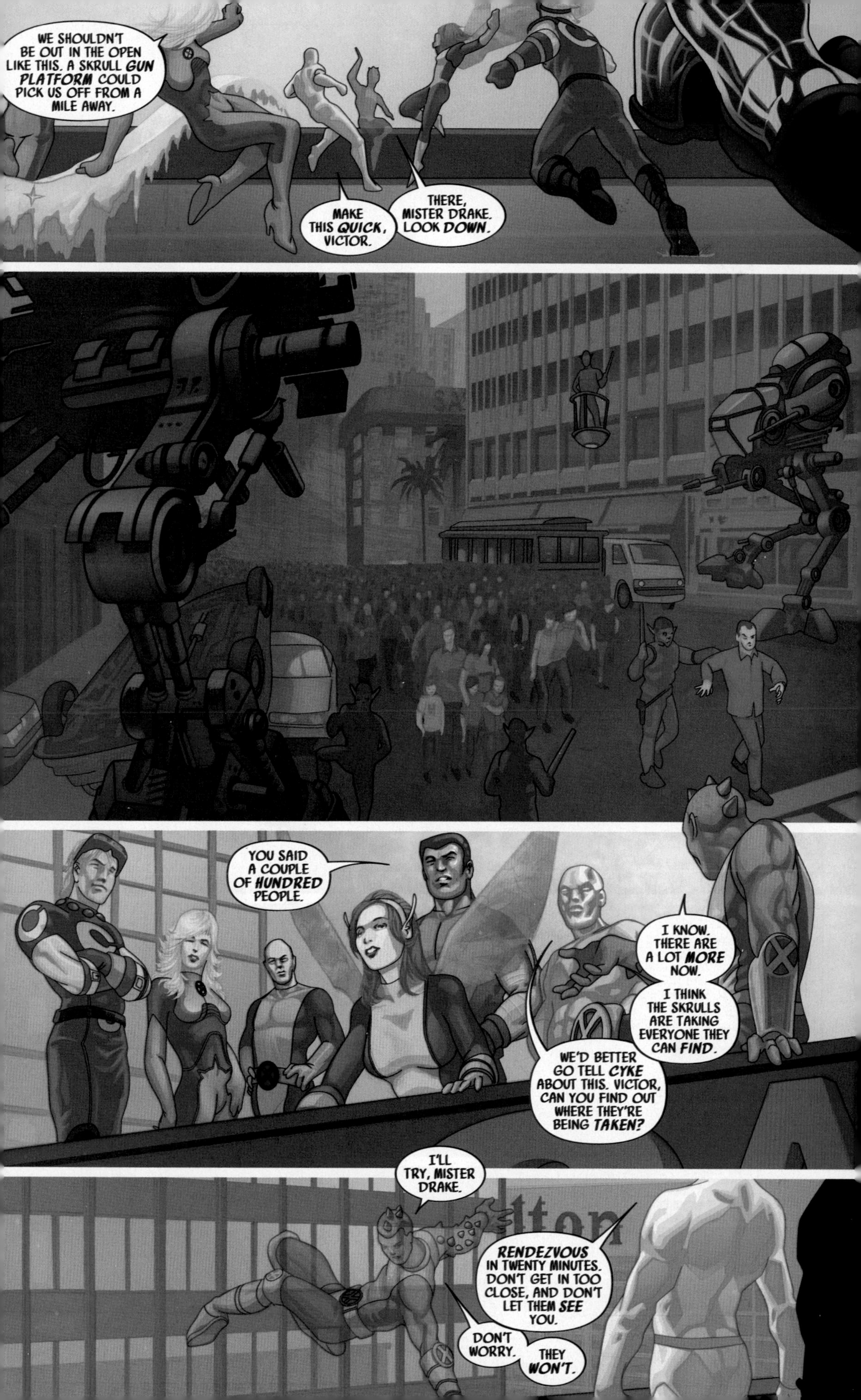
WE SHOULDN'T BE OUT IN THE OPEN LIKE THIS. A SKRULL GUN PLATFORM COULD PICK US OFF FROM A MILE AWAY.
MAKE THIS QUICK, VICTOR.
THERE, MISTER DRAKE. LOOK DOWN.
YOU SAID A COUPLE OF HUNDRED PEOPLE.
I KNOW. THERE ARE A LOT MORE NOW.
I THINK THE SKRULLS ARE TAKING EVERYONE THEY CAN FIND.
WE'D BETTER GO TELL CYKE ABOUT THIS. VICTOR, CAN YOU FIND OUT WHERE THEY'RE BEING TAKEN?
I'LL TRY, MISTER DRAKE.
RENDEZVOUS IN TWENTY MINUTES. DON'T GET IN TOO CLOSE, AND DON'T LET THEM SEE YOU.
DON'T WORRY.
THEY WON'T.

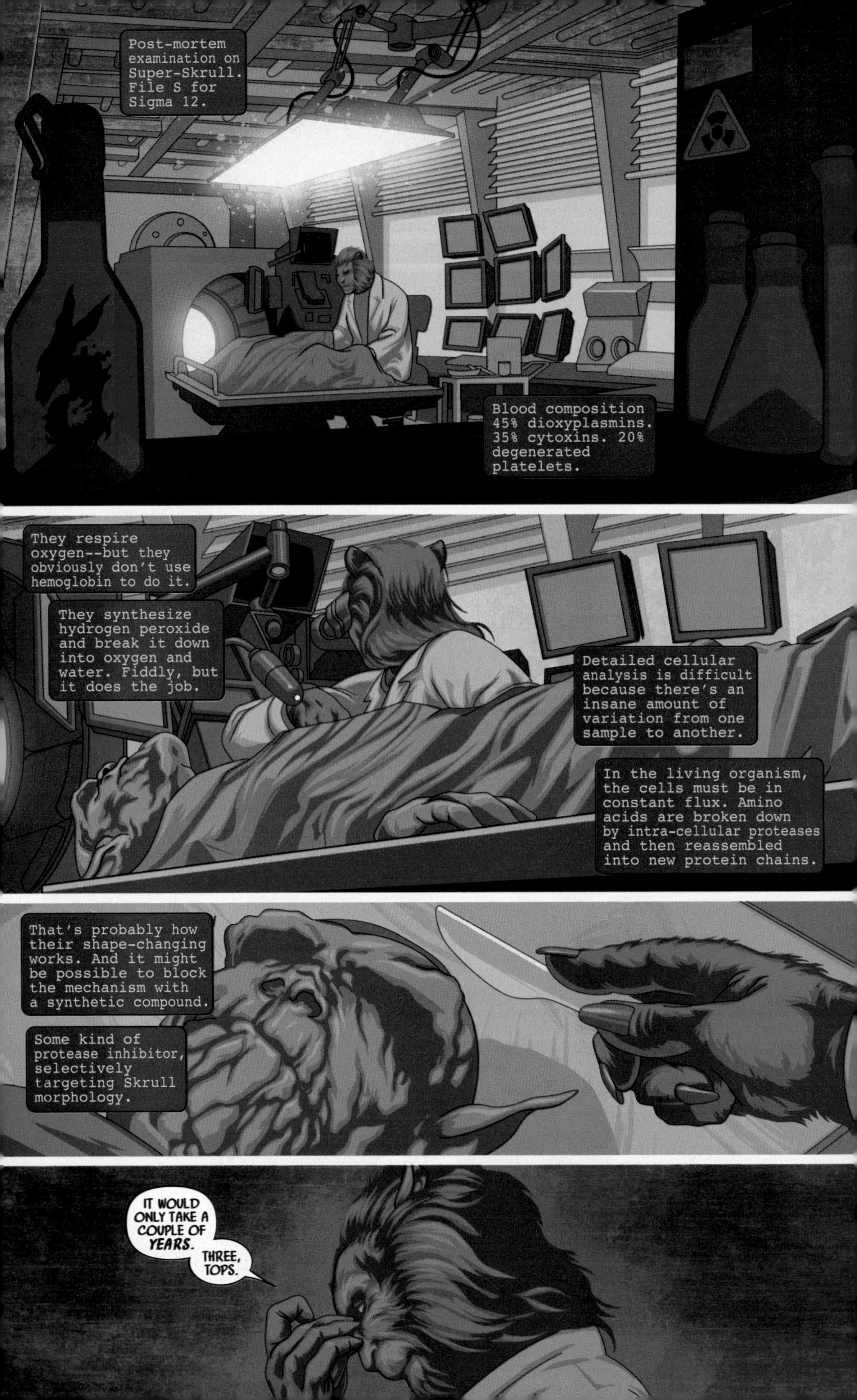

Post-mortem examination on Super-Skrull. File S for Sigma 12.
Blood composition 45% dioxyplasmins. 35% cytoxins. 20% degenerated platelets.
They respire oxygen--but they obviously don't use hemoglobin to do it.
They synthesize hydrogen peroxide and break it down into oxygen and water. Fiddly, but it does the job.
Detailed cellular analysis is difficult because there's an insane amount of variation from one sample to another.
In the living organism, the cells must be in constant flux. Amino acids are broken down by intra-cellular proteases and then reassembled into new protein chains.
That's probably how their shape-changing works. And it might be possible to block the mechanism with a synthetic compound.
Some kind of protease inhibitor, selectively targeting Skrull morphology.
IT WOULD ONLY TAKE A COUPLE OF YEARS.
THREE, TOPS.

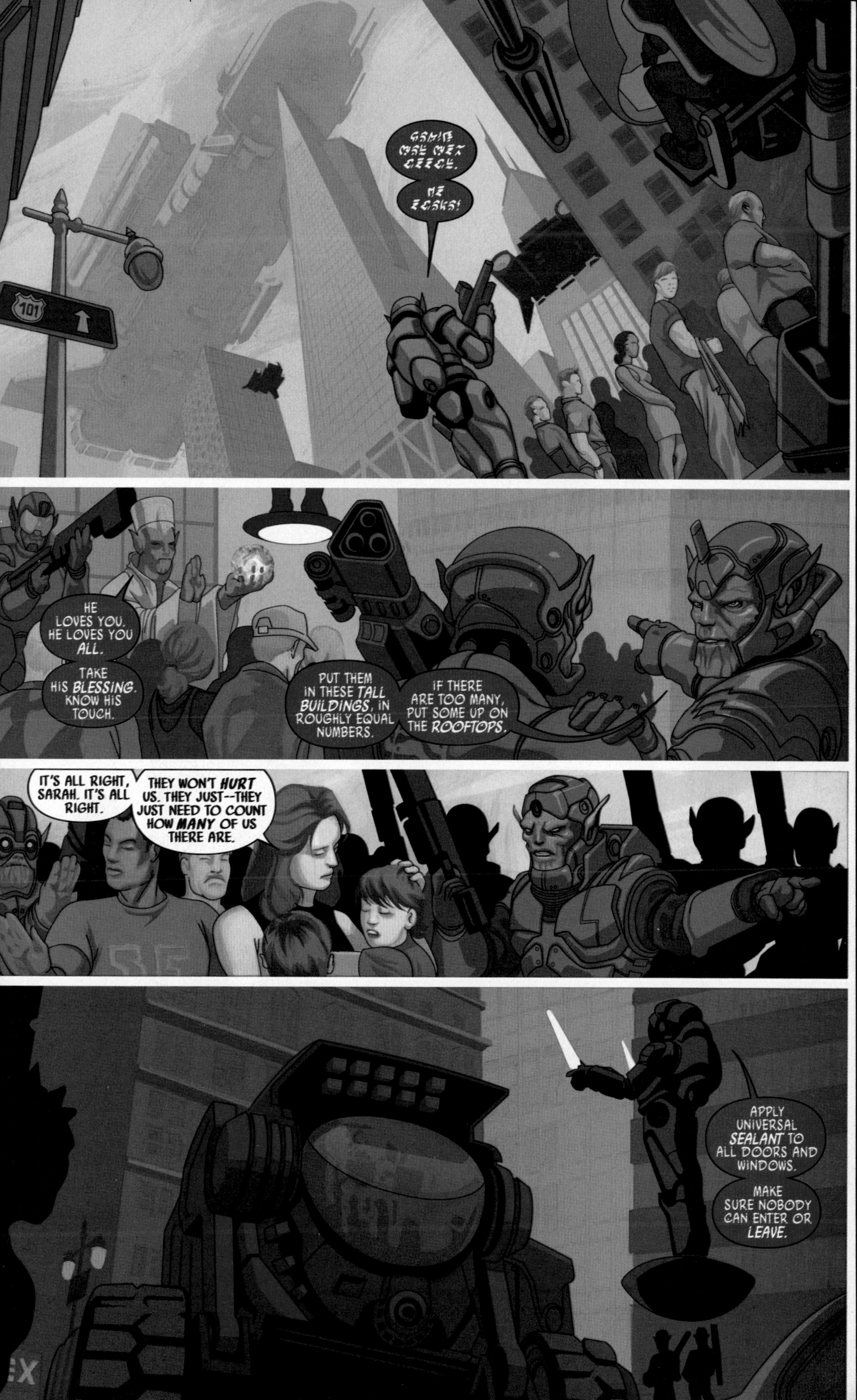
HE LOVES YOU. HE LOVES YOU ALL.
TAKE HIS BLESSING. KNOW HIS TOUCH.
PUT THEM IN THESE TALL BUILDINGS, IN ROUGHLY EQUAL NUMBERS.
IF THERE ARE TOO MANY, PUT SOME UP ON THE ROOFTOPS.
IT'S ALL RIGHT, SARAH. IT'S ALL RIGHT.
THEY WON'T HURT US. THEY JUST--THEY JUST NEED TO COUNT HOW MANY OF US THERE ARE.
APPLY UNIVERSAL SEALANT TO ALL DOORS AND WINDOWS.
MAKE SURE NOBODY CAN ENTER OR LEAVE.

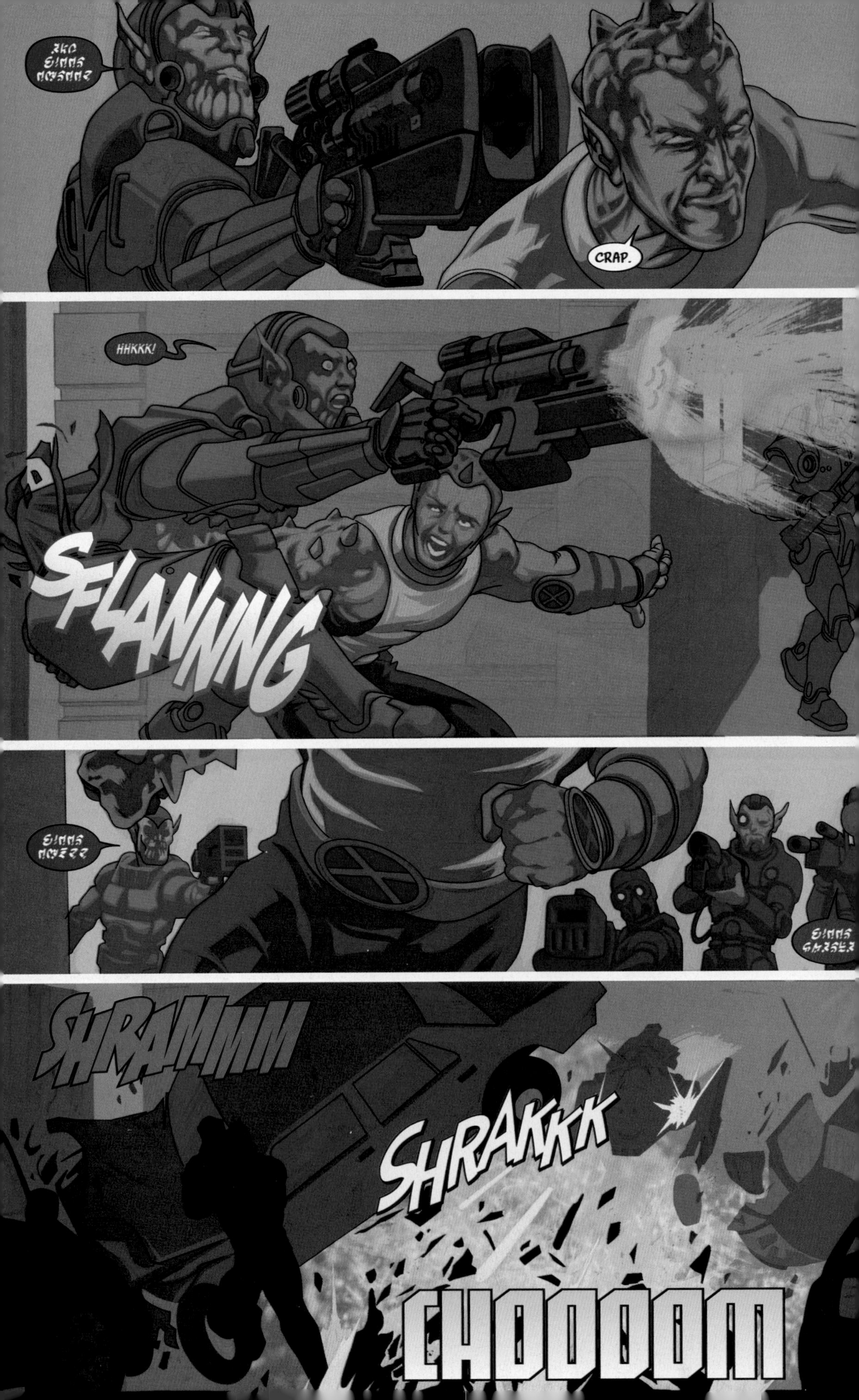
CRAP.
HHKKK!
SFLANNNG
SHRAMMMM
SHRAKKK
CHOOOOM

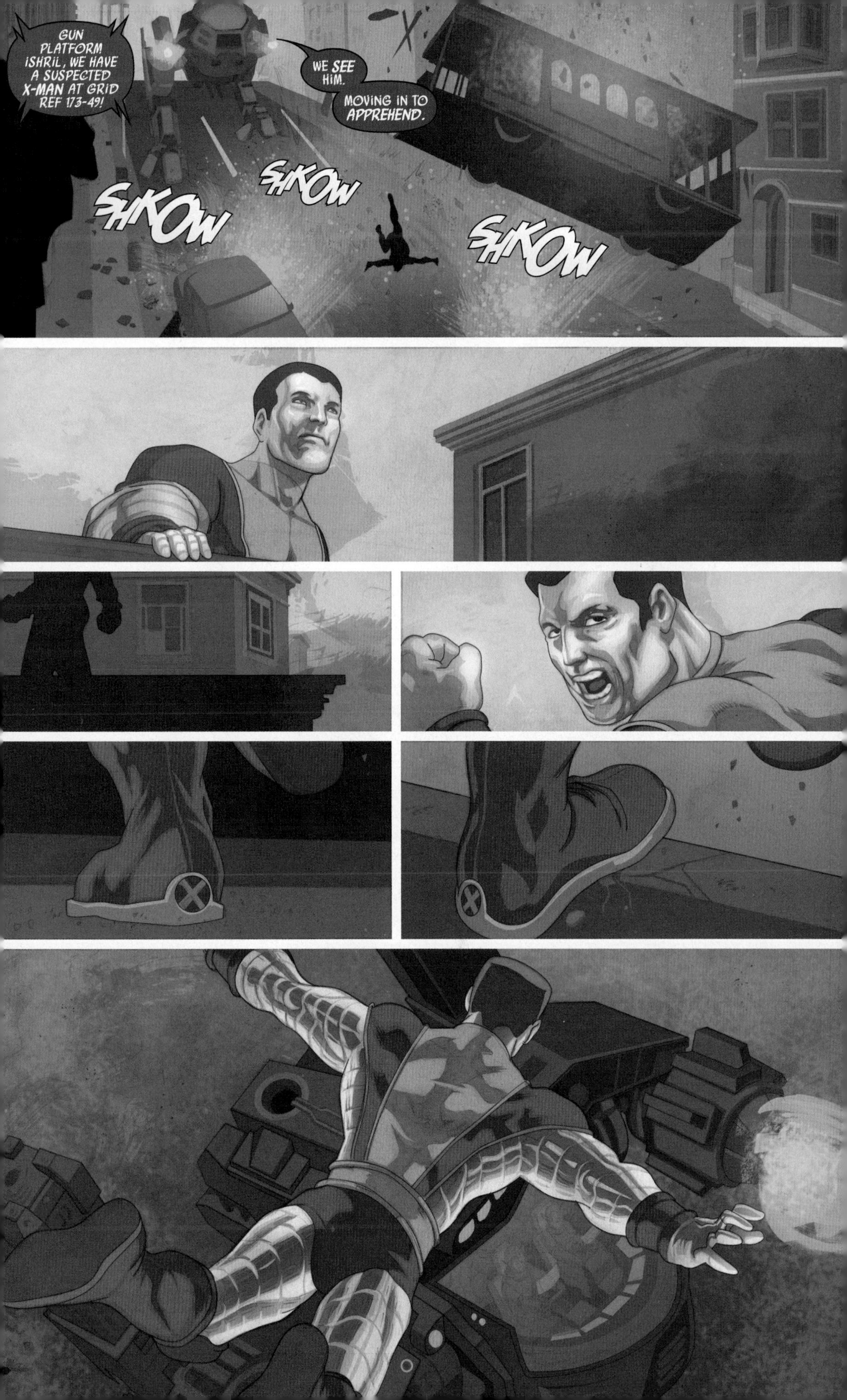
GUN PLATFORM ISHRIL, WE HAVE A SUSPECTED X-MAN AT GRID REF 173-49!
WE SEE HIM.
MOVING IN TO APPREHEND.
SHKOW
SHKOW
SHKOW

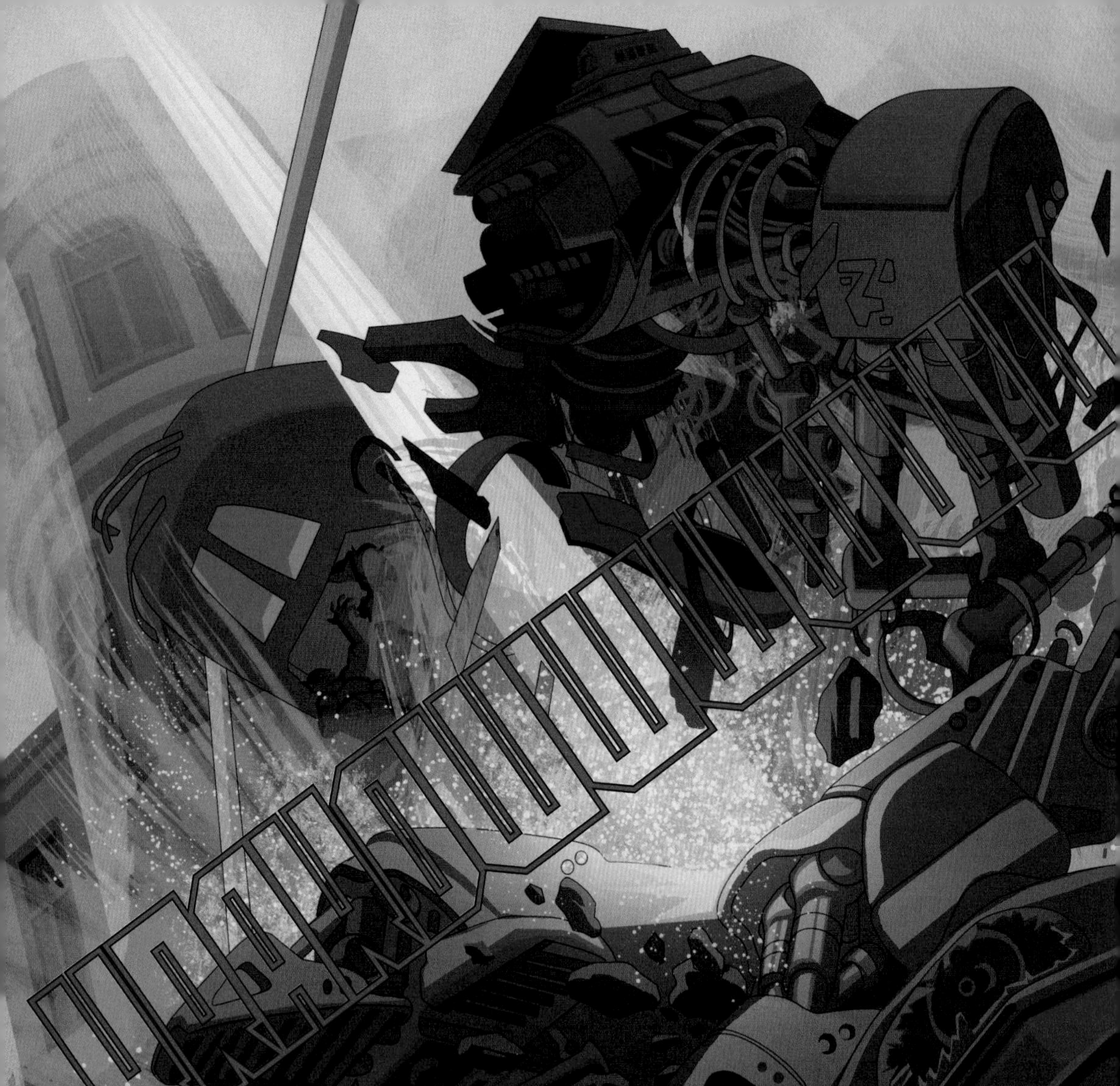

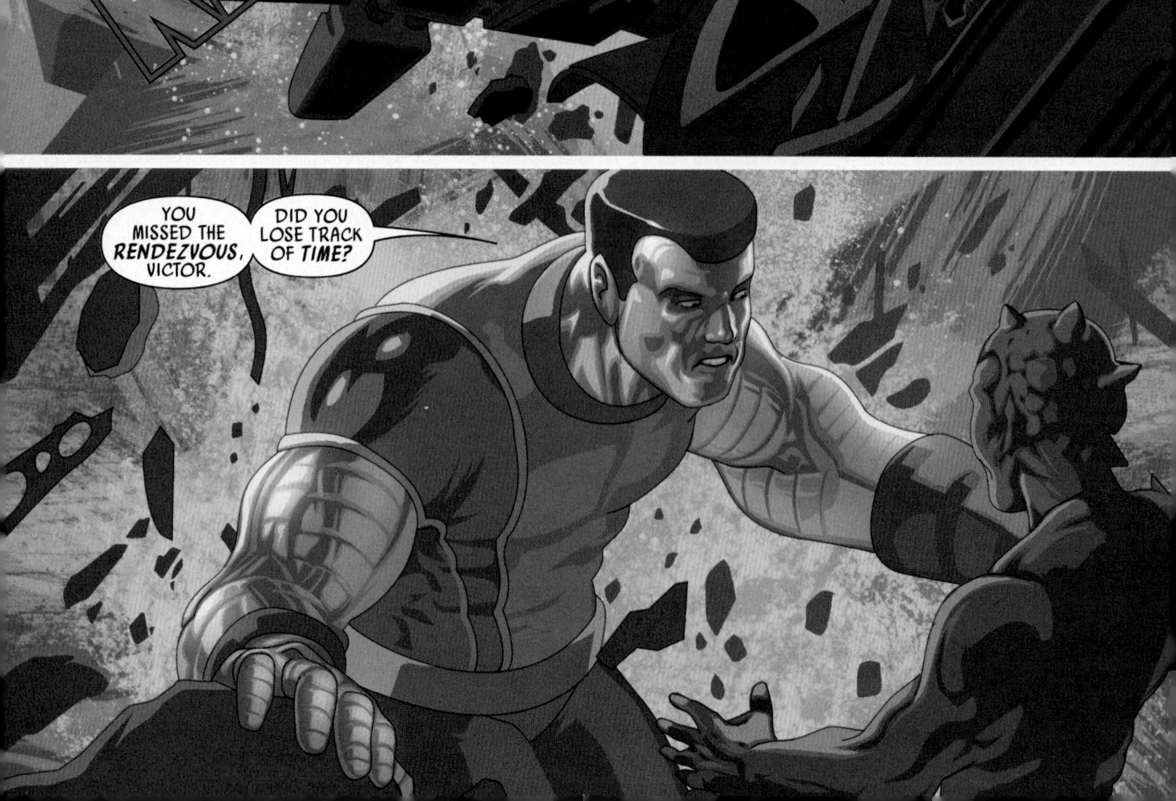
YOU MISSED THE RENDEZVOUS, VICTOR.
DID YOU LOSE TRACK OF TIME?

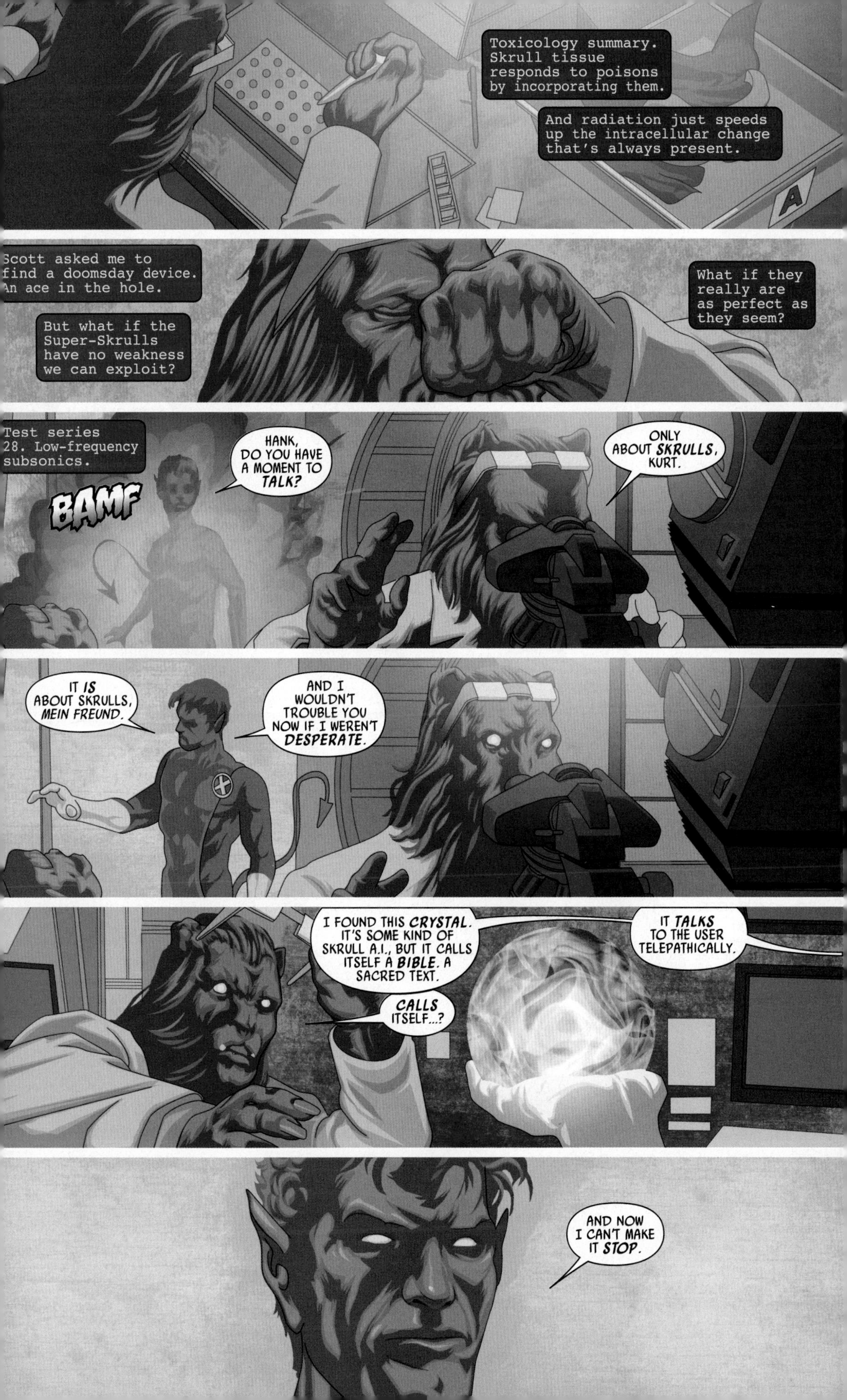
Toxicology summary. Skrull tissue responds to poisons by incorporating them.
And radiation just speeds up the intracellular change that's always present.
Scott asked me to find a doomsday device. An ace in the hole.
But what if the Super-Skrulls have no weakness we can exploit?
What if they really are as perfect as they seem?
Test series 28. Low-frequency subsonics.
BAMF
HANK, DO YOU HAVE A MOMENT TO TALK?
ONLY ABOUT SKRULLS, KURT.
IT IS ABOUT SKRULLS, MEIN FREUND.
AND I WOULDN'T TROUBLE YOU NOW IF I WEREN'T DESPERATE.
I FOUND THIS CRYSTAL. IT'S SOME KIND OF SKRULL A.I., BUT IT CALLS ITSELF A BIBLE. A SACRED TEXT.
CALLS ITSELF...?
IT TALKS TO THE USER TELEPATHICALLY.
AND NOW I CAN'T MAKE IT STOP.

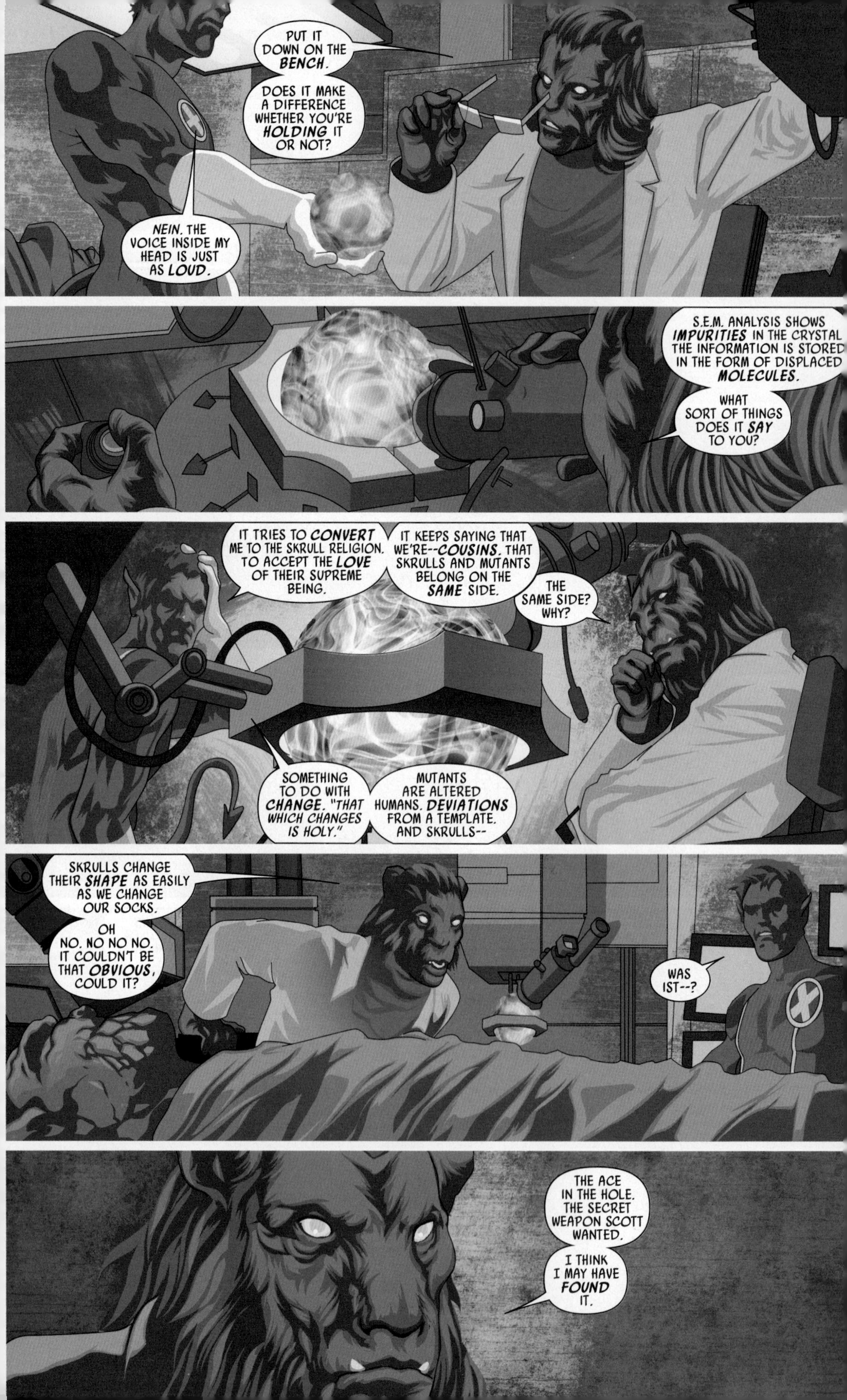
PUT IT DOWN ON THE BENCH.
DOES IT MAKE A DIFFERENCE WHETHER YOU'RE HOLDING IT OR NOT?
NEIN. THE VOICE INSIDE MY HEAD IS JUST AS LOUD.
S.E.M. ANALYSIS SHOWS IMPURITIES IN THE CRYSTAL. THE INFORMATION IS STORED IN THE FORM OF DISPLACED MOLECULES.
WHAT SORT OF THINGS DOES IT SAY TO YOU?
IT TRIES TO CONVERT ME TO THE SKRULL RELIGION. TO ACCEPT THE LOVE OF THEIR SUPREME BEING.
IT KEEPS SAYING THAT WE'RE--COUSINS. THAT SKRULLS AND MUTANTS BELONG ON THE SAME SIDE.
THE SAME SIDE? WHY?
SOMETHING TO DO WITH CHANGE. "THAT WHICH CHANGES IS HOLY."
MUTANTS ARE ALTERED HUMANS. DEVIATIONS FROM A TEMPLATE. AND SKRULLS--
SKRULLS CHANGE THEIR SHAPE AS EASILY AS WE CHANGE OUR SOCKS.
OH NO. NO NO NO. IT COULDN'T BE THAT OBVIOUS, COULD IT?
WAS IST--?
THE ACE IN THE HOLE. THE SECRET WEAPON SCOTT WANTED.
I THINK I MAY HAVE FOUND IT.

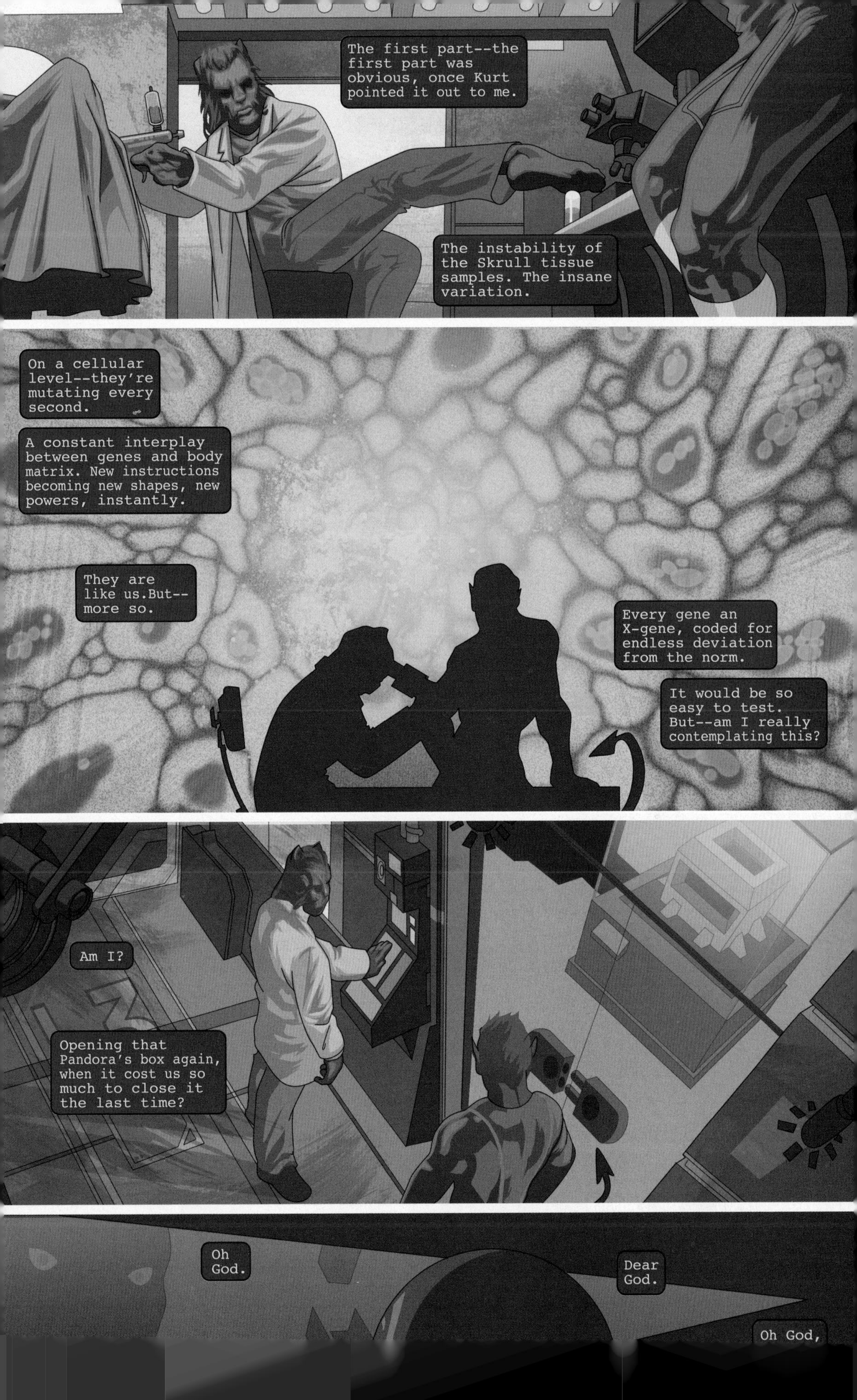
The first part--the first part was obvious, once Kurt pointed it out to me.
The instability of the Skrull tissue samples. The insane variation.
On a cellular level--they're mutating every second.
A constant interplay between genes and body matrix. New instructions becoming new shapes, new powers, instantly.
They are like us.But--more so.
Every gene an X-gene, coded for endless deviation from the norm.
It would be so easy to test. But--am I really contemplating this?
Am I?
Opening that Pandora's box again, when it cost us so much to close it the last time?
Oh God.
Dear God.
Oh God,

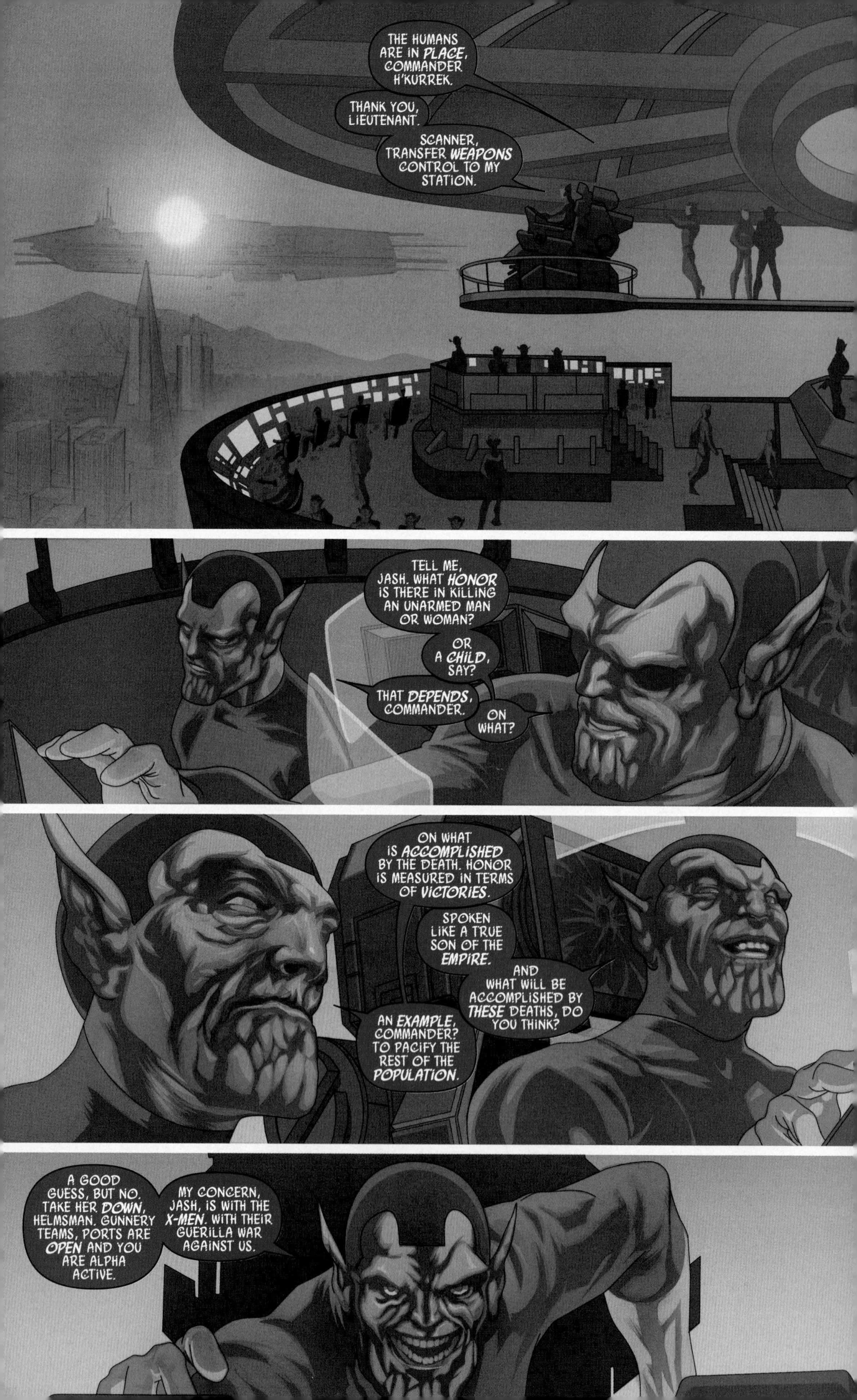
THE HUMANS ARE IN PLACE, COMMANDER H'KURREK.
THANK YOU, LIEUTENANT.
SCANNER, TRANSFER WEAPONS CONTROL TO MY STATION.
TELL ME, JASH. WHAT HONOR IS THERE IN KILLING AN UNARMED MAN OR WOMAN?
OR A CHILD, SAY?
THAT DEPENDS, COMMANDER.
ON WHAT?
ON WHAT IS ACCOMPLISHED BY THE DEATH. HONOR IS MEASURED IN TERMS OF VICTORIES.
SPOKEN LIKE A TRUE SON OF THE EMPIRE.
AND WHAT WILL BE ACCOMPLISHED BY THESE DEATHS, DO YOU THINK?
AN EXAMPLE, COMMANDER? TO PACIFY THE REST OF THE POPULATION.
A GOOD GUESS, BUT NO. TAKE HER DOWN, HELMSMAN. GUNNERY TEAMS, PORTS ARE OPEN AND YOU ARE ALPHA ACTIVE.
MY CONCERN, JASH, IS WITH THE X-MEN. WITH THEIR GUERILLA WAR AGAINST US.

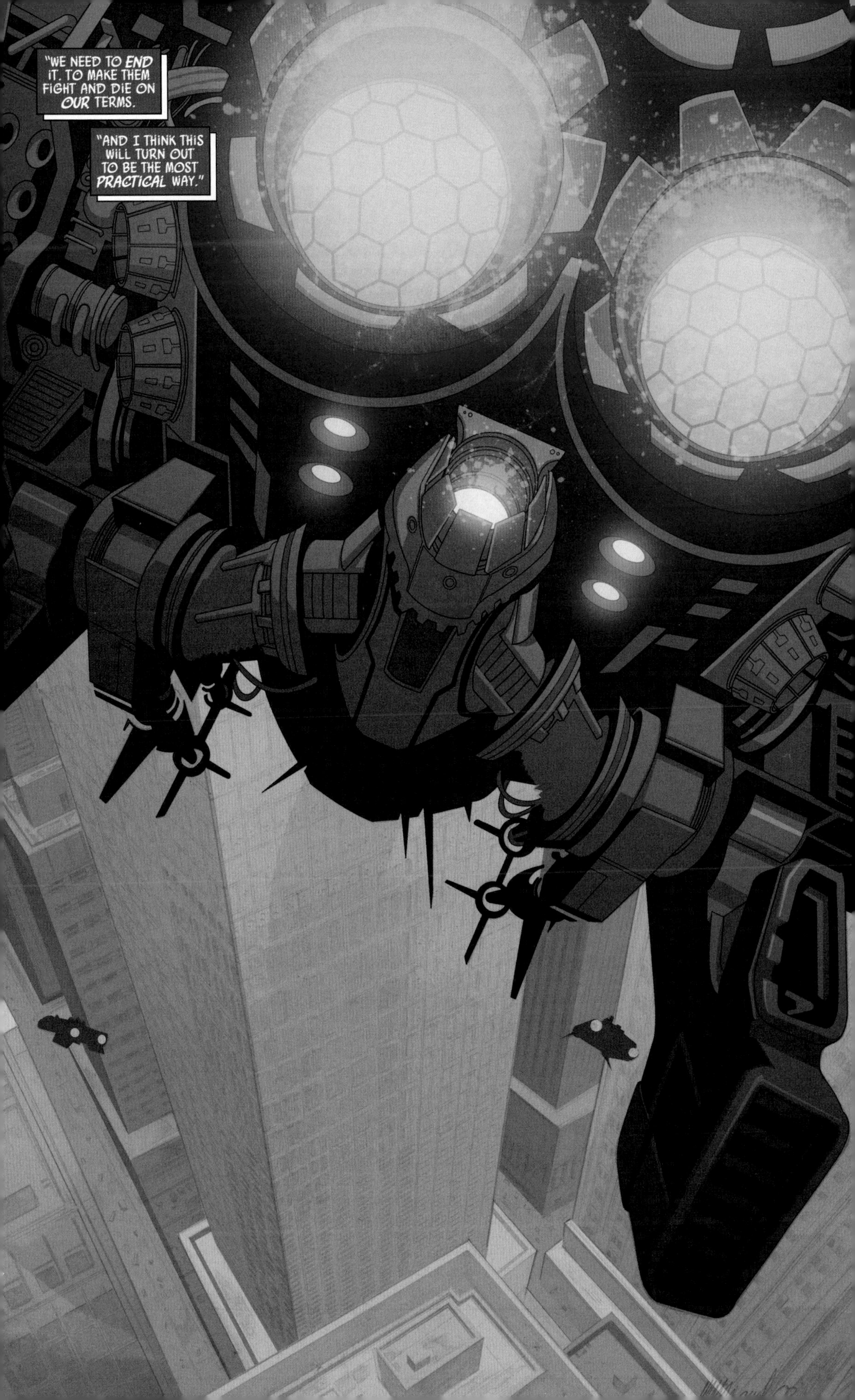
"WE NEED TO END IT. TO MAKE THEM FIGHT AND DIE ON OUR TERMS.
"AND I THINK THIS WILL TURN OUT TO BE THE MOST PRACTICAL WAY."

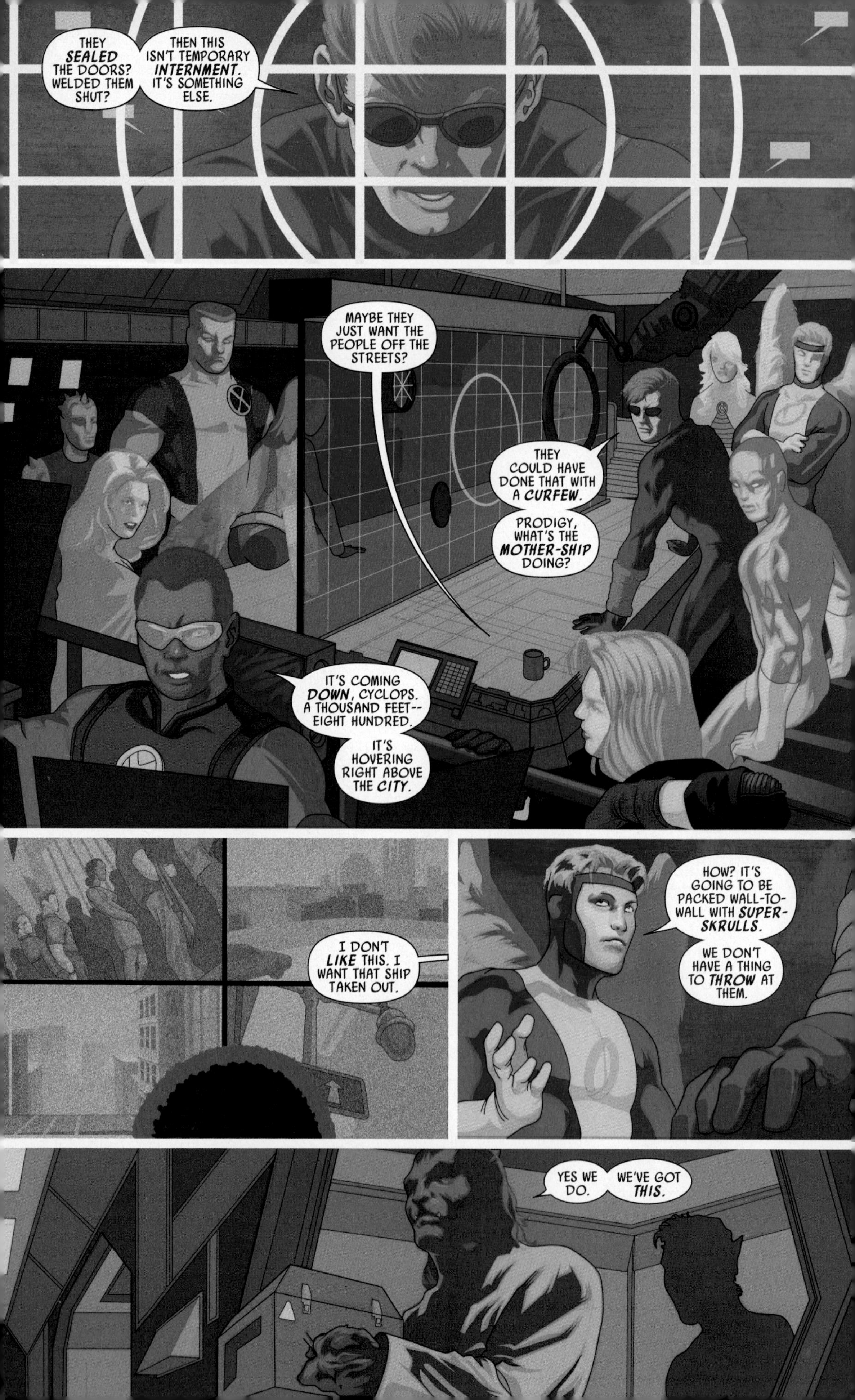
THEY SEALED THE DOORS? WELDED THEM SHUT?
THEN THIS ISN'T TEMPORARY INTERNMENT. IT'S SOMETHING ELSE.
MAYBE THEY JUST WANT THE PEOPLE OFF THE STREETS?
THEY COULD HAVE DONE THAT WITH A CURFEW.
PRODIGY, WHAT'S THE MOTHER-SHIP DOING?
IT'S COMING DOWN, CYCLOPS. A THOUSAND FEET-- EIGHT HUNDRED.
IT'S HOVERING RIGHT ABOVE THE CITY.
I DON'T LIKE THIS. I WANT THAT SHIP TAKEN OUT.
HOW? IT'S GOING TO BE PACKED WALL-TO-WALL WITH SUPER-SKRULLS.
WE DON'T HAVE A THING TO THROW AT THEM.
YES WE DO.
WE'VE GOT THIS.

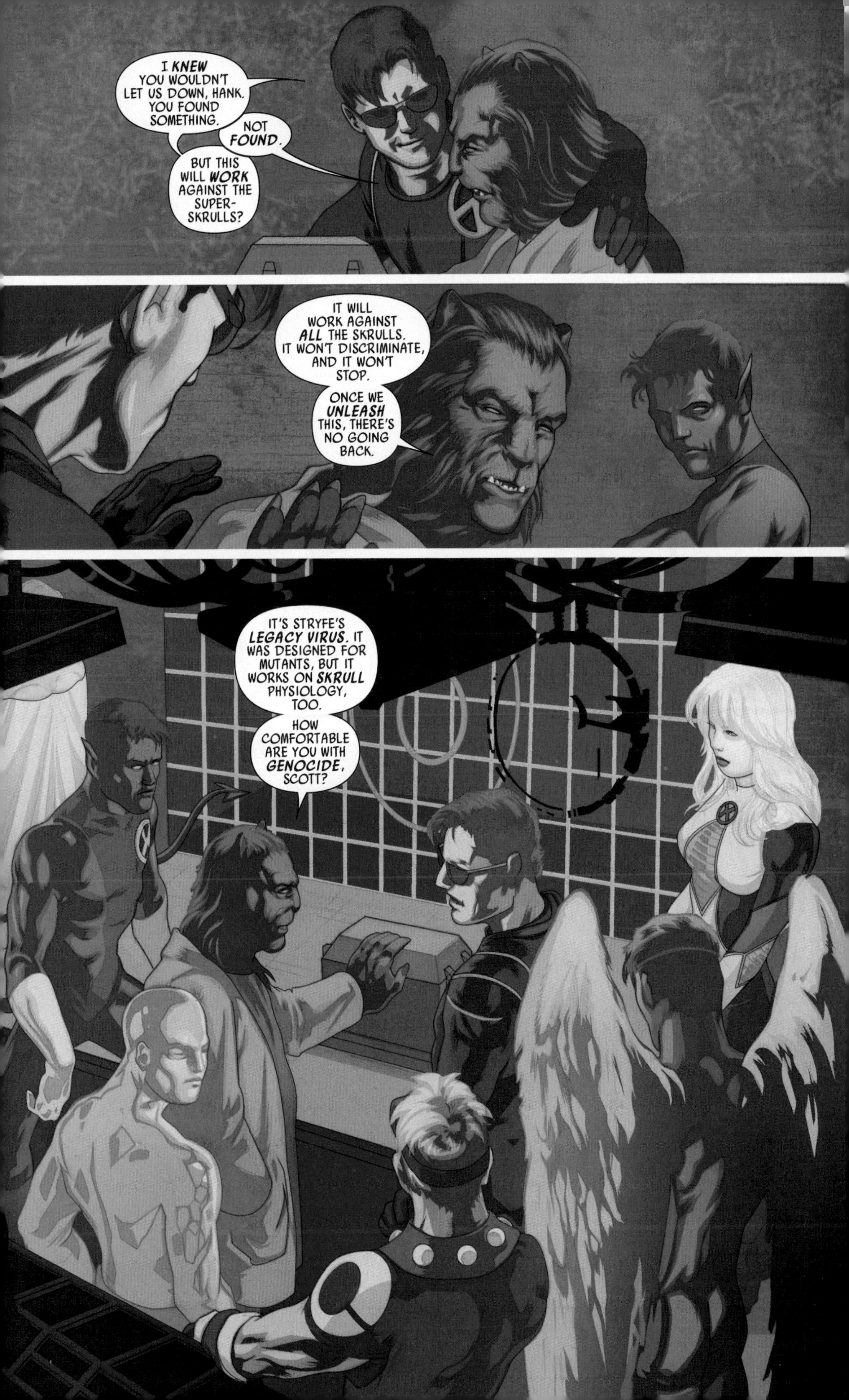
I KNEW YOU WOULDN'T LET US DOWN, HANK. YOU FOUND SOMETHING.
NOT FOUND.
BUT THIS WILL WORK AGAINST THE SUPER-SKRULLS?
IT WILL WORK AGAINST ALL THE SKRULLS. IT WON'T DISCRIMINATE, AND IT WON'T STOP.
ONCE WE UNLEASH THIS, THERE'S NO GOING BACK.
IT'S STRYFE'S LEGACY VIRUS. IT WAS DESIGNED FOR MUTANTS, BUT IT WORKS ON SKRULL PHYSIOLOGY, TOO.
HOW COMFORTABLE ARE YOU WITH GENOCIDE, SCOTT?

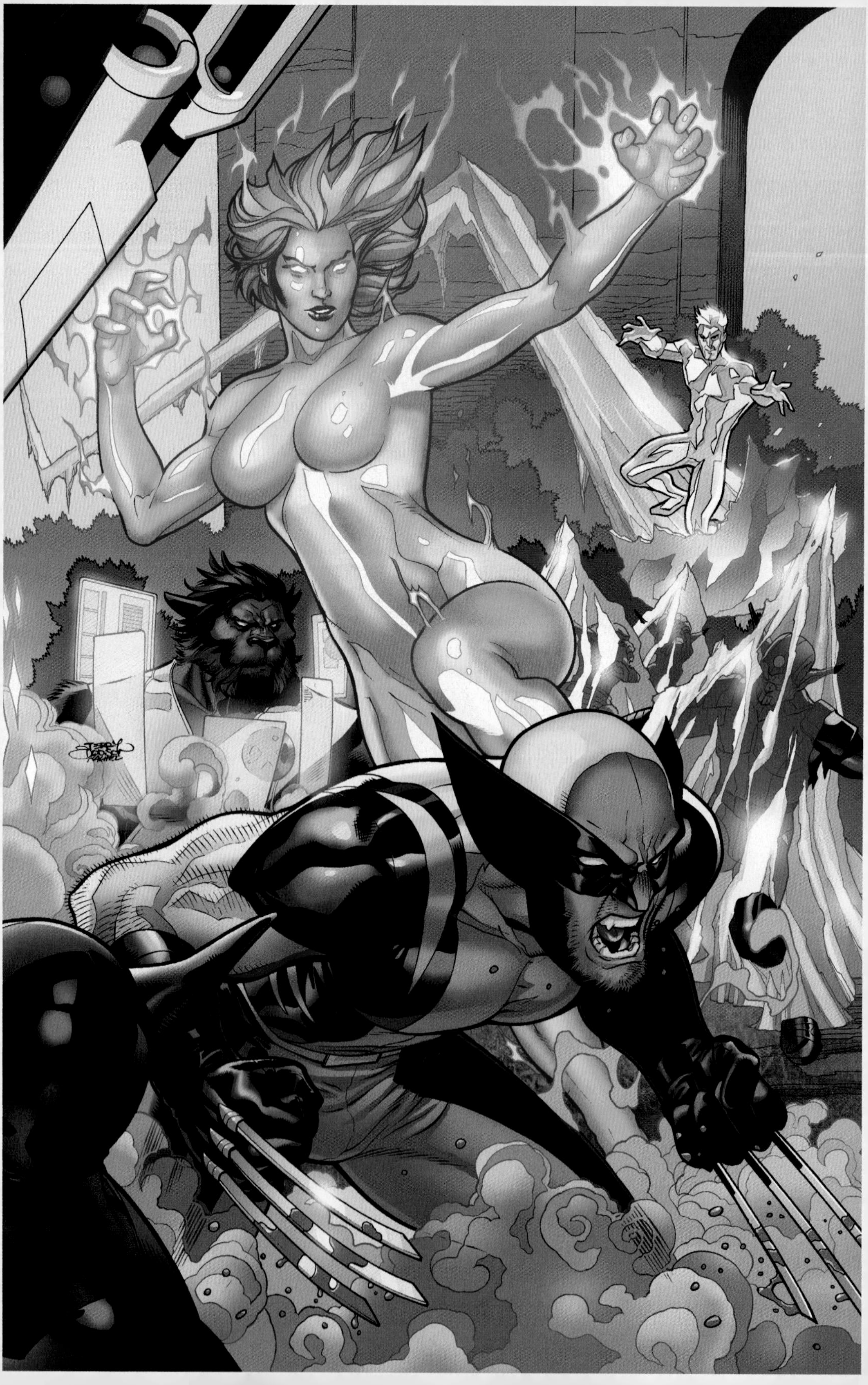

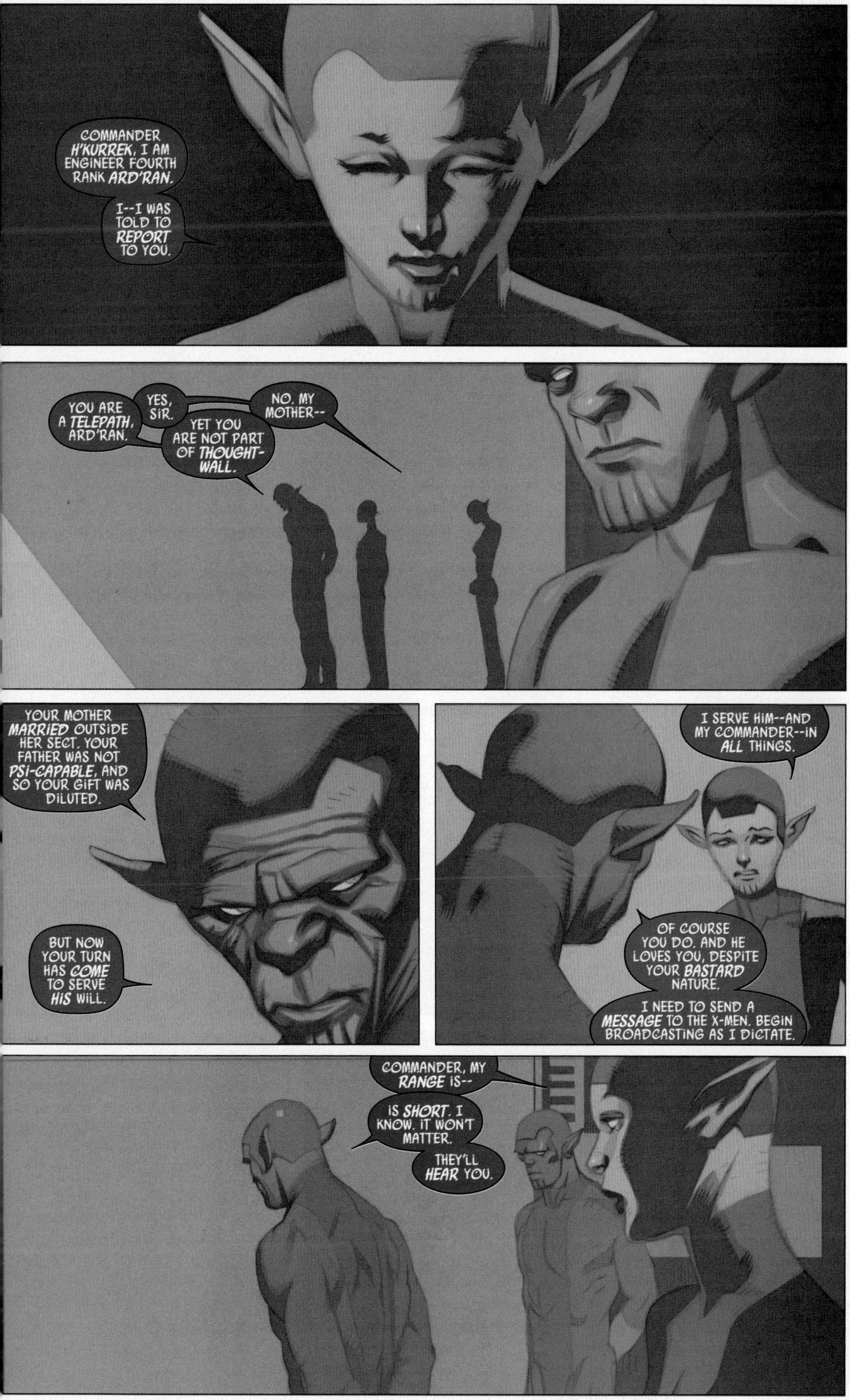
COMMANDER H'KURREK, I AM ENGINEER FOURTH RANK ARD'RAN.
I--I WAS TOLD TO REPORT TO YOU.
YOU ARE A TELEPATH, ARD'RAN.
YES, SIR.
YET YOU ARE NOT PART OF THOUGHT-WALL.
NO. MY MOTHER--
YOUR MOTHER MARRIED OUTSIDE HER SECT. YOUR FATHER WAS NOT PSI-CAPABLE, AND SO YOUR GIFT WAS DILUTED.
BUT NOW YOUR TURN HAS COME TO SERVE HIS WILL.
I SERVE HIM--AND MY COMMANDER--IN ALL THINGS.
OF COURSE YOU DO. AND HE LOVES YOU, DESPITE YOUR BASTARD NATURE.
I NEED TO SEND A MESSAGE TO THE X-MEN. BEGIN BROADCASTING AS I DICTATE.
COMMANDER, MY RANGE IS--
IS SHORT. I KNOW. IT WON'T MATTER.
THEY'LL HEAR YOU.

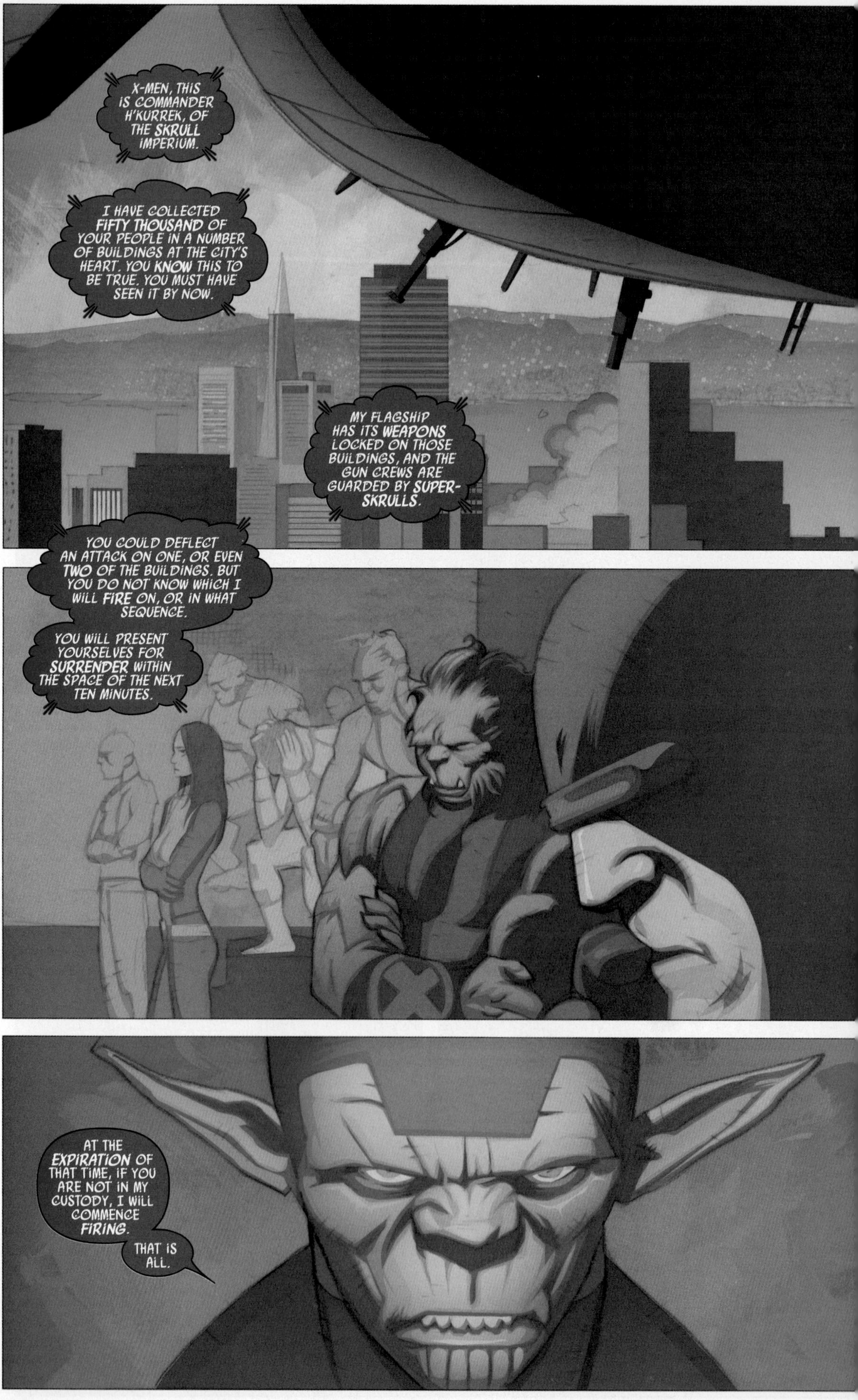
X-MEN, THIS IS COMMANDER H'KURREK, OF THE SKRULL IMPERIUM.
I HAVE COLLECTED FIFTY THOUSAND OF YOUR PEOPLE IN A NUMBER OF BUILDINGS AT THE CITY'S HEART. YOU KNOW THIS TO BE TRUE. YOU MUST HAVE SEEN IT BY NOW.
MY FLAGSHIP HAS ITS WEAPONS LOCKED ON THOSE BUILDINGS, AND THE GUN CREWS ARE GUARDED BY SUPER-SKRULLS.
YOU COULD DEFLECT AN ATTACK ON ONE, OR EVEN TWO OF THE BUILDINGS. BUT YOU DO NOT KNOW WHICH I WILL FIRE ON, OR IN WHAT SEQUENCE.
YOU WILL PRESENT YOURSELVES FOR SURRENDER WITHIN THE SPACE OF THE NEXT TEN MINUTES.
AT THE EXPIRATION OF THAT TIME, IF YOU ARE NOT IN MY CUSTODY, I WILL COMMENCE FIRING.
THAT IS ALL.

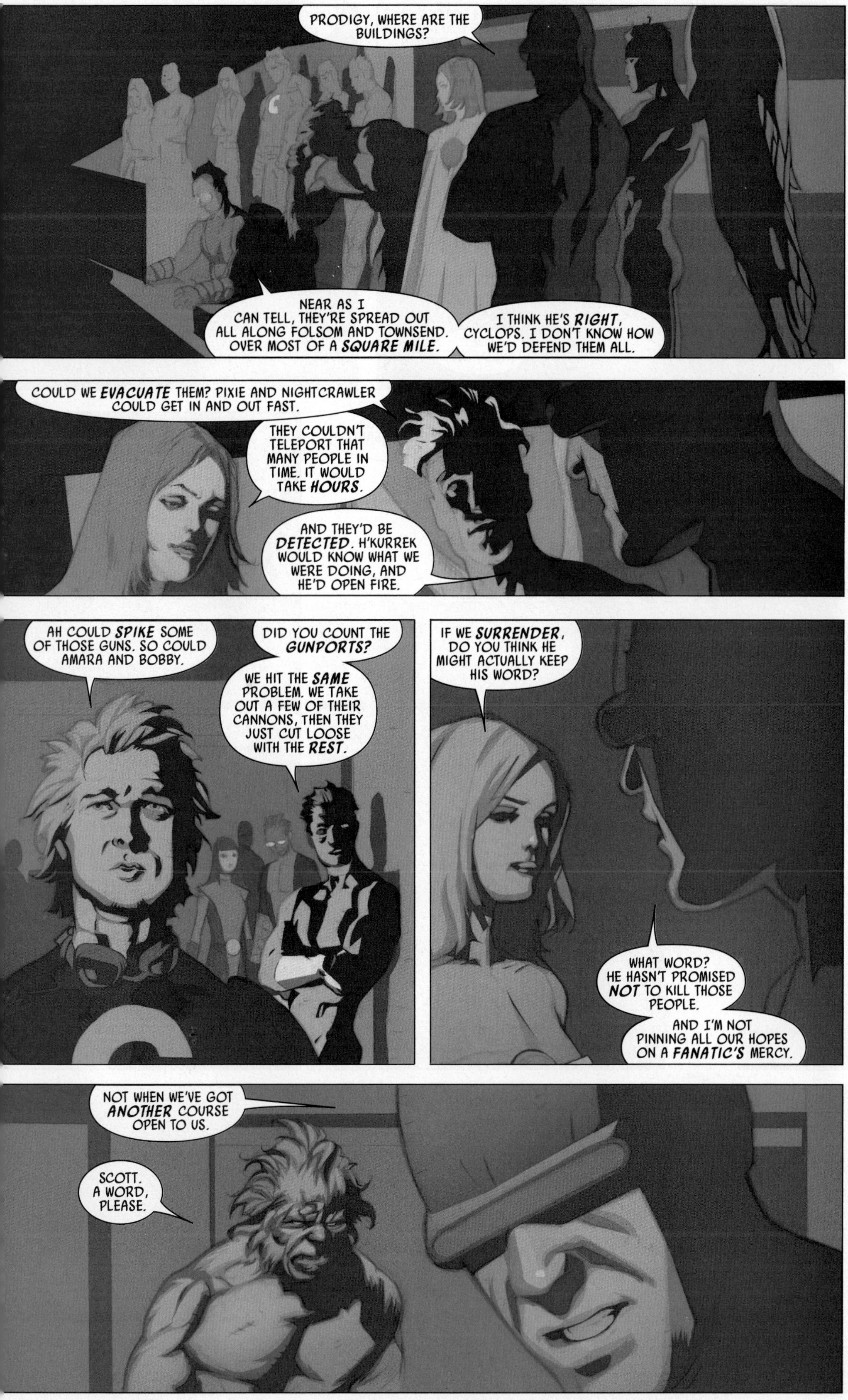
PRODIGY, WHERE ARE THE BUILDINGS?
NEAR AS I CAN TELL, THEY'RE SPREAD OUT ALL ALONG FOLSOM AND TOWNSEND. OVER MOST OF A SQUARE MILE.
I THINK HE'S RIGHT, CYCLOPS. I DON'T KNOW HOW WE'D DEFEND THEM ALL.
COULD WE EVACUATE THEM? PIXIE AND NIGHTCRAWLER COULD GET IN AND OUT FAST.
THEY COULDN'T TELEPORT THAT MANY PEOPLE IN TIME. IT WOULD TAKE HOURS.
AND THEY'D BE DETECTED. H'KURREK WOULD KNOW WHAT WE WERE DOING, AND HE'D OPEN FIRE.
AH COULD SPIKE SOME OF THOSE GUNS. SO COULD AMARA AND BOBBY.
DID YOU COUNT THE GUNPORTS?
WE HIT THE SAME PROBLEM. WE TAKE OUT A FEW OF THEIR CANNONS, THEN THEY JUST CUT LOOSE WITH THE REST.
IF WE SURRENDER, DO YOU THINK HE MIGHT ACTUALLY KEEP HIS WORD?
WHAT WORD? HE HASN'T PROMISED NOT TO KILL THOSE PEOPLE.
AND I'M NOT PINNING ALL OUR HOPES ON A FANATIC'S MERCY.
NOT WHEN WE'VE GOT ANOTHER COURSE OPEN TO US.
SCOTT. A WORD, PLEASE.

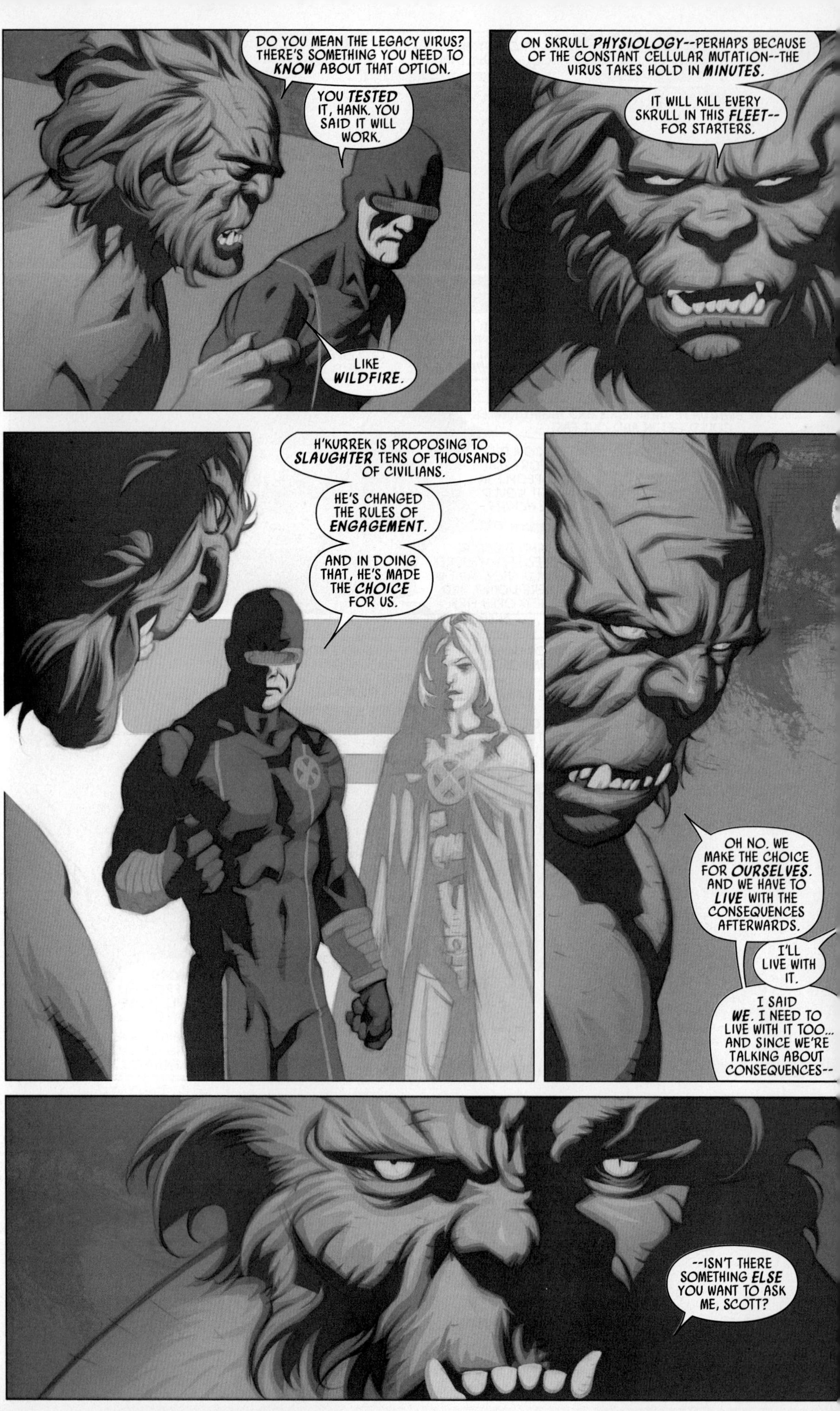
DO YOU MEAN THE LEGACY VIRUS? THERE'S SOMETHING YOU NEED TO KNOW ABOUT THAT OPTION.
YOU TESTED IT, HANK. YOU SAID IT WILL WORK.
LIKE WILDFIRE.
ON SKRULL PHYSIOLOGY--PERHAPS BECAUSE OF THE CONSTANT CELLULAR MUTATION--THE VIRUS TAKES HOLD IN MINUTES.
IT WILL KILL EVERY SKRULL IN THIS FLEET--FOR STARTERS.
H'KURREK IS PROPOSING TO SLAUGHTER TENS OF THOUSANDS OF CIVILIANS.
HE'S CHANGED THE RULES OF ENGAGEMENT.
AND IN DOING THAT, HE'S MADE THE CHOICE FOR US.
OH NO. WE MAKE THE CHOICE FOR OURSELVES. AND WE HAVE TO LIVE WITH THE CONSEQUENCES AFTERWARDS.
I'LL LIVE WITH IT.
I SAID WE. I NEED TO LIVE WITH IT TOO... AND SINCE WE'RE TALKING ABOUT CONSEQUENCES--
--ISN'T THERE SOMETHING ELSE YOU WANT TO ASK ME, SCOTT?

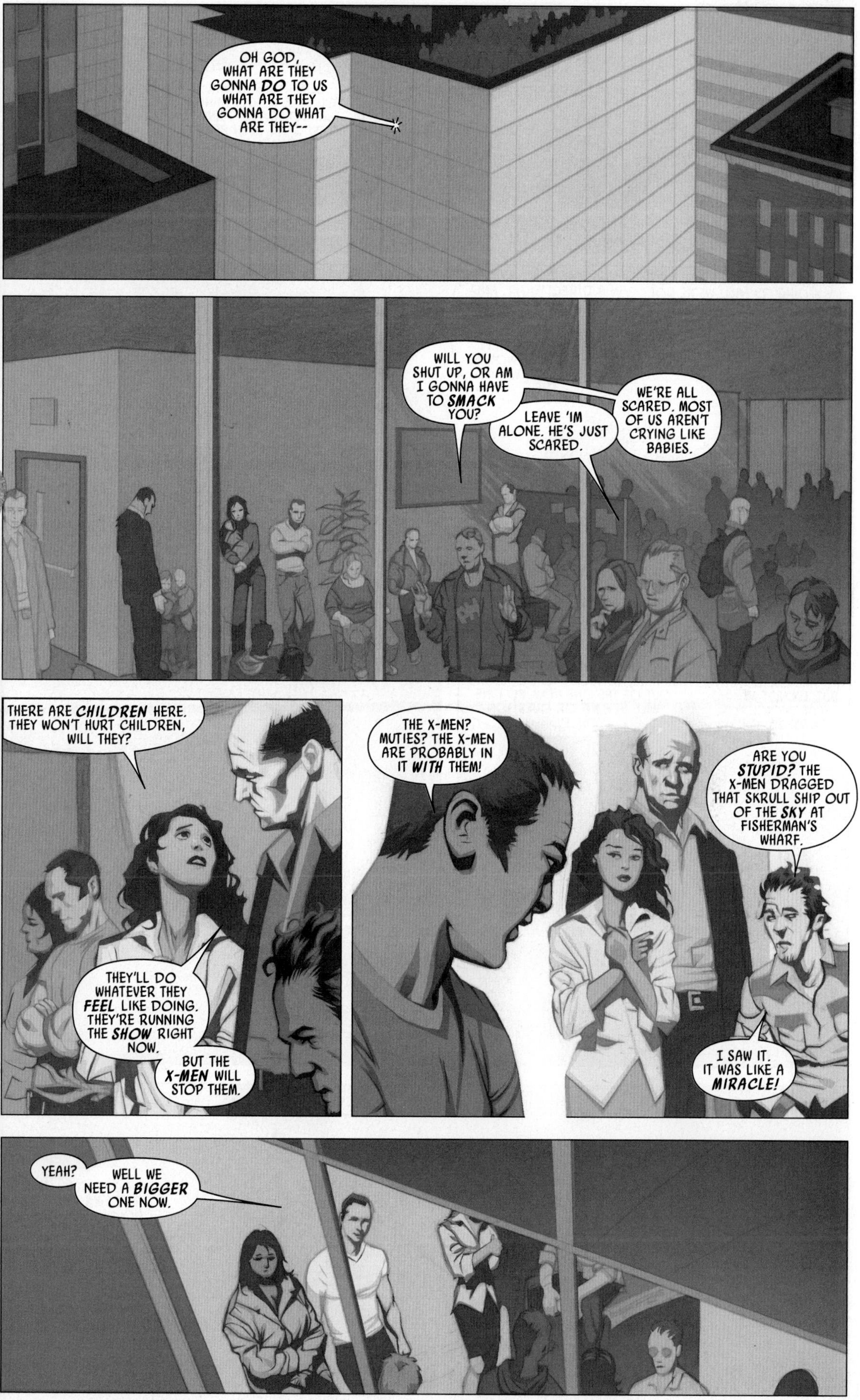
OH GOD, WHAT ARE THEY GONNA DO TO US WHAT ARE THEY GONNA DO WHAT ARE THEY--
WILL YOU SHUT UP, OR AM I GONNA HAVE TO SMACK YOU?
LEAVE 'IM ALONE. HE'S JUST SCARED.
WE'RE ALL SCARED. MOST OF US AREN'T CRYING LIKE BABIES.
THERE ARE CHILDREN HERE. THEY WON'T HURT CHILDREN, WILL THEY?
THEY'LL DO WHATEVER THEY FEEL LIKE DOING. THEY'RE RUNNING THE SHOW RIGHT NOW.
BUT THE X-MEN WILL STOP THEM.
THE X-MEN? MUTIES? THE X-MEN ARE PROBABLY IN IT WITH THEM!
ARE YOU STUPID? THE X-MEN DRAGGED THAT SKRULL SHIP OUT OF THE SKY AT FISHERMAN'S WHARF.
I SAW IT. IT WAS LIKE A MIRACLE!
YEAH?
WELL WE NEED A BIGGER ONE NOW.

SOMETIMES IN WAR YOU HAVE TO DO THINGS THAT YOU *HATE*. THINGS YOU CAN'T EVEN BEAR TO *THINK* ABOUT.

THIS IS ONE OF THOSE TIMES.

THOSE BUILDINGS ARE *NOT* GOING TO FALL. WE'RE NOT GOING TO LET THEM.

BUT WE CAN'T *WIN* IN A DIRECT FIGHT. AND EVEN IF WE COULD, THE SKRULL GUNS WOULD STILL FIRE BEFORE WE COULD *DISABLE* THEM. FIFTY THOUSAND MEN, WOMEN AND CHILDREN WOULD DIE.

SO THE WAY I SEE IT, IT'S THIS OR *NOTHING*. BUT I'M NOT MAKING THAT CHOICE FOR *ANY* OF YOU.

IF YOU HAVE ANY *DOUBTS* ABOUT WHAT WE'RE ABOUT TO DO, STAND OUT OF THE LINE NOW. NO ONE WILL *BLAME* OR QUESTION YOU. EVER.

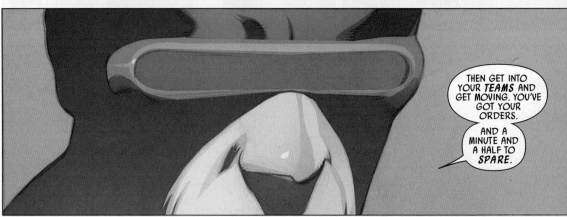

THEN GET INTO YOUR *TEAMS* AND GET MOVING. YOU'VE GOT YOUR ORDERS.

AND A MINUTE AND A HALF TO *SPARE*.

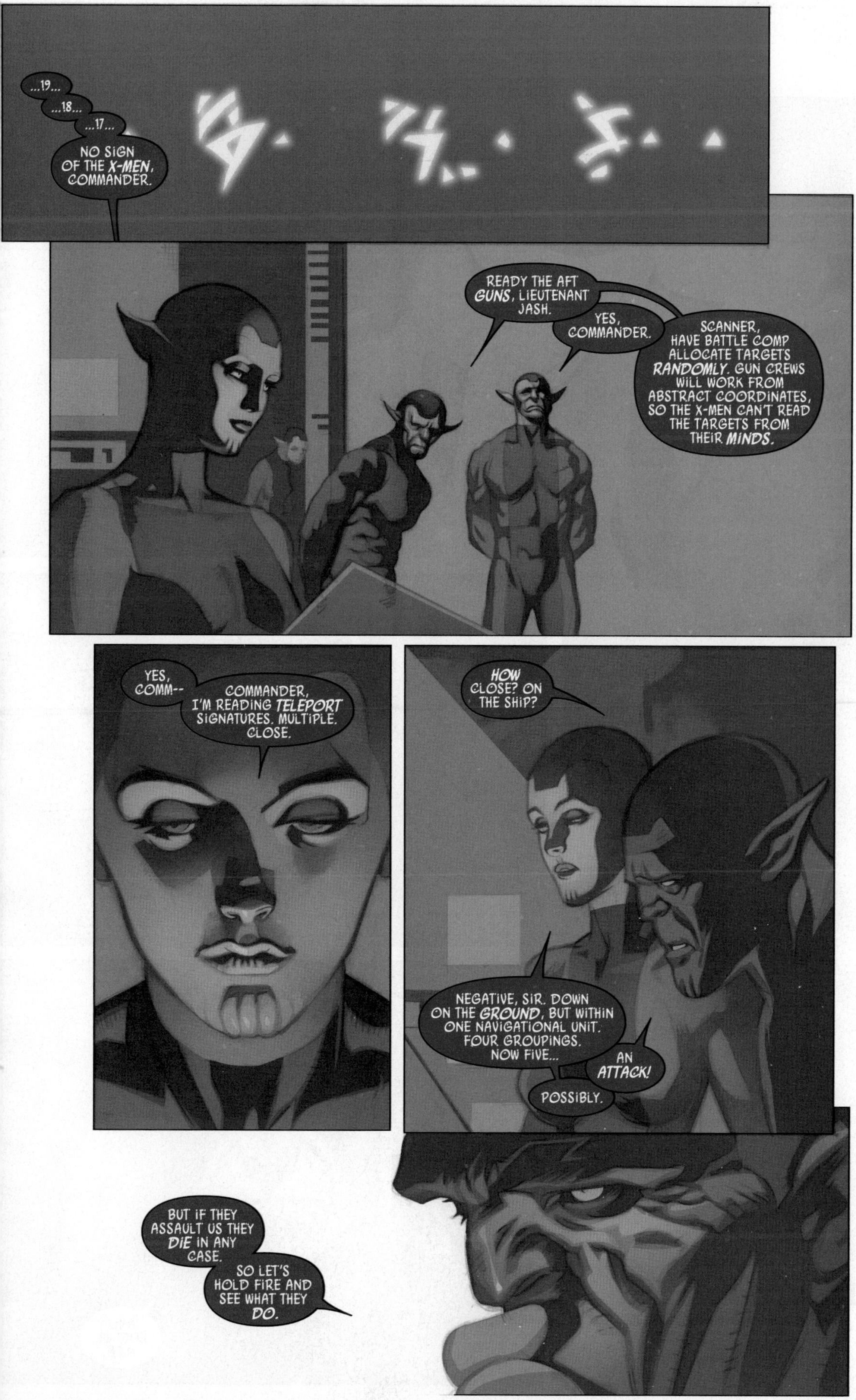
...19...
...18...
...17...
NO SIGN OF THE X-MEN, COMMANDER.
READY THE AFT GUNS, LIEUTENANT JASH.
YES, COMMANDER.
SCANNER, HAVE BATTLE COMP ALLOCATE TARGETS RANDOMLY. GUN CREWS WILL WORK FROM ABSTRACT COORDINATES, SO THE X-MEN CAN'T READ THE TARGETS FROM THEIR MINDS.
YES, COMM--
COMMANDER, I'M READING TELEPORT SIGNATURES. MULTIPLE. CLOSE.
HOW CLOSE? ON THE SHIP?
NEGATIVE, SIR. DOWN ON THE GROUND, BUT WITHIN ONE NAVIGATIONAL UNIT. FOUR GROUPINGS. NOW FIVE...
AN ATTACK!
POSSIBLY.
BUT IF THEY ASSAULT US THEY DIE IN ANY CASE.
SO LET'S HOLD FIRE AND SEE WHAT THEY DO.

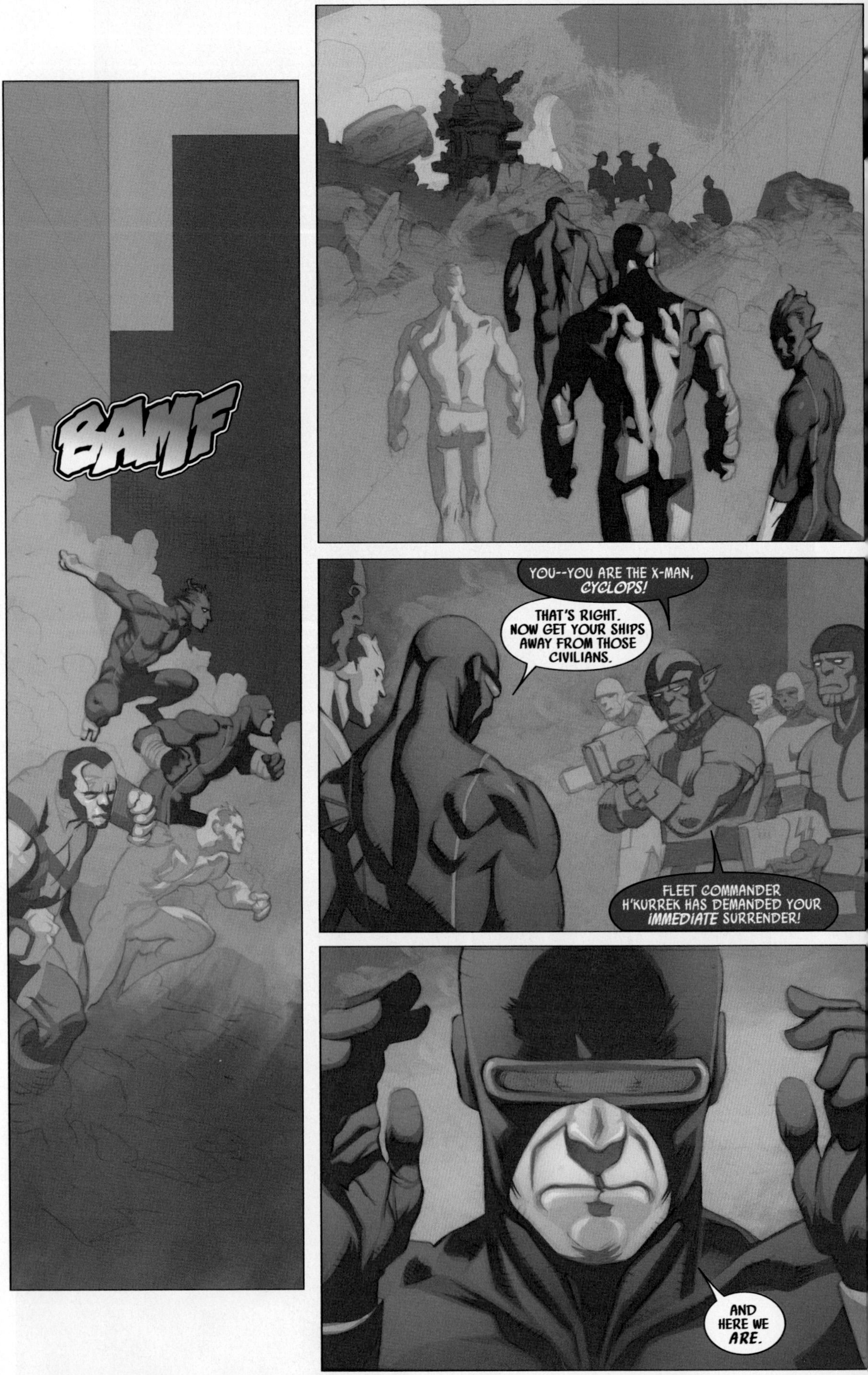
BAMF
YOU--YOU ARE THE X-MAN, *CYCLOPS!*
THAT'S RIGHT. NOW GET YOUR SHIPS AWAY FROM THOSE CIVILIANS.
FLEET COMMANDER H'KURREK HAS DEMANDED YOUR *IMMEDIATE* SURRENDER!
AND HERE WE *ARE.*

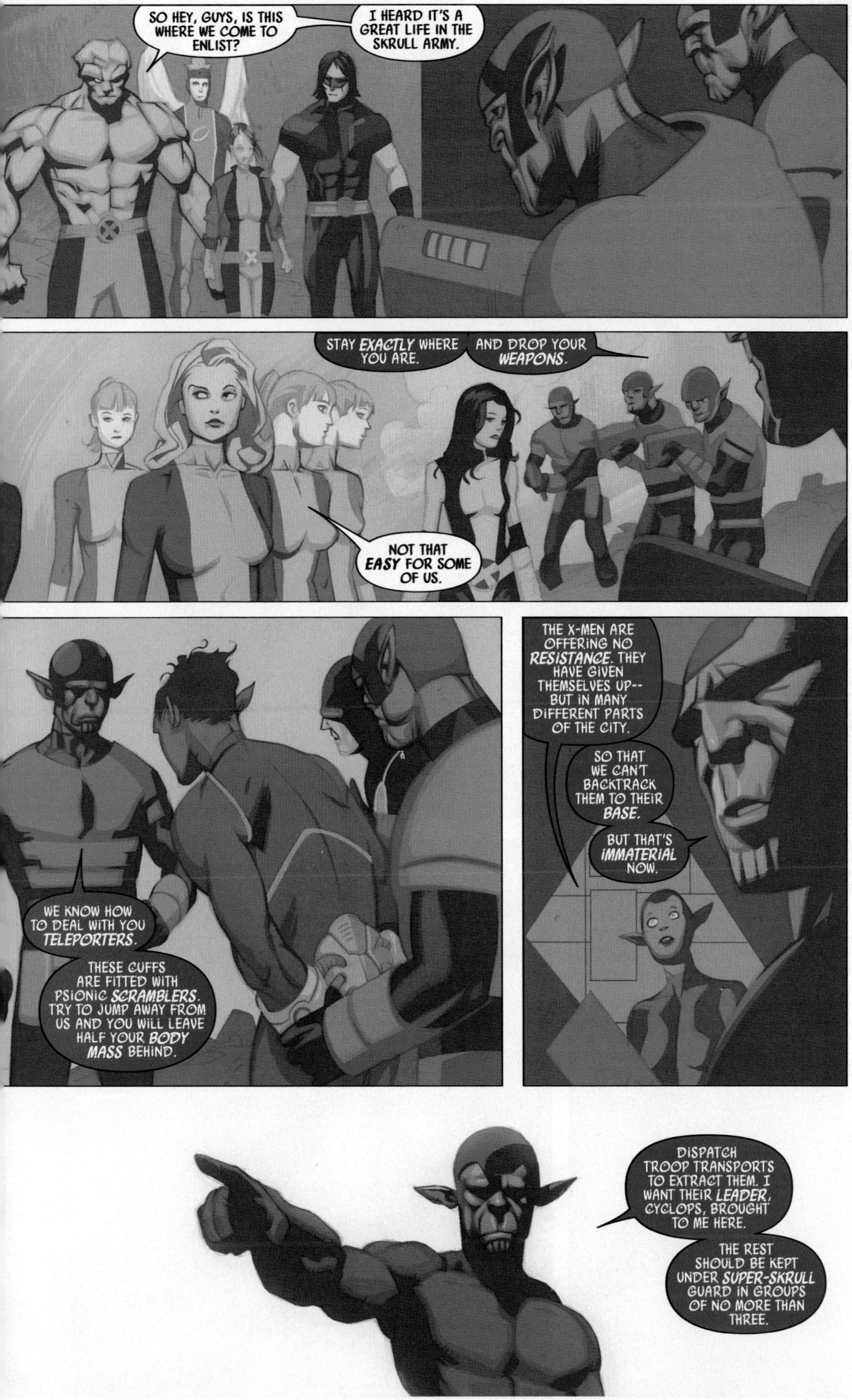
SO HEY, GUYS, IS THIS WHERE WE COME TO ENLIST?
I HEARD IT'S A GREAT LIFE IN THE SKRULL ARMY.
STAY EXACTLY WHERE YOU ARE.
AND DROP YOUR WEAPONS.
NOT THAT EASY FOR SOME OF US.
WE KNOW HOW TO DEAL WITH YOU TELEPORTERS.
THESE CUFFS ARE FITTED WITH PSIONIC SCRAMBLERS. TRY TO JUMP AWAY FROM US AND YOU WILL LEAVE HALF YOUR BODY MASS BEHIND.
THE X-MEN ARE OFFERING NO RESISTANCE. THEY HAVE GIVEN THEMSELVES UP-- BUT IN MANY DIFFERENT PARTS OF THE CITY.
SO THAT WE CAN'T BACKTRACK THEM TO THEIR BASE.
BUT THAT'S IMMATERIAL NOW.
DISPATCH TROOP TRANSPORTS TO EXTRACT THEM. I WANT THEIR LEADER, CYCLOPS, BROUGHT TO ME HERE.
THE REST SHOULD BE KEPT UNDER SUPER-SKRULL GUARD IN GROUPS OF NO MORE THAN THREE.

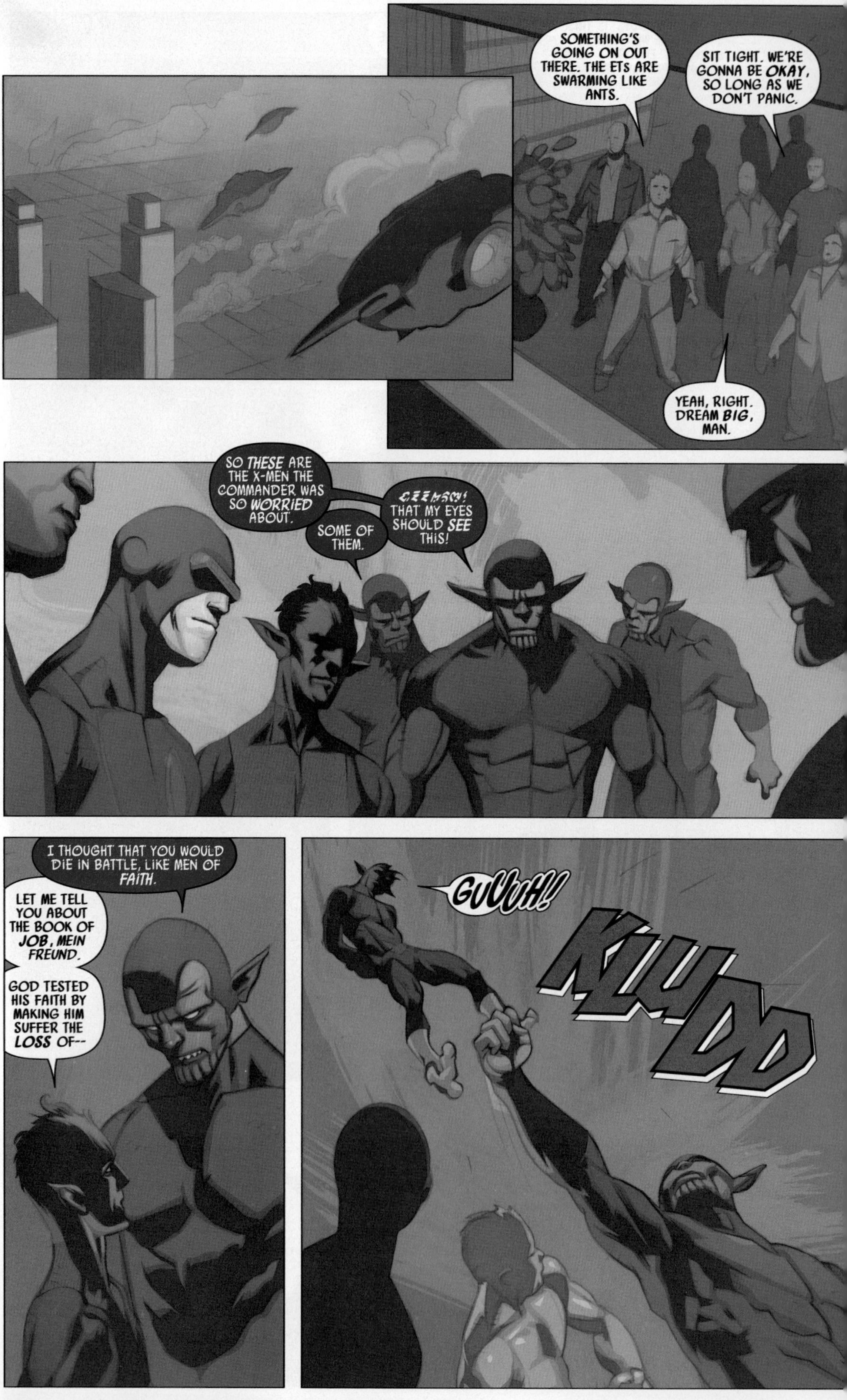
SOMETHING'S GOING ON OUT THERE. THE ETS ARE SWARMING LIKE ANTS.
SIT TIGHT. WE'RE GONNA BE OKAY, SO LONG AS WE DON'T PANIC.
YEAH, RIGHT. DREAM BIG, MAN.
SO THESE ARE THE X-MEN THE COMMANDER WAS SO WORRIED ABOUT.
SOME OF THEM.
THAT MY EYES SHOULD SEE THIS!
I THOUGHT THAT YOU WOULD DIE IN BATTLE, LIKE MEN OF FAITH.
LET ME TELL YOU ABOUT THE BOOK OF JOB, MEIN FREUND.
GOD TESTED HIS FAITH BY MAKING HIM SUFFER THE LOSS OF--
GUUUH!
KLUDD

I'LL TAKE THAT *BIG* ONE.

YOU MAY TAKE WHAT'S *LEFT* OF HIM, *TOVARISCH.*

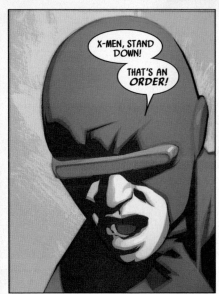

X-MEN, STAND *DOWN!*

THAT'S AN *ORDER!*

YOU OKAY, *KURT?*

I'LL BE-- *UHH!*--FINE, *SCOTT.*

CAN YOU *HELP* ME TO *STAND?*

F SUFFERING IS A TEST OF FAITH, HE SHOULD *THANK* ME.

WE CAN SWAP *BIBLE STORIES* LATER, SKRULL.

I THINK YOUR *COMMANDER* MENTIONED A *DEADLINE.*

THE X-MAN *CYCLOPS*, COMMANDER. AS YOU ORDERED.

THANK YOU, JASH.

STAND *OFF*, ALL OF YOU.

I *CONGRATULATE* YOU ON THE GUERRILLA WAR YOU WAGED. YOU HELD AN OVERWHELMINGLY SUPERIOR *FORCE* OFF FOR FAR LONGER THAN SHOULD HAVE BEEN POSSIBLE.

WE MEET AS *BROTHERS* AND EQUALS.

WE DO?

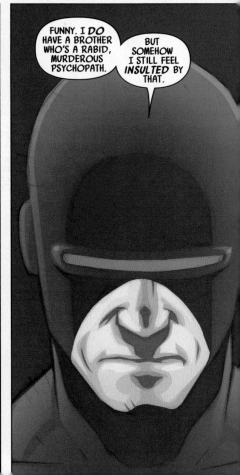

FUNNY. I *DO* HAVE A BROTHER WHO'S A RABID, MURDEROUS PSYCHOPATH.

BUT SOMEHOW I STILL FEEL *INSULTED* BY THAT.

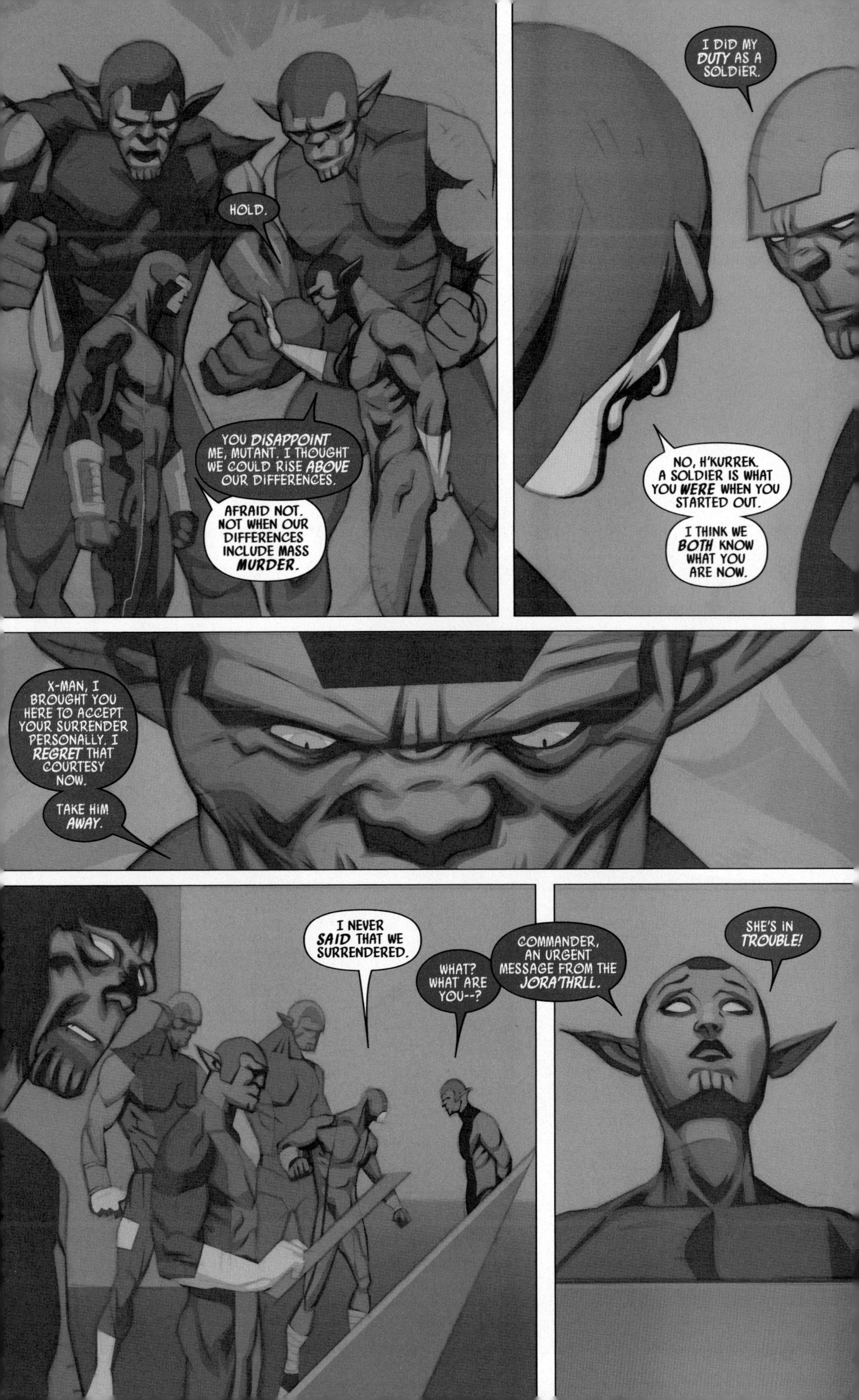
HOLD.
YOU DISAPPOINT ME, MUTANT. I THOUGHT WE COULD RISE ABOVE OUR DIFFERENCES.
AFRAID NOT. NOT WHEN OUR DIFFERENCES INCLUDE MASS MURDER.
I DID MY DUTY AS A SOLDIER.
NO, H'KURREK. A SOLDIER IS WHAT YOU WERE WHEN YOU STARTED OUT.
I THINK WE BOTH KNOW WHAT YOU ARE NOW.
X-MAN, I BROUGHT YOU HERE TO ACCEPT YOUR SURRENDER PERSONALLY. I REGRET THAT COURTESY NOW.
TAKE HIM AWAY.
I NEVER SAID THAT WE SURRENDERED.
WHAT? WHAT ARE YOU--?
COMMANDER, AN URGENT MESSAGE FROM THE JORA'THRLL.
SHE'S IN TROUBLE!

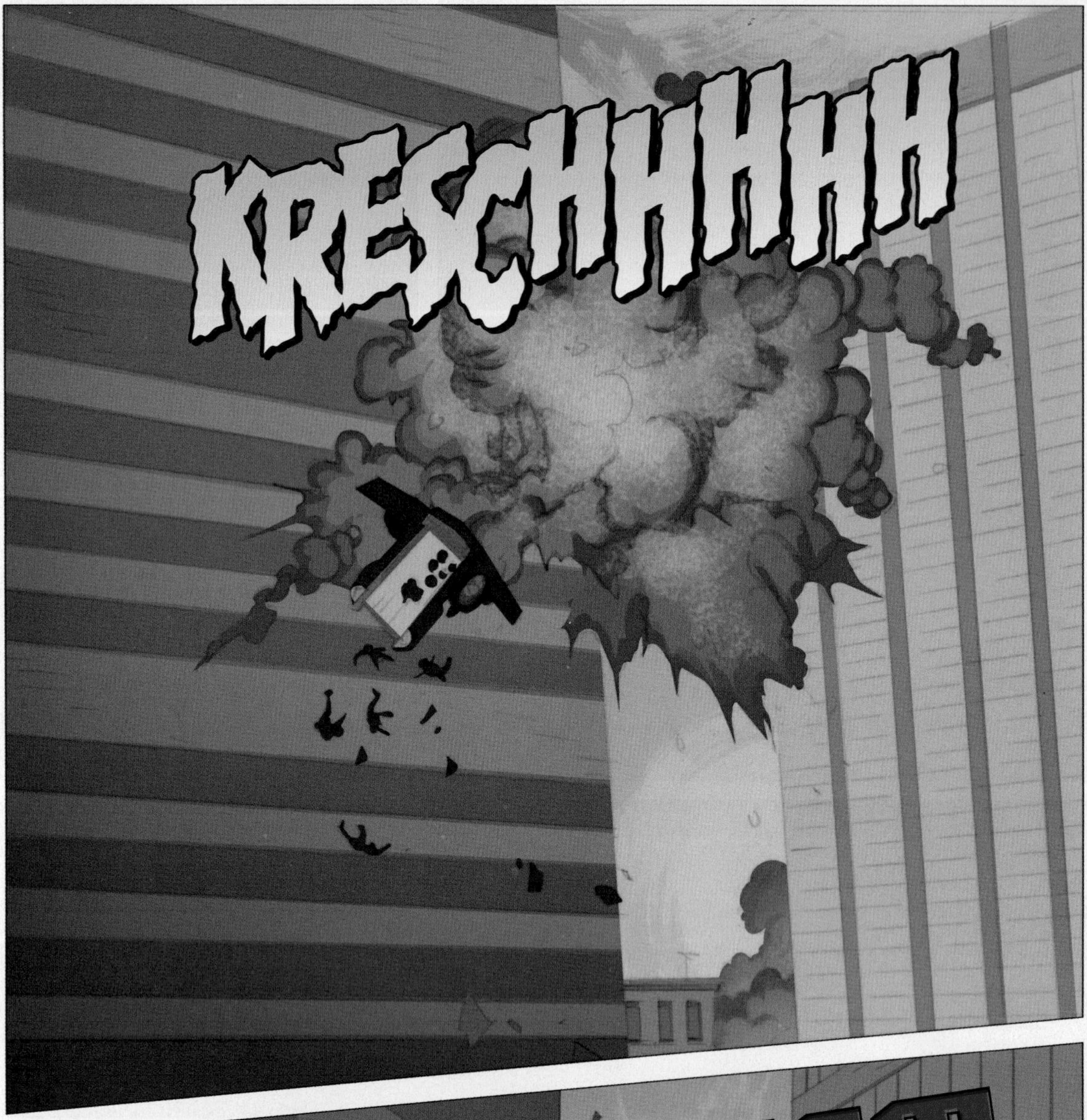
KRESCHHHHHH

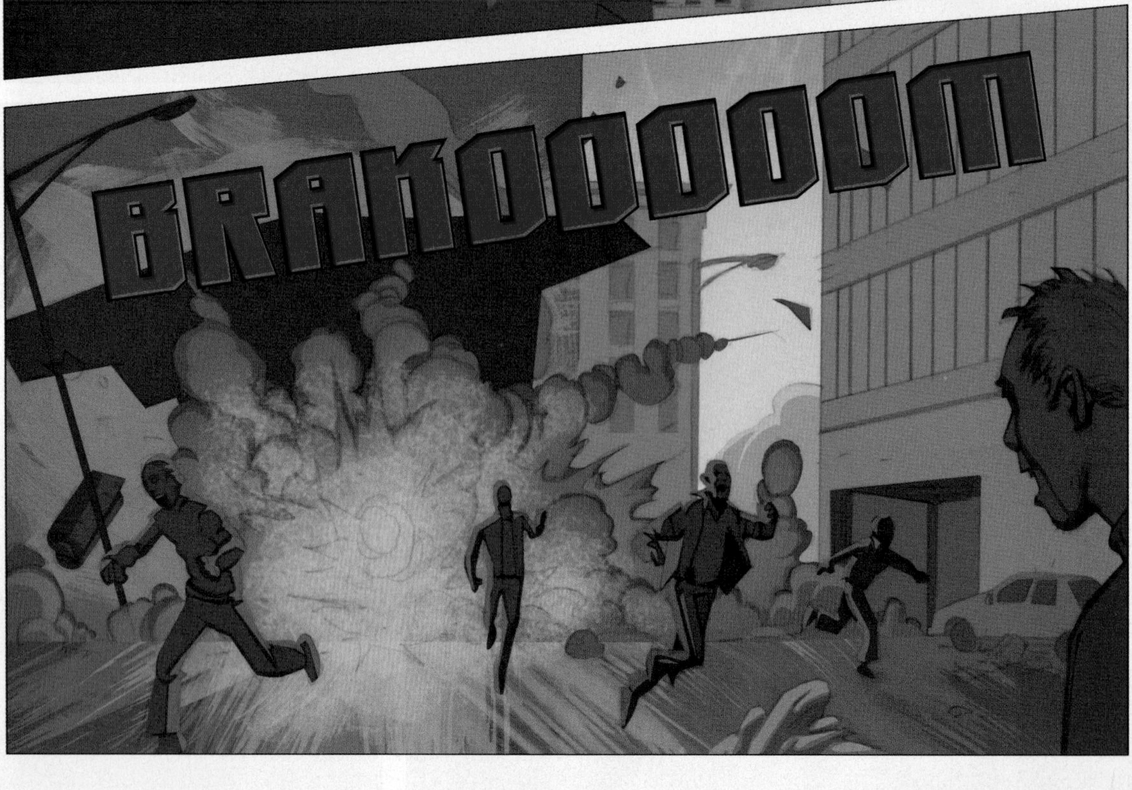
BRANOOOOOOM

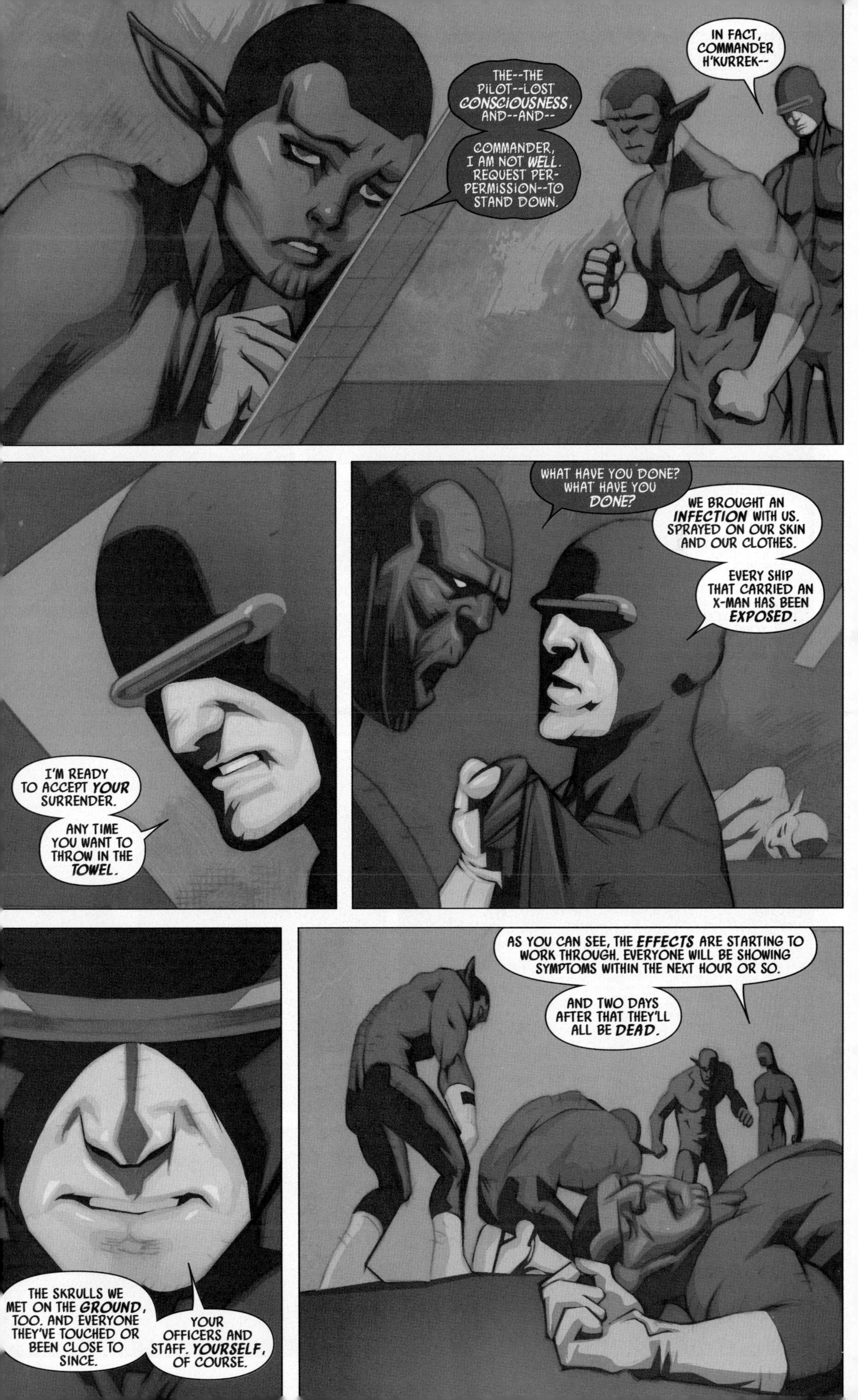
THE--THE PILOT--LOST CONSCIOUSNESS, AND--AND--
COMMANDER, I AM NOT WELL. REQUEST PER-PERMISSION--TO STAND DOWN.
IN FACT, COMMANDER H'KURREK--
I'M READY TO ACCEPT YOUR SURRENDER.
ANY TIME YOU WANT TO THROW IN THE TOWEL.
WHAT HAVE YOU DONE? WHAT HAVE YOU DONE?
WE BROUGHT AN INFECTION WITH US. SPRAYED ON OUR SKIN AND OUR CLOTHES.
EVERY SHIP THAT CARRIED AN X-MAN HAS BEEN EXPOSED.
THE SKRULLS WE MET ON THE GROUND, TOO. AND EVERYONE THEY'VE TOUCHED OR BEEN CLOSE TO SINCE.
YOUR OFFICERS AND STAFF. YOURSELF, OF COURSE.
AS YOU CAN SEE, THE EFFECTS ARE STARTING TO WORK THROUGH. EVERYONE WILL BE SHOWING SYMPTOMS WITHIN THE NEXT HOUR OR SO.
AND TWO DAYS AFTER THAT THEY'LL ALL BE DEAD.

LIEUTENANT JASH!

COMM-- COMMANDER?

FIND THE *TELEPATH* ARD'RAN. BRING HER HERE YOURSELF.

YOU UPBRAID ME FOR MURDER, AND THEN USE *PLAGUE* AS A WEAPON?

HEAR ME OUT. NOBODY HAS TO *DIE* HERE.

WE HAVE AN *ANTIDOTE*. AND WE'VE ADAPTED IT TO SKRULL MORPHOLOGY.

YOU CAN *HAVE* IT IF YOU STAND YOUR FLEET DOWN. OTHERWISE YOU'LL CARRY A *DEATH SENTENCE* TO EVERY SKRULL YOU MEET.

FOURTH ENGINEER ARD'RAN REPORTING, COMMANDER.

READ THIS MAN'S *MIND*.

TELL ME IF HE SPEAKS THE TRUTH!

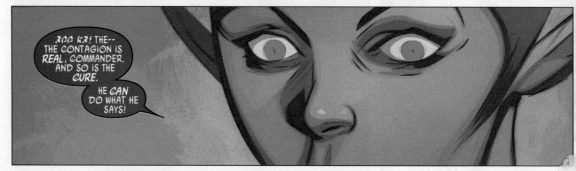

300 k3! THE-- THE CONTAGION IS *REAL*, COMMANDER. AND SO IS THE *CURE.*

HE *CAN* DO WHAT HE SAYS!

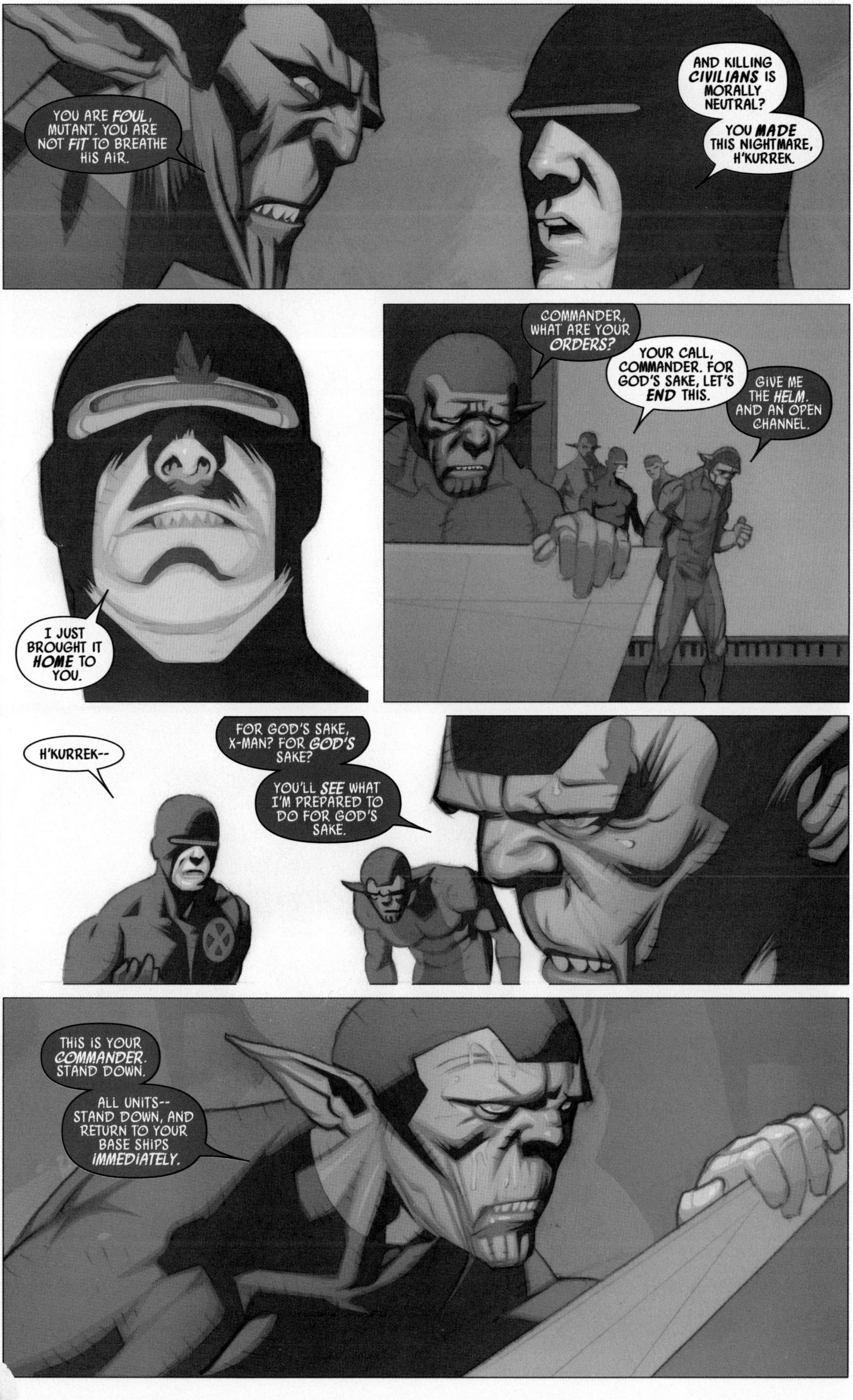
YOU ARE FOUL, MUTANT. YOU ARE NOT FIT TO BREATHE HIS AIR.
AND KILLING CIVILIANS IS MORALLY NEUTRAL?
YOU MADE THIS NIGHTMARE, H'KURREK.
I JUST BROUGHT IT HOME TO YOU.
COMMANDER, WHAT ARE YOUR ORDERS?
YOUR CALL, COMMANDER. FOR GOD'S SAKE, LET'S END THIS.
GIVE ME THE HELM. AND AN OPEN CHANNEL.
H'KURREK--
FOR GOD'S SAKE, X-MAN? FOR GOD'S SAKE?
YOU'LL SEE WHAT I'M PREPARED TO DO FOR GOD'S SAKE.
THIS IS YOUR COMMANDER. STAND DOWN.
ALL UNITS-- STAND DOWN, AND RETURN TO YOUR BASE SHIPS IMMEDIATELY.

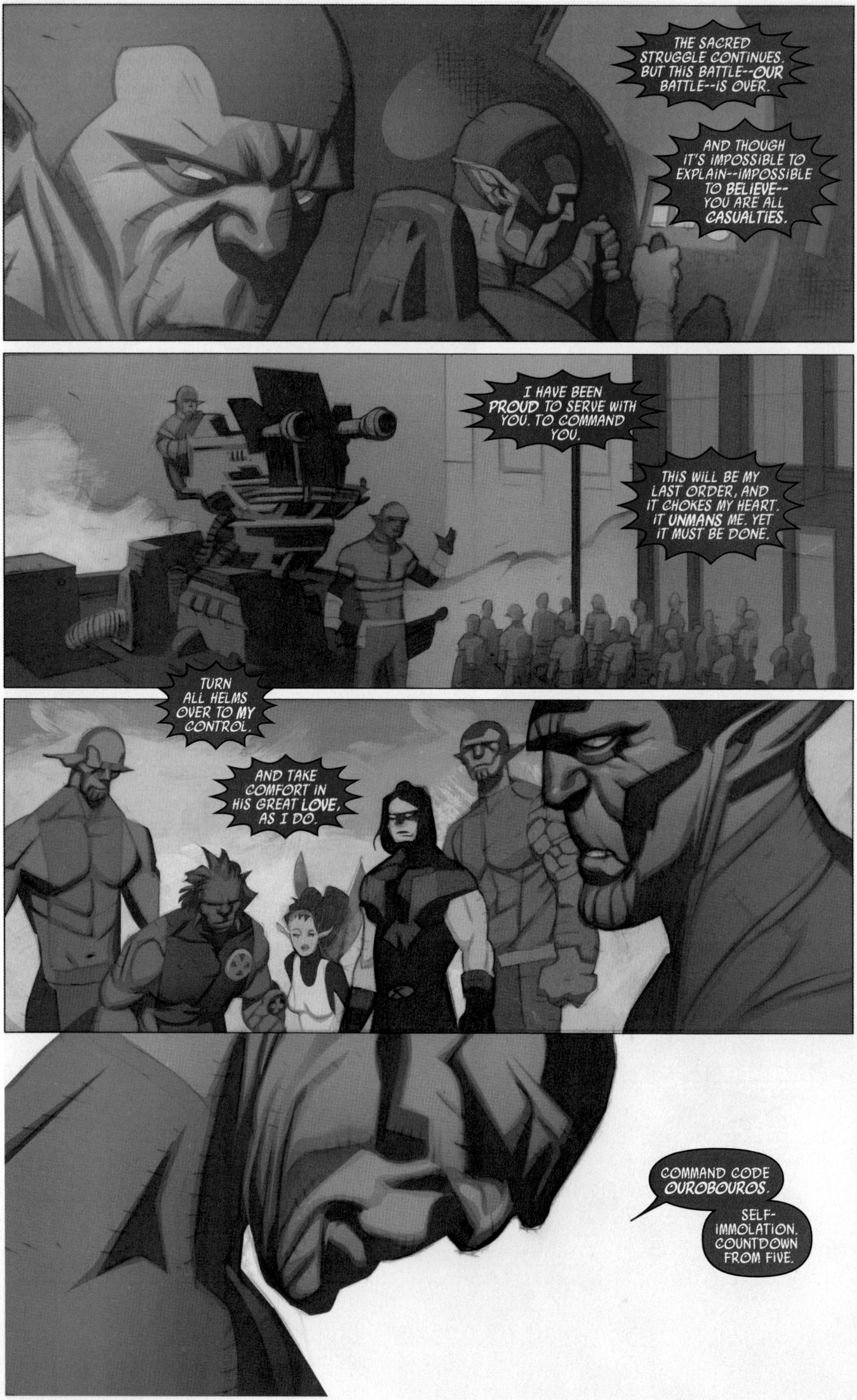
THE SACRED STRUGGLE CONTINUES. BUT THIS BATTLE--OUR BATTLE--IS OVER.
AND THOUGH IT'S IMPOSSIBLE TO EXPLAIN--IMPOSSIBLE TO BELIEVE--YOU ARE ALL CASUALTIES.
I HAVE BEEN PROUD TO SERVE WITH YOU. TO COMMAND YOU.
THIS WILL BE MY LAST ORDER, AND IT CHOKES MY HEART. IT UNMANS ME. YET IT MUST BE DONE.
TURN ALL HELMS OVER TO MY CONTROL.
AND TAKE COMFORT IN HIS GREAT LOVE, AS I DO.
COMMAND CODE OUROBOUROS.
SELF-IMMOLATION. COUNTDOWN FROM FIVE.

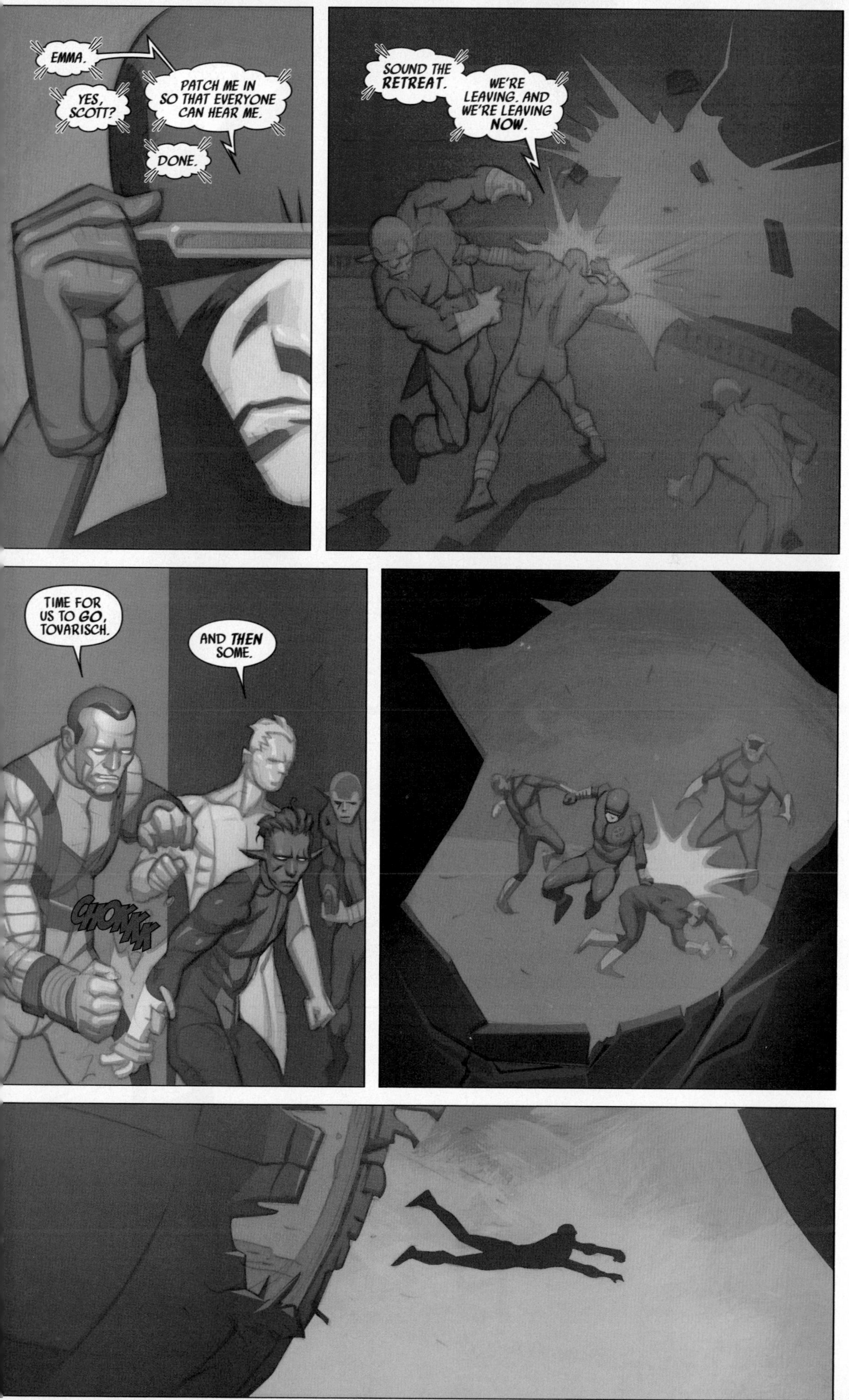
EMMA.
YES, SCOTT?
PATCH ME IN SO THAT EVERYONE CAN HEAR ME.
DONE.
SOUND THE RETREAT.
WE'RE LEAVING. AND WE'RE LEAVING NOW.
TIME FOR US TO GO, TOVARISCH.
AND THEN SOME.
CHOKKK

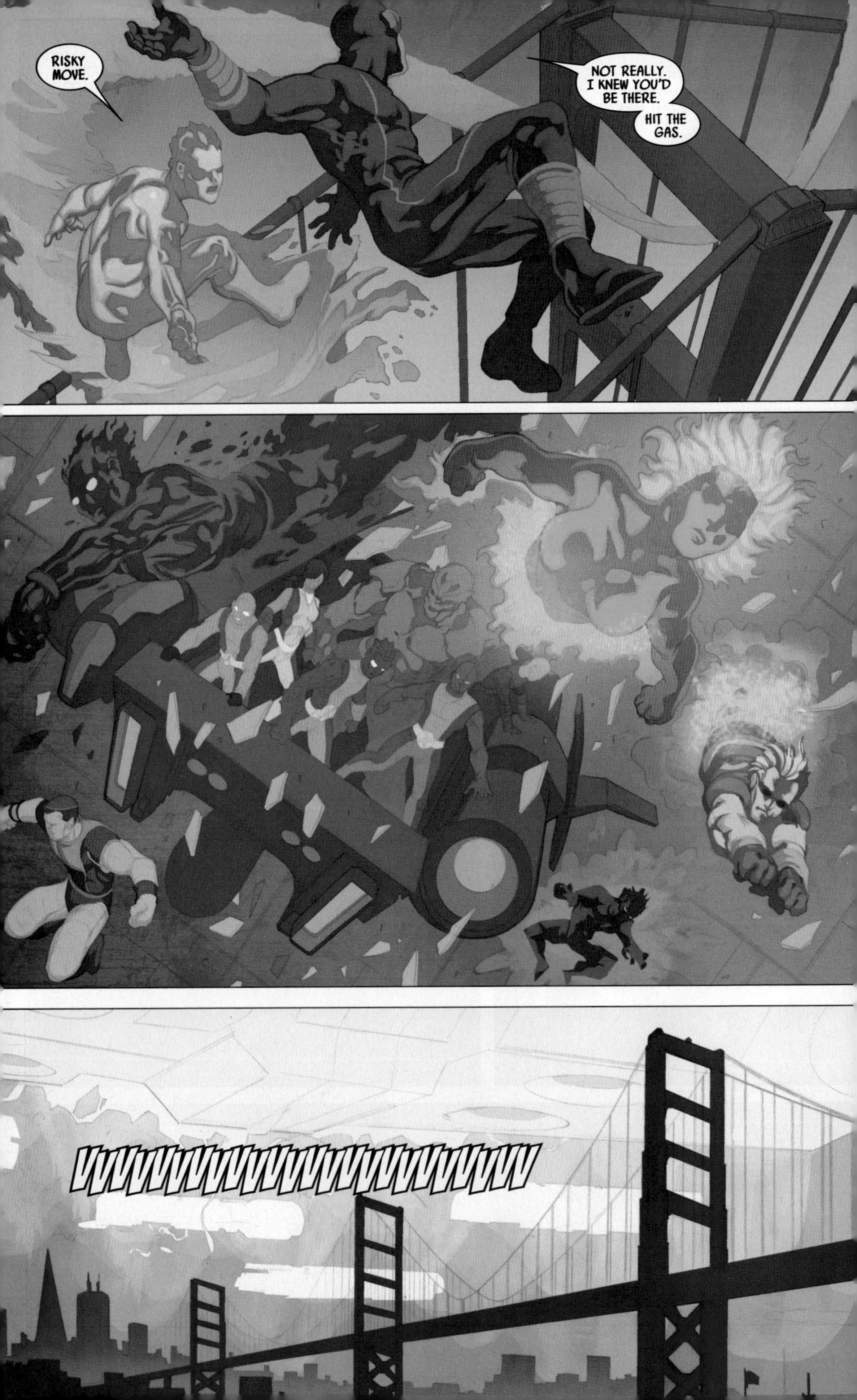
RISKY MOVE.
NOT REALLY. I KNEW YOU'D BE THERE.
HIT THE GAS.
VVVVVVVVVVVVVVVVVVVVVVVVVVVVVV

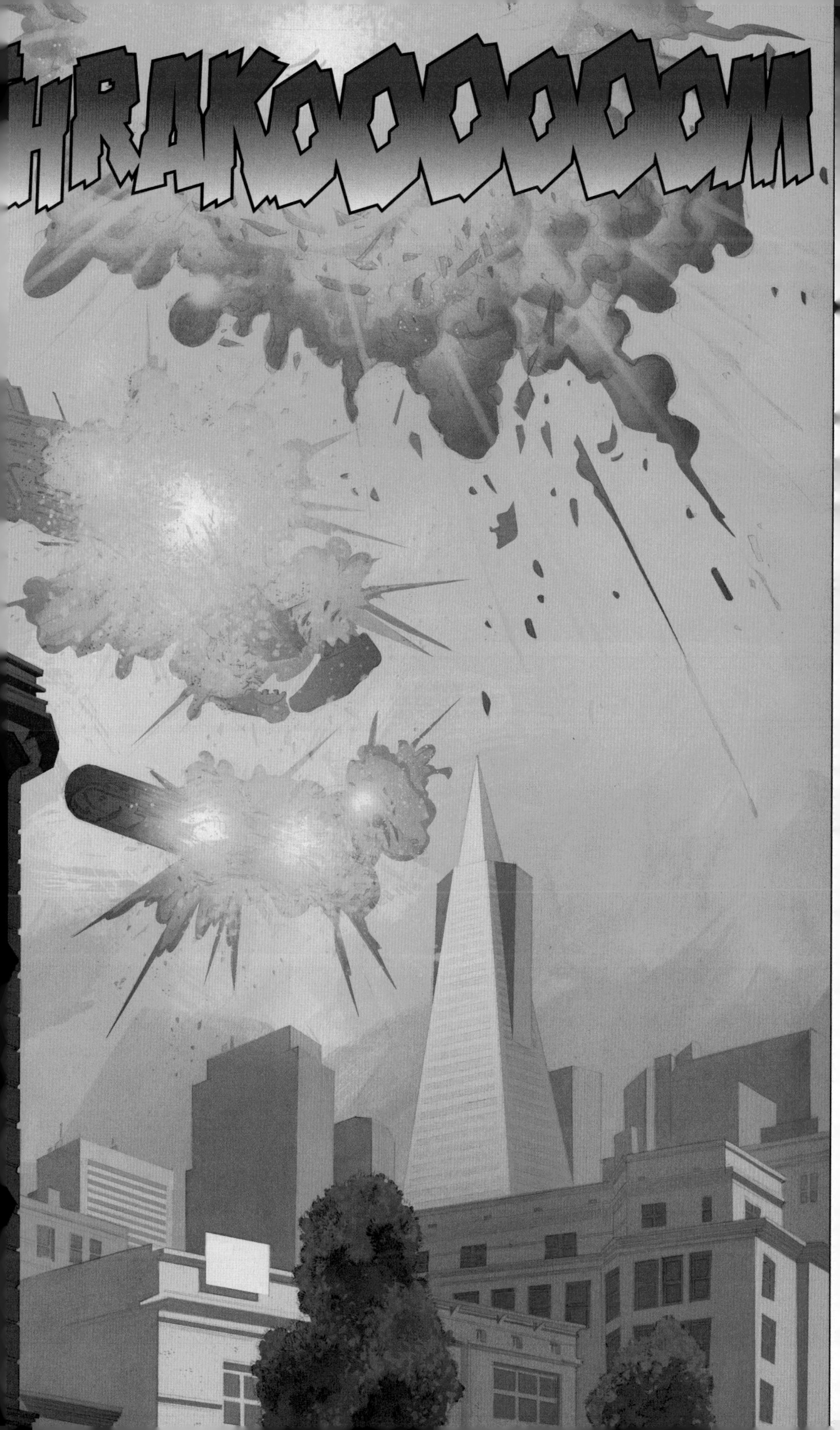
HRAKOOOOOM

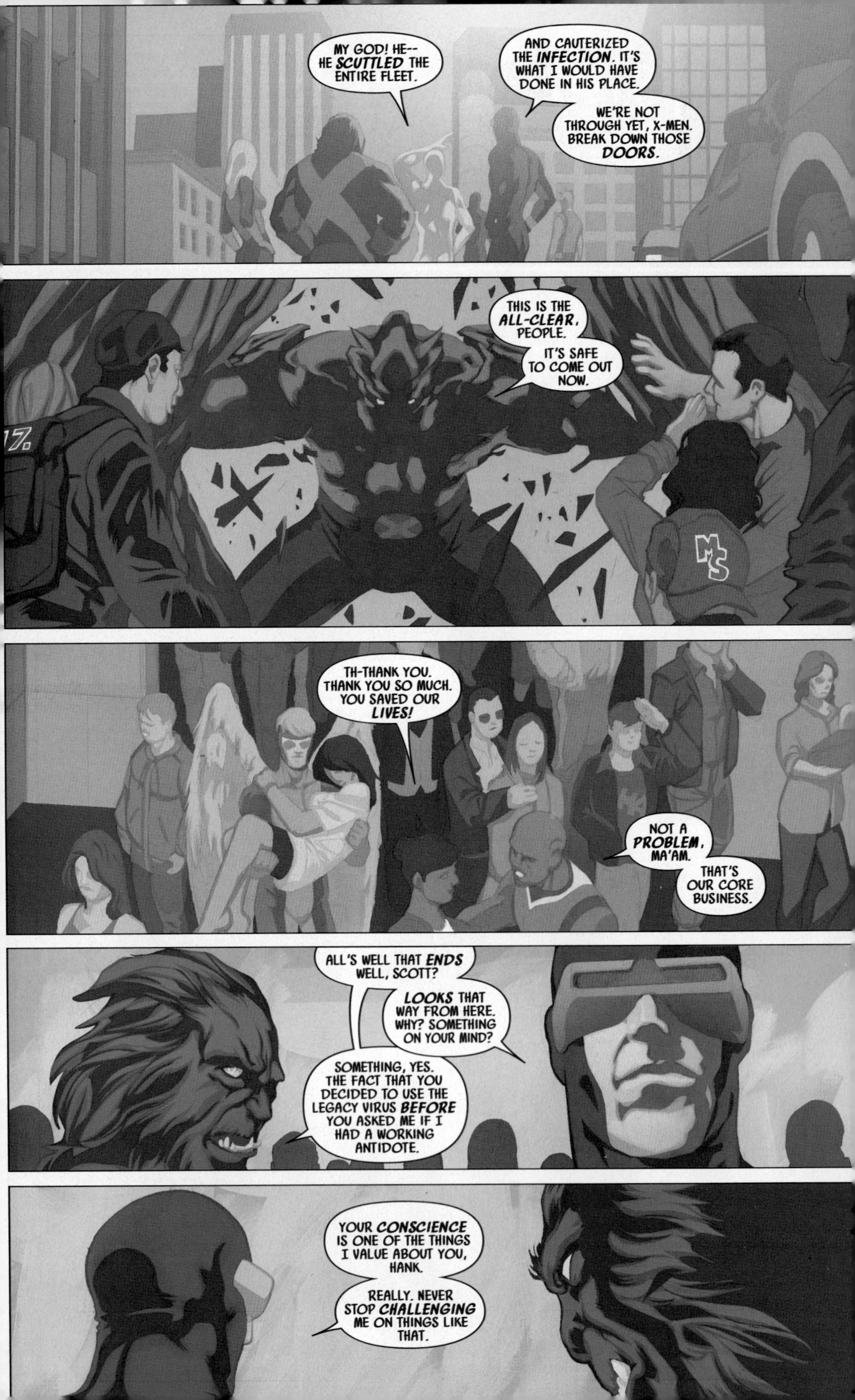
MY GOD! HE-- HE SCUTTLED THE ENTIRE FLEET.
AND CAUTERIZED THE INFECTION. IT'S WHAT I WOULD HAVE DONE IN HIS PLACE.
WE'RE NOT THROUGH YET, X-MEN. BREAK DOWN THOSE DOORS.
THIS IS THE ALL-CLEAR, PEOPLE.
IT'S SAFE TO COME OUT NOW.
TH-THANK YOU. THANK YOU SO MUCH. YOU SAVED OUR LIVES!
NOT A PROBLEM, MA'AM.
THAT'S OUR CORE BUSINESS.
ALL'S WELL THAT ENDS WELL, SCOTT?
LOOKS THAT WAY FROM HERE. WHY? SOMETHING ON YOUR MIND?
SOMETHING, YES. THE FACT THAT YOU DECIDED TO USE THE LEGACY VIRUS BEFORE YOU ASKED ME IF I HAD A WORKING ANTIDOTE.
YOUR CONSCIENCE IS ONE OF THE THINGS I VALUE ABOUT YOU, HANK.
REALLY. NEVER STOP CHALLENGING ME ON THINGS LIKE THAT.

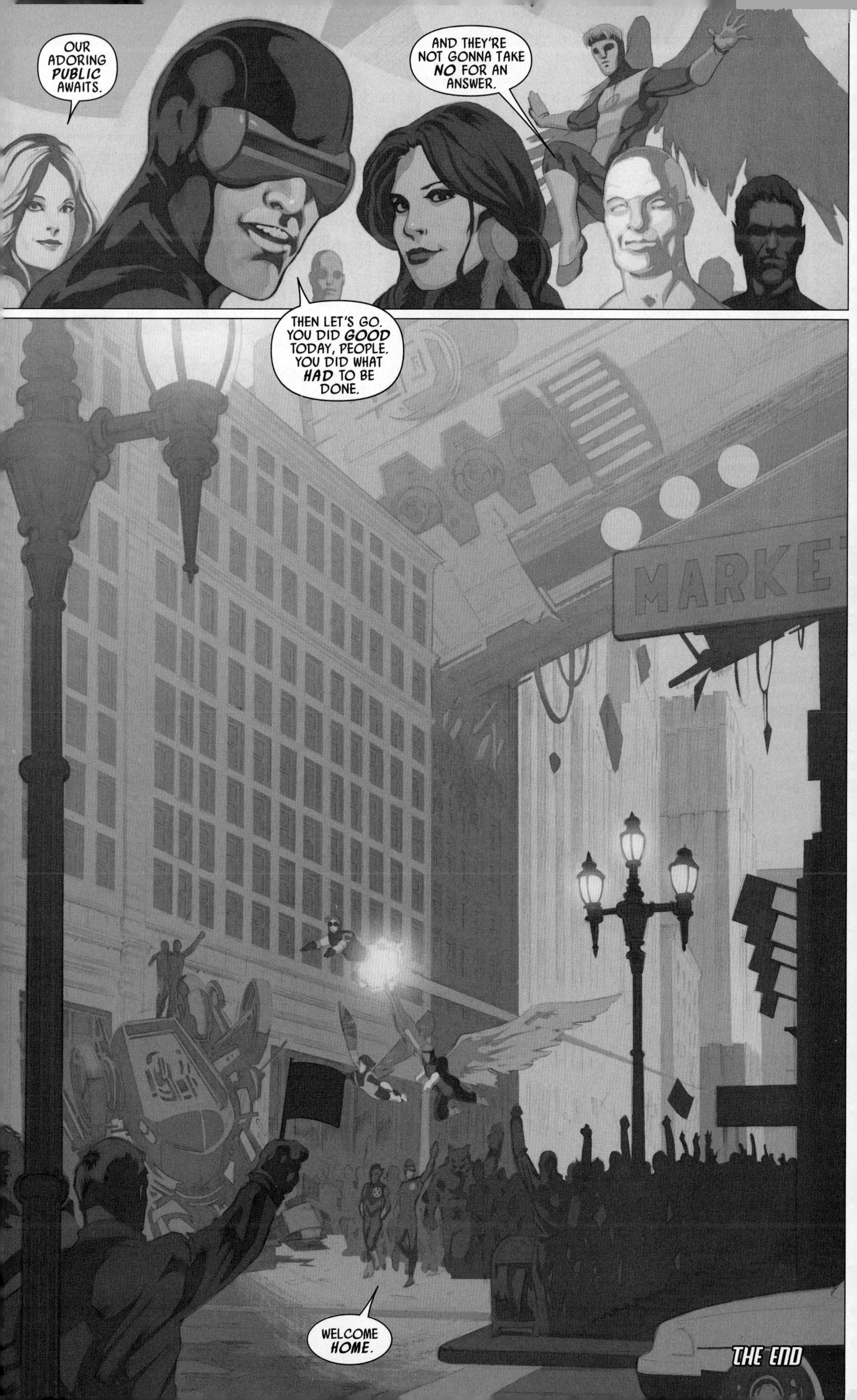
OUR ADORING PUBLIC AWAITS.
AND THEY'RE NOT GONNA TAKE NO FOR AN ANSWER.
THEN LET'S GO. YOU DID GOOD TODAY, PEOPLE. YOU DID WHAT HAD TO BE DONE.
MARKE
WELCOME HOME.
THE END

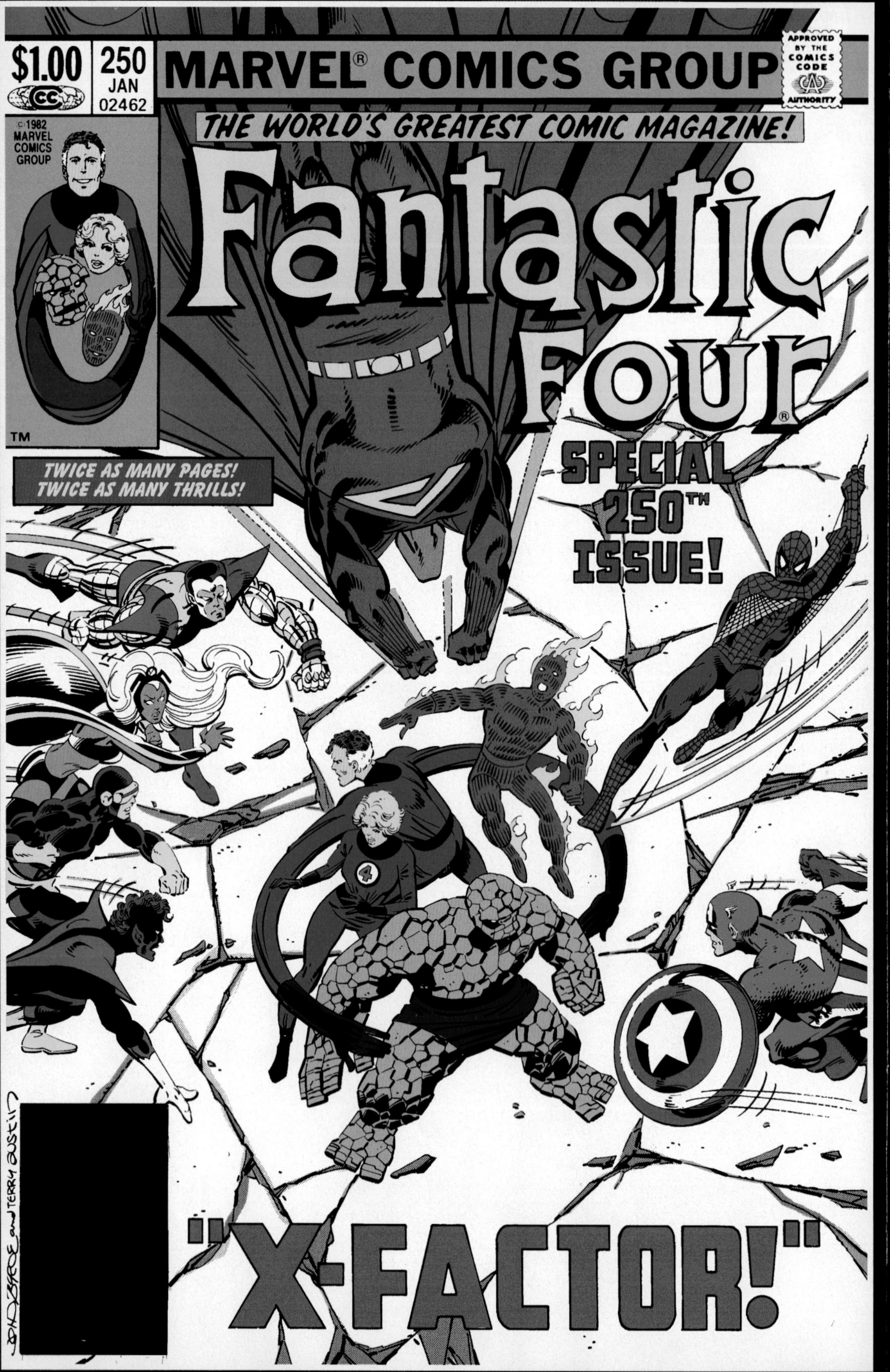
$1.00
250
JAN
02462
MARVEL® COMICS GROUP
APPROVED BY THE COMICS CODE AUTHORITY
THE WORLD'S GREATEST COMIC MAGAZINE!
©1982 MARVEL COMICS GROUP
TM
Fantastic Four®
TWICE AS MANY PAGES!
TWICE AS MANY THRILLS!
SPECIAL 250TH ISSUE!
"X-FACTOR!"

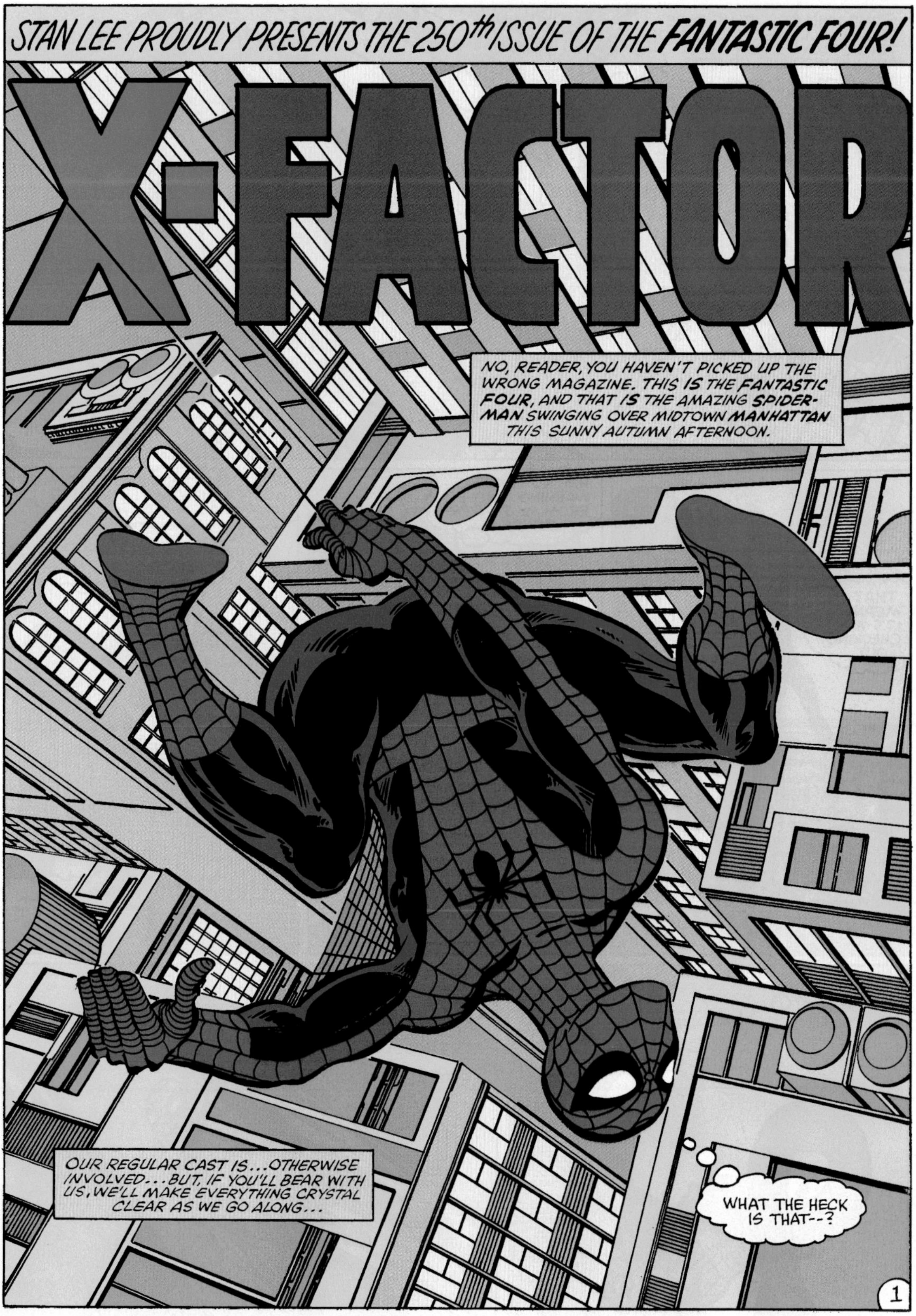
STAN LEE PROUDLY PRESENTS THE 250th ISSUE OF THE FANTASTIC FOUR!
X-FACTOR
NO, READER, YOU HAVEN'T PICKED UP THE WRONG MAGAZINE. THIS IS THE FANTASTIC FOUR, AND THAT IS THE AMAZING SPIDER-MAN SWINGING OVER MIDTOWN MANHATTAN THIS SUNNY AUTUMN AFTERNOON.
OUR REGULAR CAST IS...OTHERWISE INVOLVED...BUT, IF YOU'LL BEAR WITH US, WE'LL MAKE EVERYTHING CRYSTAL CLEAR AS WE GO ALONG...
WHAT THE HECK IS THAT--?
1

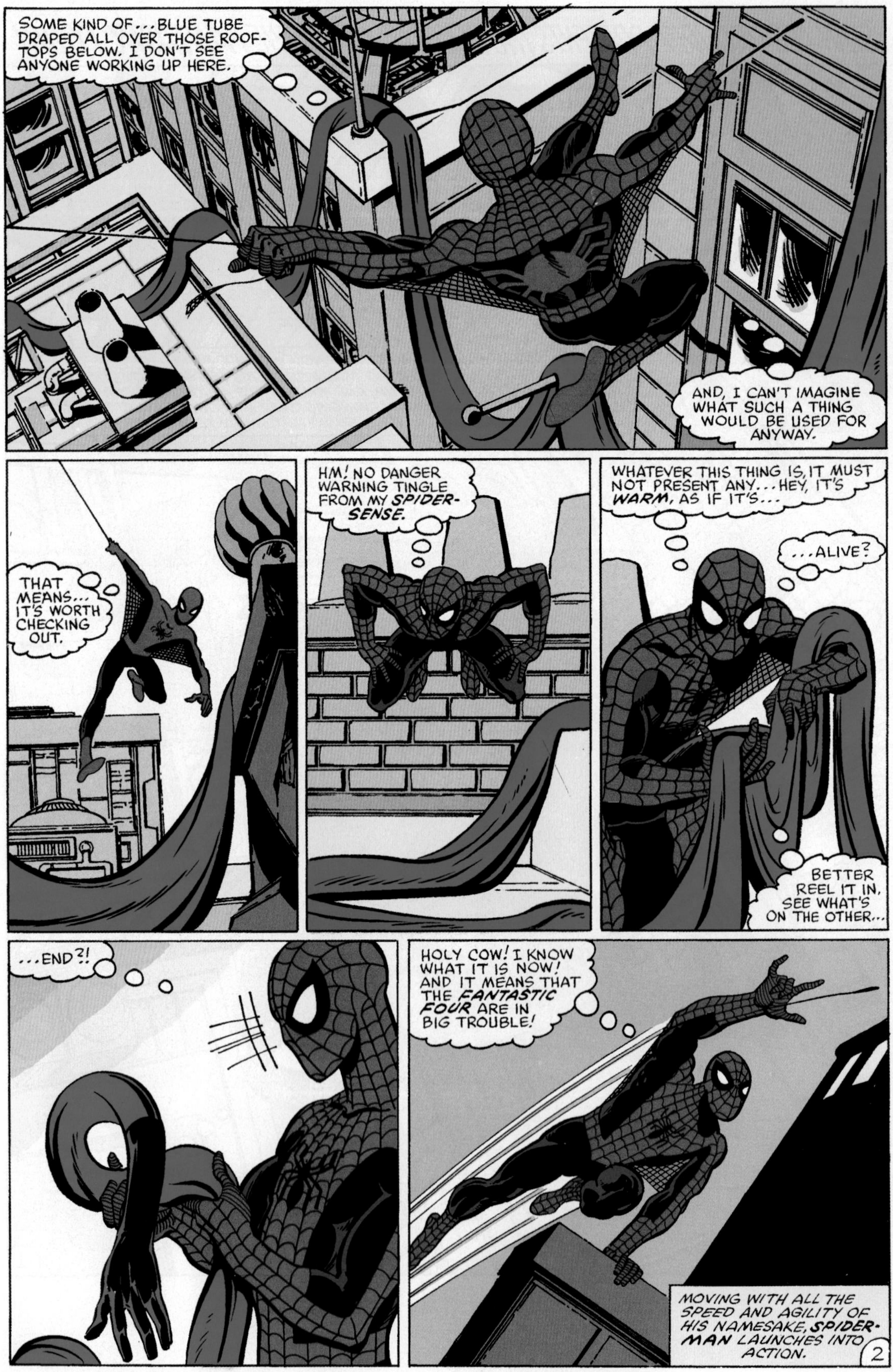
SOME KIND OF... BLUE TUBE DRAPED ALL OVER THOSE ROOF-TOPS BELOW. I DON'T SEE ANYONE WORKING UP HERE.
AND, I CAN'T IMAGINE WHAT SUCH A THING WOULD BE USED FOR ANYWAY.
THAT MEANS... IT'S WORTH CHECKING OUT.
HM! NO DANGER WARNING TINGLE FROM MY SPIDER-SENSE.
WHATEVER THIS THING IS, IT MUST NOT PRESENT ANY... HEY, IT'S WARM, AS IF IT'S...
...ALIVE?
BETTER REEL IT IN, SEE WHAT'S ON THE OTHER...
...END?!
HOLY COW! I KNOW WHAT IT IS NOW! AND IT MEANS THAT THE FANTASTIC FOUR ARE IN BIG TROUBLE!
MOVING WITH ALL THE SPEED AND AGILITY OF HIS NAMESAKE, SPIDER-MAN LAUNCHES INTO ACTION.

AND, WITHIN A HEARTBEAT...

THERE HE IS! *MISTER FANTASTIC*, THE *FF'S* HEAD HONCHO!

BOY, HE LOOKS IN MISERABLE SHAPE!

PROFESSOR *RICHARDS*... REED... ARE YOU OKAY?

WH-WHAT... S-SPIDER-MAN? WHAT ARE YOU DOING HERE? WHAT HAPPENED TO ME?

I THINK THAT'S MY QUESTION, FRIEND.

YES--YES, I REMEMBER. I WAS *ATTACKED*-- ALL OF THE FANTASTIC FOUR WERE ATTACKED--BY AN INCREDIBLE BEING.

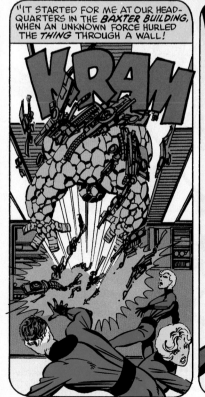

"IT STARTED FOR ME AT OUR HEADQUARTERS IN THE *BAXTER BUILDING*, WHEN AN UNKNOWN FORCE HURLED THE *THING* THROUGH A WALL!

KRAM

"THAT FORCE DID NOT STAY UNKNOWN FOR LONG. SUDDENLY THE WHOLE BUILDING WAS ROCKING...

"...BECAUSE A COSTUMED MAN HAD *PICKED IT UP* BY ONE CORNER!

"THAT SHOULD HAVE BEEN IMPOSSIBLE--THE BUILDING SHOULD HAVE FALLEN APART--BUT BEFORE I COULD ANALYZE FURTHER...

I AM *GLADIATOR*, PRAETOR OF THE IMPERIAL GUARD OF THE SH'IAR EMPIRE. I HAVE COME TO DESTROY YOU, *SKRULLS!**

*AS TRANSLATED LAST ISSUE BY REED'S UNIVERSAL TRANSLATOR!

3

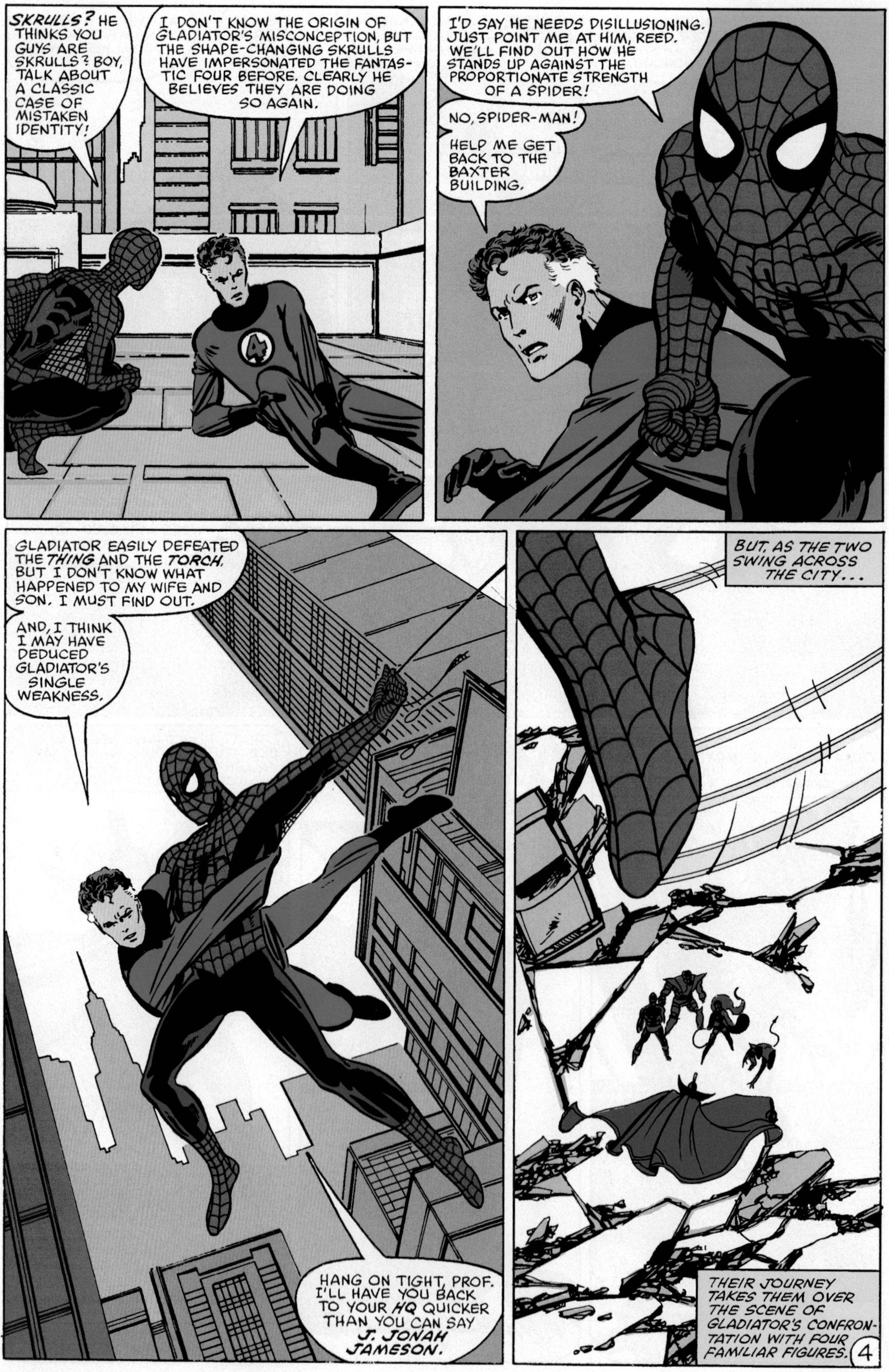
SKRULLS? HE THINKS YOU GUYS ARE SKRULLS? BOY, TALK ABOUT A CLASSIC CASE OF MISTAKEN IDENTITY!
I DON'T KNOW THE ORIGIN OF GLADIATOR'S MISCONCEPTION, BUT THE SHAPE-CHANGING SKRULLS HAVE IMPERSONATED THE FANTASTIC FOUR BEFORE. CLEARLY HE BELIEVES THEY ARE DOING SO AGAIN.
I'D SAY HE NEEDS DISILLUSIONING. JUST POINT ME AT HIM, REED. WE'LL FIND OUT HOW HE STANDS UP AGAINST THE PROPORTIONATE STRENGTH OF A SPIDER!
NO, SPIDER-MAN!
HELP ME GET BACK TO THE BAXTER BUILDING.
GLADIATOR EASILY DEFEATED THE THING AND THE TORCH, BUT I DON'T KNOW WHAT HAPPENED TO MY WIFE AND SON. I MUST FIND OUT.
AND, I THINK I MAY HAVE DEDUCED GLADIATOR'S SINGLE WEAKNESS.
HANG ON TIGHT, PROF. I'LL HAVE YOU BACK TO YOUR HQ QUICKER THAN YOU CAN SAY J. JONAH JAMESON.
BUT, AS THE TWO SWING ACROSS THE CITY...
THEIR JOURNEY TAKES THEM OVER THE SCENE OF GLADIATOR'S CONFRONTATION WITH FOUR FAMILIAR FIGURES.
4

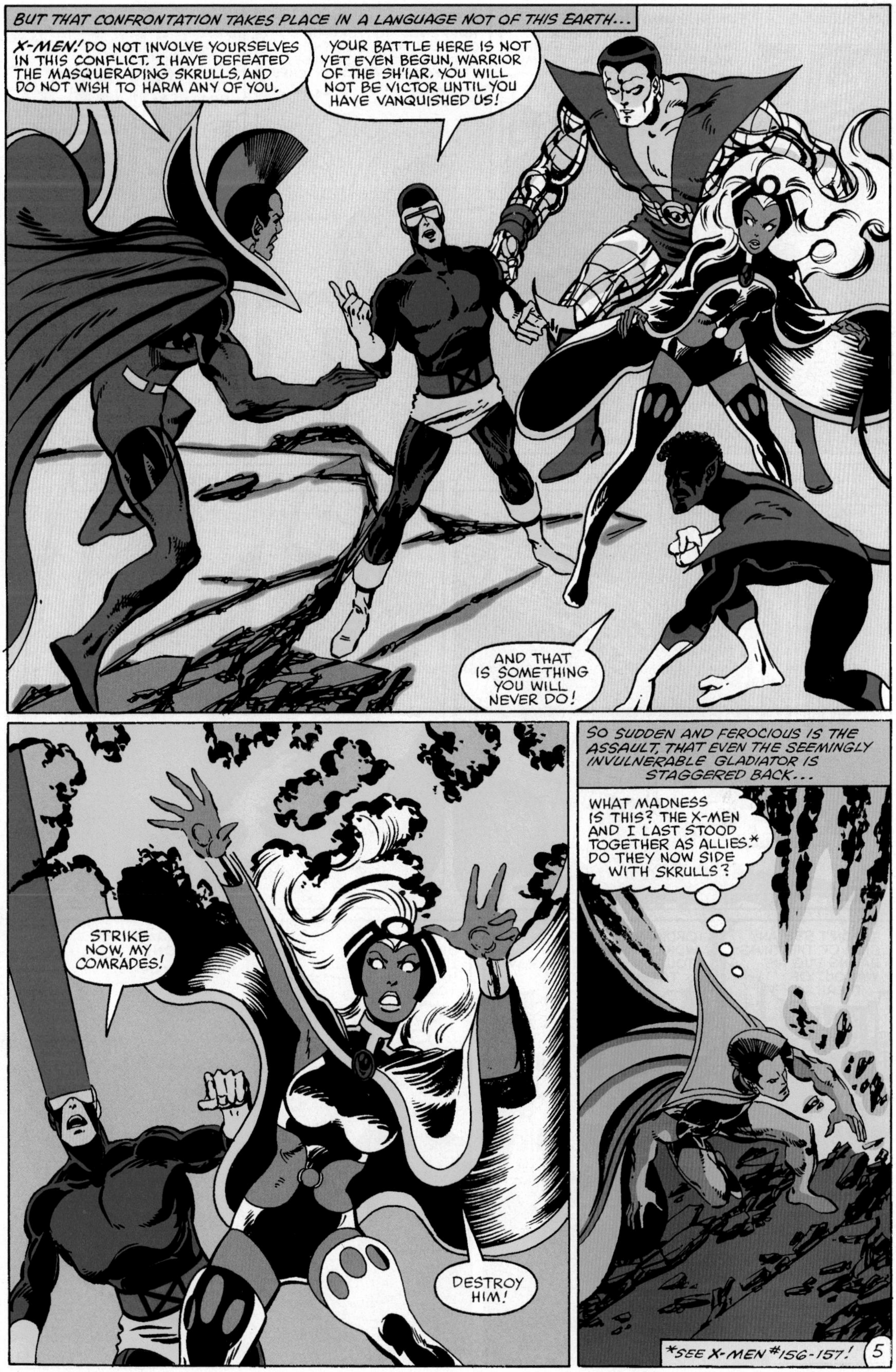
BUT THAT CONFRONTATION TAKES PLACE IN A LANGUAGE NOT OF THIS EARTH...
X-MEN! DO NOT INVOLVE YOURSELVES IN THIS CONFLICT. I HAVE DEFEATED THE MASQUERADING SKRULLS, AND DO NOT WISH TO HARM ANY OF YOU.
YOUR BATTLE HERE IS NOT YET EVEN BEGUN, WARRIOR OF THE SH'IAR. YOU WILL NOT BE VICTOR UNTIL YOU HAVE VANQUISHED US!
AND THAT IS SOMETHING YOU WILL NEVER DO!
STRIKE NOW, MY COMRADES!
DESTROY HIM!
SO SUDDEN AND FEROCIOUS IS THE ASSAULT, THAT EVEN THE SEEMINGLY INVULNERABLE GLADIATOR IS STAGGERED BACK...
WHAT MADNESS IS THIS? THE X-MEN AND I LAST STOOD TOGETHER AS ALLIES.* DO THEY NOW SIDE WITH SKRULLS?
*SEE X-MEN #156-157!

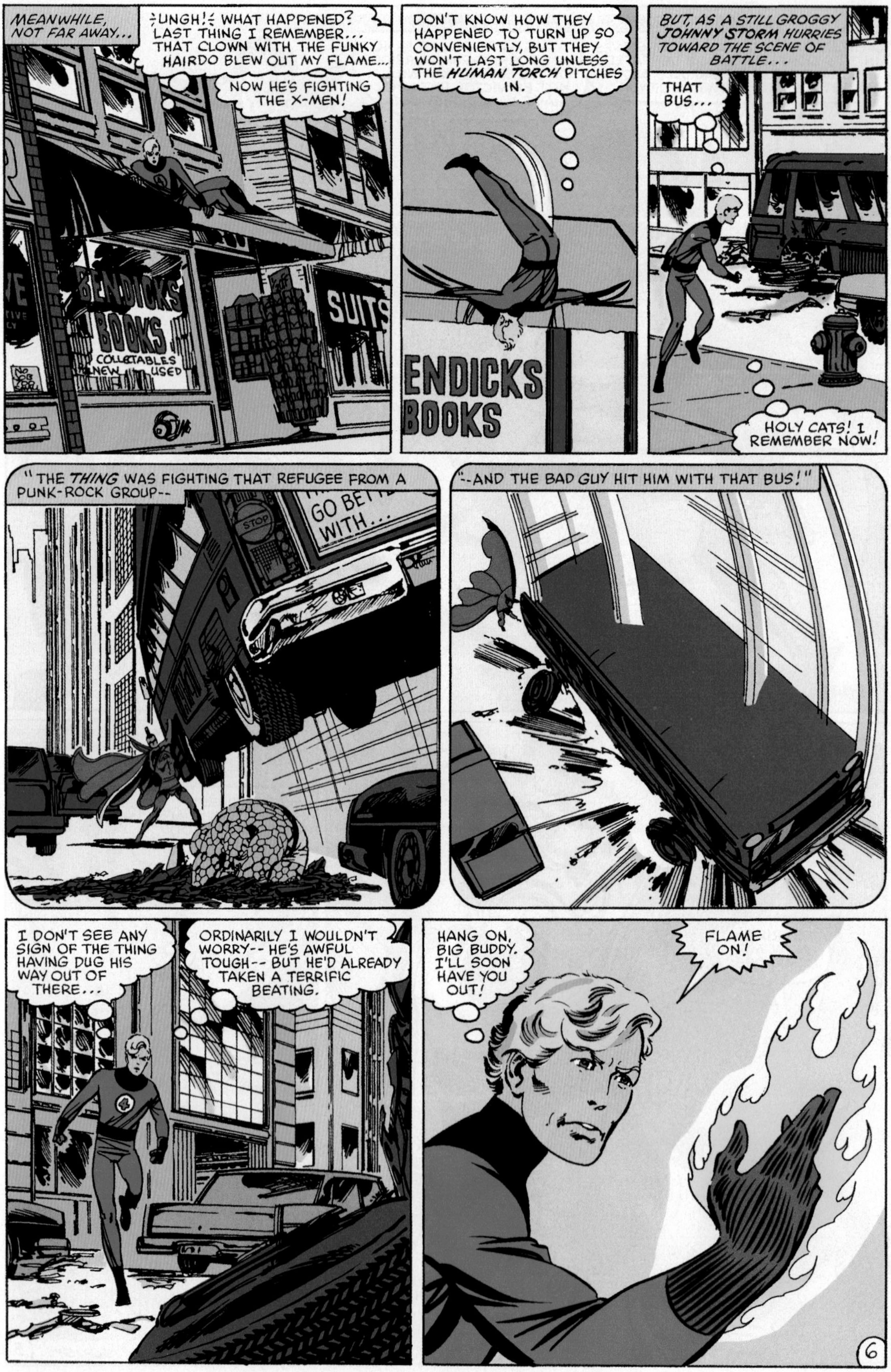
MEANWHILE, NOT FAR AWAY...
UNGH! WHAT HAPPENED? LAST THING I REMEMBER... THAT CLOWN WITH THE FUNKY HAIRDO BLEW OUT MY FLAME...
NOW HE'S FIGHTING THE X-MEN!
BENDICKS BOOKS
COLLECTABLES NEW USED
SUITS
DON'T KNOW HOW THEY HAPPENED TO TURN UP SO CONVENIENTLY, BUT THEY WON'T LAST LONG UNLESS THE HUMAN TORCH PITCHES IN.
ENDICKS BOOKS
BUT, AS A STILL GROGGY JOHNNY STORM HURRIES TOWARD THE SCENE OF BATTLE...
THAT BUS...
HOLY CATS! I REMEMBER NOW!
"THE THING WAS FIGHTING THAT REFUGEE FROM A PUNK-ROCK GROUP--
STOP
GO BETT WITH...
"--AND THE BAD GUY HIT HIM WITH THAT BUS!"
I DON'T SEE ANY SIGN OF THE THING HAVING DUG HIS WAY OUT OF THERE...
ORDINARILY I WOULDN'T WORRY-- HE'S AWFUL TOUGH-- BUT HE'D ALREADY TAKEN A TERRIFIC BEATING.
HANG ON, BIG BUDDY. I'LL SOON HAVE YOU OUT!
FLAME ON!
6

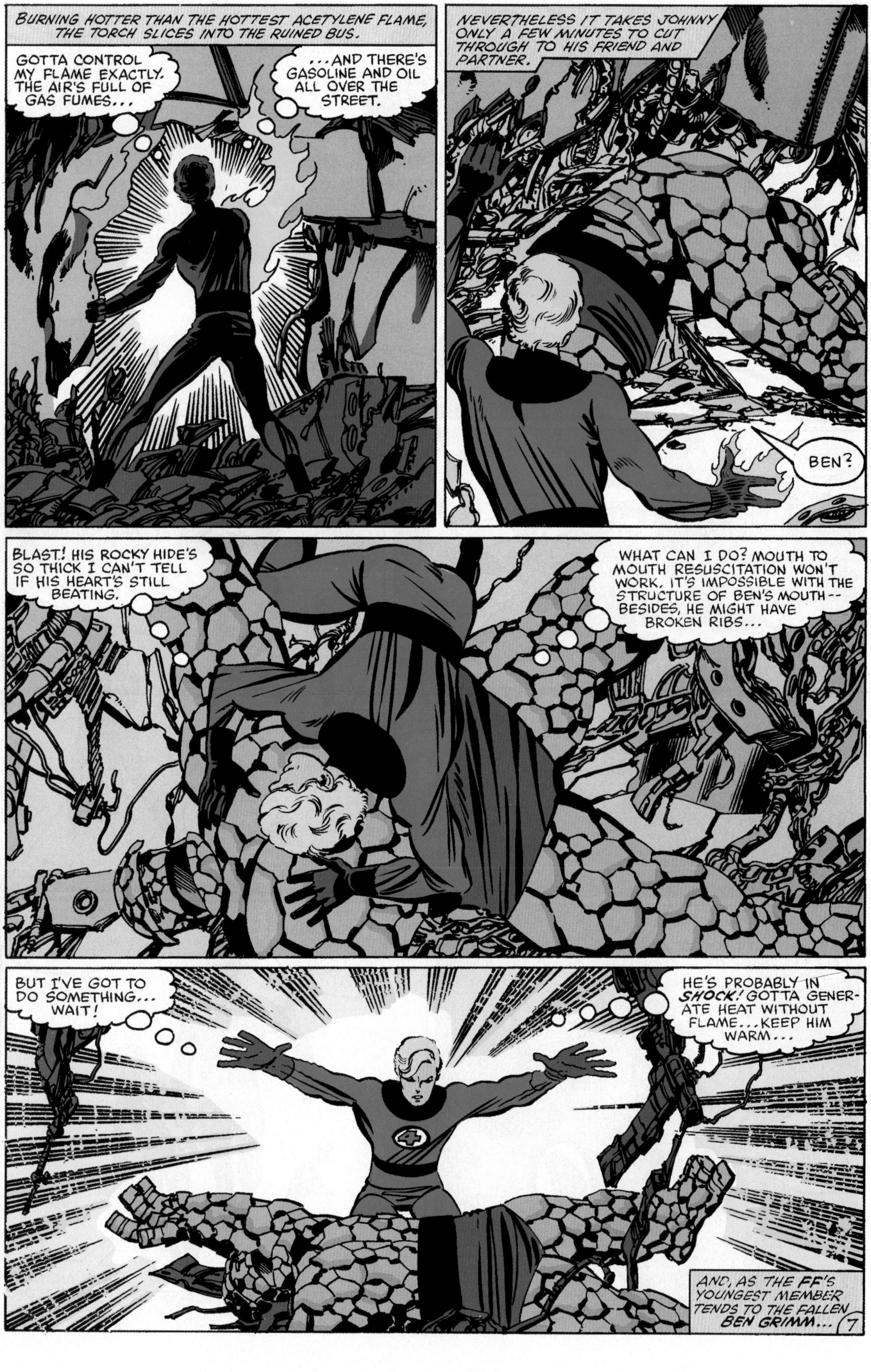
BURNING HOTTER THAN THE HOTTEST ACETYLENE FLAME, THE TORCH SLICES INTO THE RUINED BUS.
GOTTA CONTROL MY FLAME EXACTLY. THE AIR'S FULL OF GAS FUMES...
...AND THERE'S GASOLINE AND OIL ALL OVER THE STREET.
NEVERTHELESS IT TAKES JOHNNY ONLY A FEW MINUTES TO CUT THROUGH TO HIS FRIEND AND PARTNER.
BEN?
BLAST! HIS ROCKY HIDE'S SO THICK I CAN'T TELL IF HIS HEART'S STILL BEATING.
WHAT CAN I DO? MOUTH TO MOUTH RESUSCITATION WON'T WORK, IT'S IMPOSSIBLE WITH THE STRUCTURE OF BEN'S MOUTH-- BESIDES, HE MIGHT HAVE BROKEN RIBS...
BUT I'VE GOT TO DO SOMETHING... WAIT!
HE'S PROBABLY IN SHOCK! GOTTA GENERATE HEAT WITHOUT FLAME... KEEP HIM WARM...
AND, AS THE FF'S YOUNGEST MEMBER TENDS TO THE FALLEN BEN GRIMM...

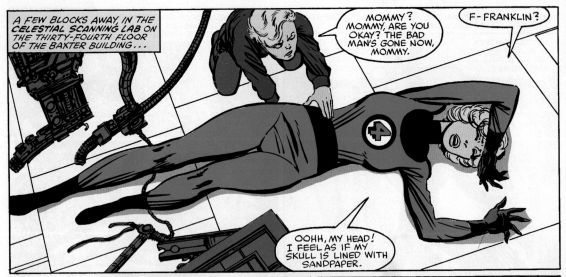

A FEW BLOCKS AWAY, IN THE CELESTIAL SCANNING LAB ON THE THIRTY-FOURTH FLOOR OF THE BAXTER BUILDING...

MOMMY? MOMMY, ARE YOU OKAY? THE BAD MAN'S GONE NOW, MOMMY.

F- FRANKLIN?

OOHH, MY HEAD! I FEEL AS IF MY SKULL IS LINED WITH SANDPAPER.

SUE! FRANKLIN! WHERE'S BEN?

SPIDEY-MAN!

R- REED? IS THAT YOU?

"SPIDEY-MAN"? I SHOULD HAVE KNOWN THAT WOULD HAPPEN WHEN I LET THE ELECTRIC COMPANY CALL ME "SPIDEY."

ER...THAT'S SPIDER-MAN, FRANKLIN.

SUE, DARLING, ARE YOU ALL RIGHT?

I- I THINK SO. I ENCASED GLADIATOR IN ONE OF MY INVISIBLE FORCE FIELDS, BUT HE FOUGHT BACK AGAINST IT. SOME KIND OF... FEEDBACK KNOCKED ME OUT.

FEEDBACK? SUSAN, DO YOU REMEMBER THE NATURE OF IT? HOW IT FELT? IT COULD BE IMPORTANT...

WHY, YES, I THINK I DO RE-MEMBER.

I THOUGHT AT THE TIME THAT IT WAS MORE THAN PHYSICAL FORCE. A...PSYCHIC PRESSURE...

THAT'S IT! IT ALL FITS! IT EXPLAINS EVERYTHING! COME ON, SUE, WE HAVE WORK TO DO!

BUT, REED, WHAT IS IT? WHAT HAVE YOU DEDUCED?

THE ANSWER, SUSAN! THE ONLY POSSIBLE ANSWER!

8

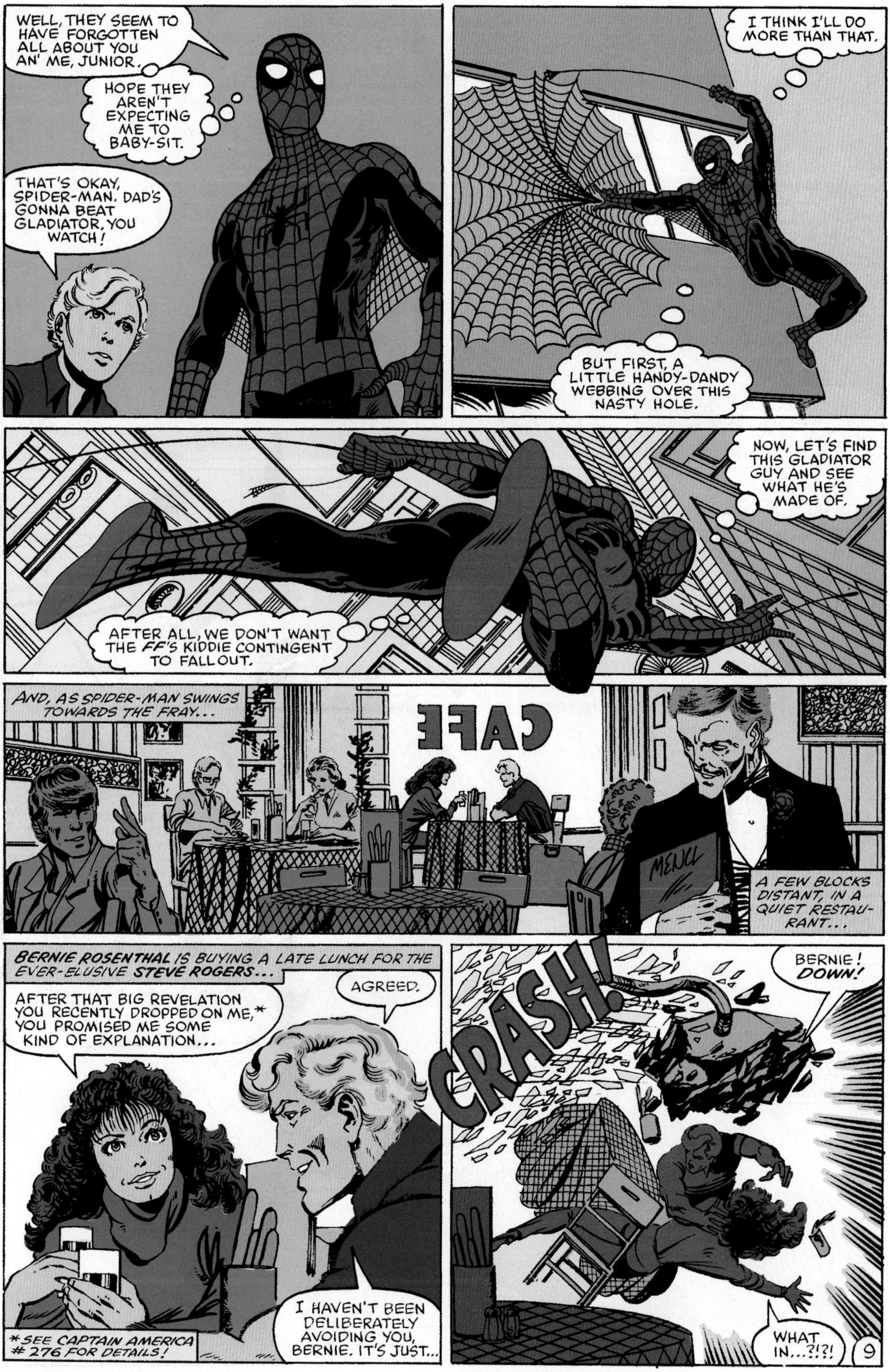
WELL, THEY SEEM TO HAVE FORGOTTEN ALL ABOUT YOU AN' ME, JUNIOR.
HOPE THEY AREN'T EXPECTING ME TO BABY-SIT.
THAT'S OKAY, SPIDER-MAN. DAD'S GONNA BEAT GLADIATOR, YOU WATCH!
I THINK I'LL DO MORE THAN THAT.
BUT FIRST, A LITTLE HANDY-DANDY WEBBING OVER THIS NASTY HOLE.
NOW, LET'S FIND THIS GLADIATOR GUY AND SEE WHAT HE'S MADE OF.
AFTER ALL, WE DON'T WANT THE FF'S KIDDIE CONTINGENT TO FALL OUT.
AND, AS SPIDER-MAN SWINGS TOWARDS THE FRAY...
CAFE
MENU
A FEW BLOCKS DISTANT, IN A QUIET RESTAURANT...
BERNIE ROSENTHAL IS BUYING A LATE LUNCH FOR THE EVER-ELUSIVE STEVE ROGERS...
AFTER THAT BIG REVELATION YOU RECENTLY DROPPED ON ME,* YOU PROMISED ME SOME KIND OF EXPLANATION...
AGREED.
I HAVEN'T BEEN DELIBERATELY AVOIDING YOU, BERNIE. IT'S JUST...
*SEE CAPTAIN AMERICA #276 FOR DETAILS!
CRASH!
BERNIE! DOWN!
WHAT IN...?!?!
9

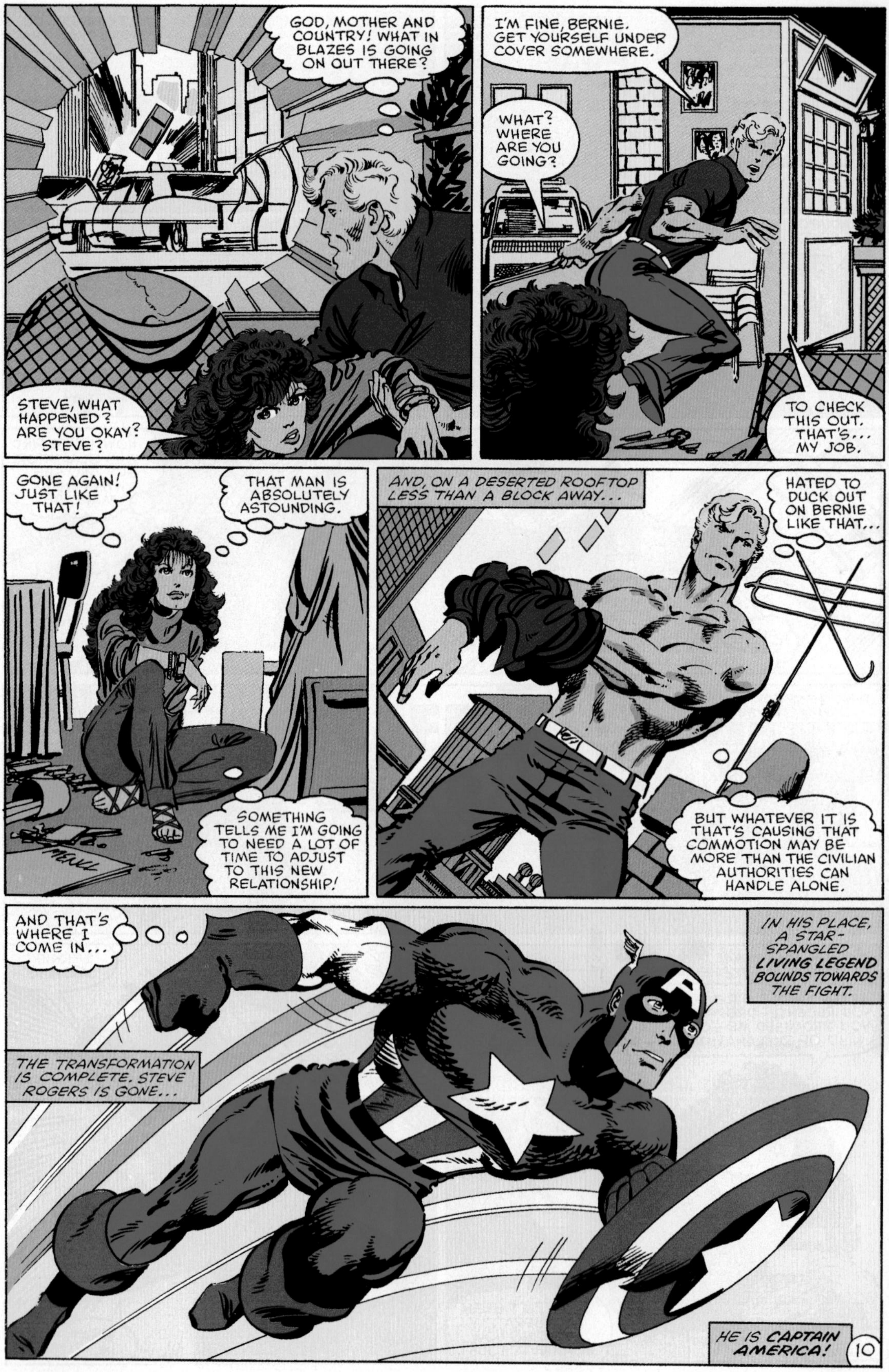
GOD, MOTHER AND COUNTRY! WHAT IN BLAZES IS GOING ON OUT THERE?
STEVE, WHAT HAPPENED? ARE YOU OKAY? STEVE?
I'M FINE, BERNIE. GET YOURSELF UNDER COVER SOMEWHERE.
WHAT? WHERE ARE YOU GOING?
TO CHECK THIS OUT. THAT'S... MY JOB.
GONE AGAIN! JUST LIKE THAT!
THAT MAN IS ABSOLUTELY ASTOUNDING.
SOMETHING TELLS ME I'M GOING TO NEED A LOT OF TIME TO ADJUST TO THIS NEW RELATIONSHIP!
AND, ON A DESERTED ROOFTOP LESS THAN A BLOCK AWAY...
HATED TO DUCK OUT ON BERNIE LIKE THAT...
BUT WHATEVER IT IS THAT'S CAUSING THAT COMMOTION MAY BE MORE THAN THE CIVILIAN AUTHORITIES CAN HANDLE ALONE.
AND THAT'S WHERE I COME IN...
THE TRANSFORMATION IS COMPLETE. STEVE ROGERS IS GONE...
IN HIS PLACE, A STAR-SPANGLED LIVING LEGEND BOUNDS TOWARDS THE FIGHT.
HE IS CAPTAIN AMERICA!

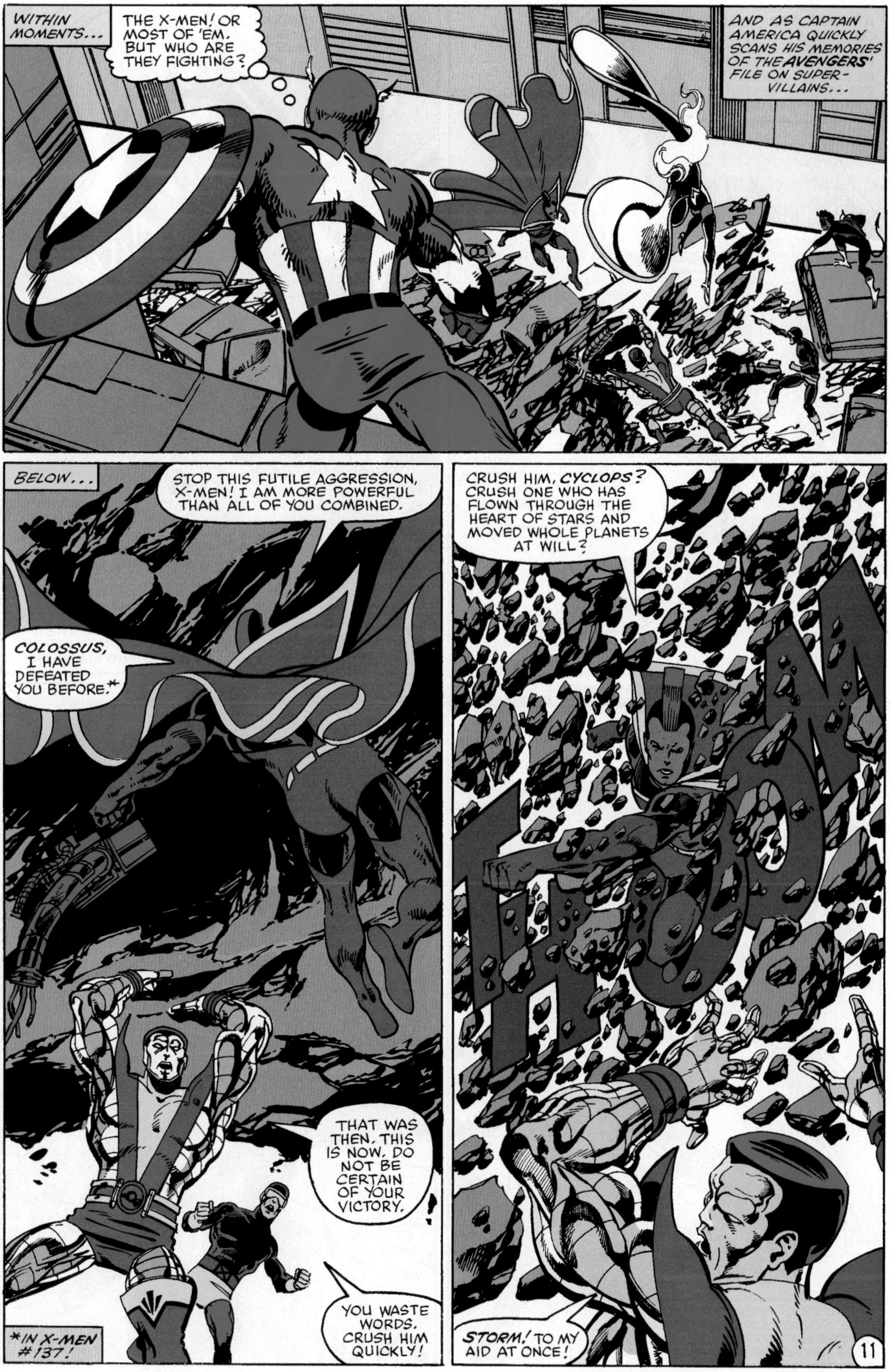
WITHIN MOMENTS...
THE X-MEN! OR MOST OF 'EM. BUT WHO ARE THEY FIGHTING?
AND AS CAPTAIN AMERICA QUICKLY SCANS HIS MEMORIES OF THE AVENGERS' FILE ON SUPER-VILLAINS...
BELOW...
STOP THIS FUTILE AGGRESSION, X-MEN! I AM MORE POWERFUL THAN ALL OF YOU COMBINED.
COLOSSUS, I HAVE DEFEATED YOU BEFORE.*
THAT WAS THEN. THIS IS NOW. DO NOT BE CERTAIN OF YOUR VICTORY.
YOU WASTE WORDS. CRUSH HIM QUICKLY!
*IN X-MEN #137!
CRUSH HIM, CYCLOPS? CRUSH ONE WHO HAS FLOWN THROUGH THE HEART OF STARS AND MOVED WHOLE PLANETS AT WILL?
THOOM
STORM! TO MY AID AT ONCE!

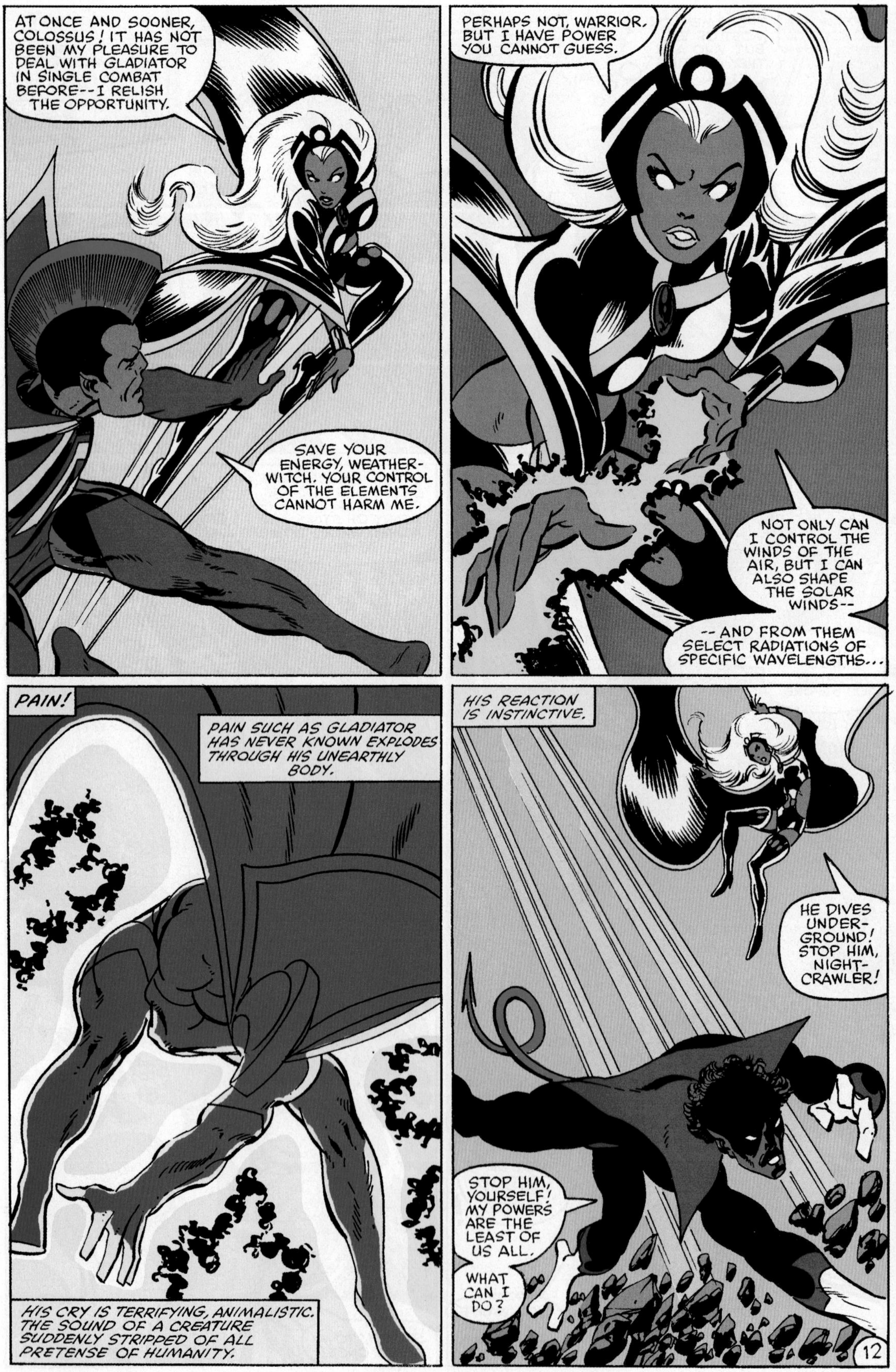
AT ONCE AND SOONER, COLOSSUS! IT HAS NOT BEEN MY PLEASURE TO DEAL WITH GLADIATOR IN SINGLE COMBAT BEFORE--I RELISH THE OPPORTUNITY.
SAVE YOUR ENERGY, WEATHER-WITCH. YOUR CONTROL OF THE ELEMENTS CANNOT HARM ME.
PERHAPS NOT, WARRIOR. BUT I HAVE POWER YOU CANNOT GUESS.
NOT ONLY CAN I CONTROL THE WINDS OF THE AIR, BUT I CAN ALSO SHAPE THE SOLAR WINDS--
--AND FROM THEM SELECT RADIATIONS OF SPECIFIC WAVELENGTHS...
PAIN!
PAIN SUCH AS GLADIATOR HAS NEVER KNOWN EXPLODES THROUGH HIS UNEARTHLY BODY.
HIS CRY IS TERRIFYING, ANIMALISTIC. THE SOUND OF A CREATURE SUDDENLY STRIPPED OF ALL PRETENSE OF HUMANITY.
HIS REACTION IS INSTINCTIVE.
HE DIVES UNDER-GROUND! STOP HIM, NIGHT-CRAWLER!
STOP HIM, YOURSELF! MY POWERS ARE THE LEAST OF US ALL.
WHAT CAN I DO?
12

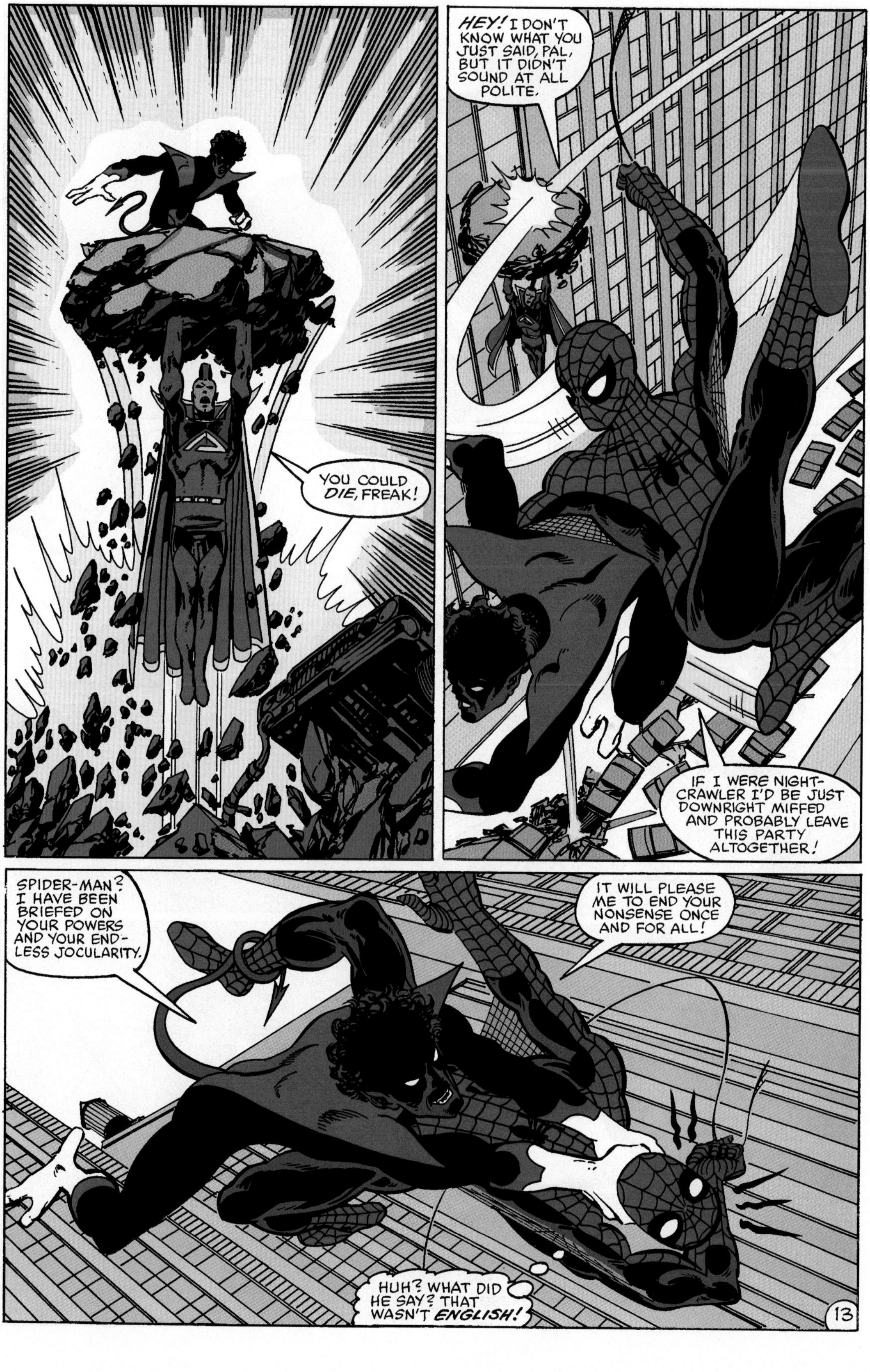
YOU COULD DIE, FREAK!
HEY! I DON'T KNOW WHAT YOU JUST SAID, PAL, BUT IT DIDN'T SOUND AT ALL POLITE.
IF I WERE NIGHT-CRAWLER I'D BE JUST DOWNRIGHT MIFFED AND PROBABLY LEAVE THIS PARTY ALTOGETHER!
SPIDER-MAN? I HAVE BEEN BRIEFED ON YOUR POWERS AND YOUR END-LESS JOCULARITY.
IT WILL PLEASE ME TO END YOUR NONSENSE ONCE AND FOR ALL!
HUH? WHAT DID HE SAY? THAT WASN'T ENGLISH!

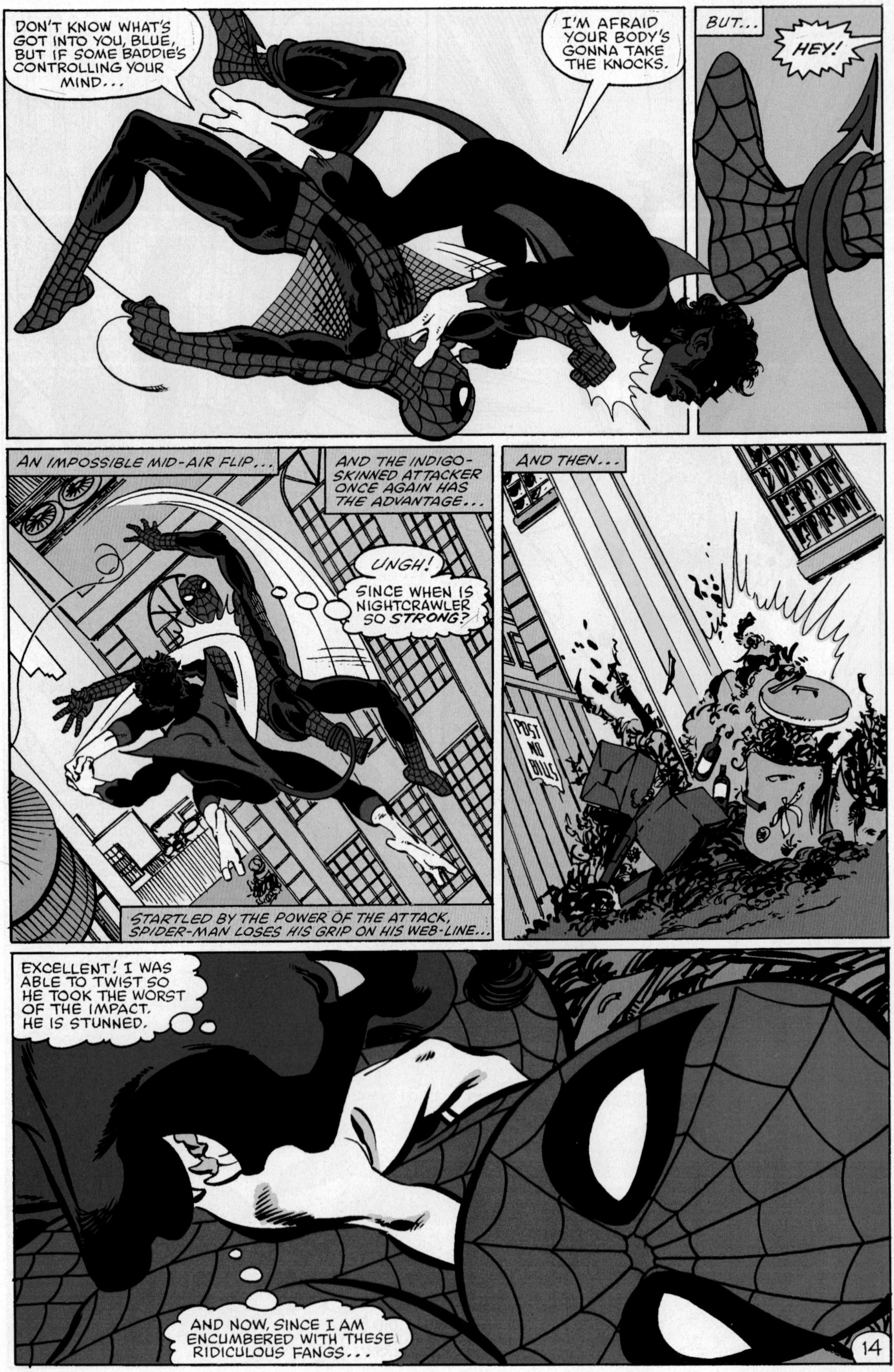
DON'T KNOW WHAT'S GOT INTO YOU, BLUE, BUT IF SOME BADDIE'S CONTROLLING YOUR MIND...
I'M AFRAID YOUR BODY'S GONNA TAKE THE KNOCKS.
BUT...
HEY!
AN IMPOSSIBLE MID-AIR FLIP...
AND THE INDIGO-SKINNED ATTACKER ONCE AGAIN HAS THE ADVANTAGE...
UNGH!
SINCE WHEN IS NIGHTCRAWLER SO STRONG?
STARTLED BY THE POWER OF THE ATTACK, SPIDER-MAN LOSES HIS GRIP ON HIS WEB-LINE...
AND THEN...
POST NO BILLS
EXCELLENT! I WAS ABLE TO TWIST SO HE TOOK THE WORST OF THE IMPACT. HE IS STUNNED.
AND NOW, SINCE I AM ENCUMBERED WITH THESE RIDICULOUS FANGS...
14

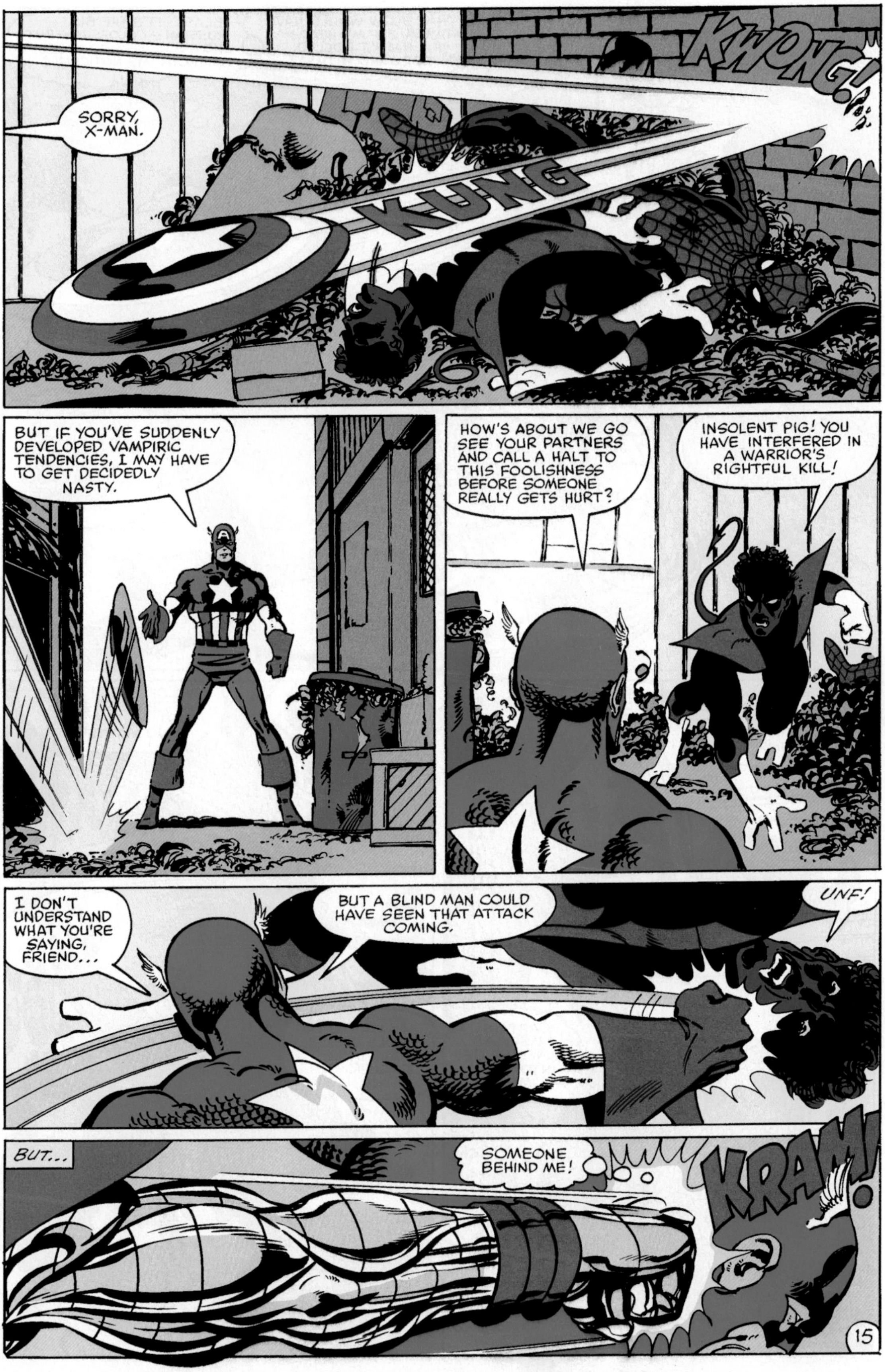

KWONG!
SORRY, X-MAN.
KUNG
BUT IF YOU'VE SUDDENLY DEVELOPED VAMPIRIC TENDENCIES, I MAY HAVE TO GET DECIDEDLY NASTY.
HOW'S ABOUT WE GO SEE YOUR PARTNERS AND CALL A HALT TO THIS FOOLISHNESS BEFORE SOMEONE REALLY GETS HURT?
INSOLENT PIG! YOU HAVE INTERFERED IN A WARRIOR'S RIGHTFUL KILL!
I DON'T UNDERSTAND WHAT YOU'RE SAYING, FRIEND...
BUT A BLIND MAN COULD HAVE SEEN THAT ATTACK COMING.
UNF!
BUT...
SOMEONE BEHIND ME!
KRAM!

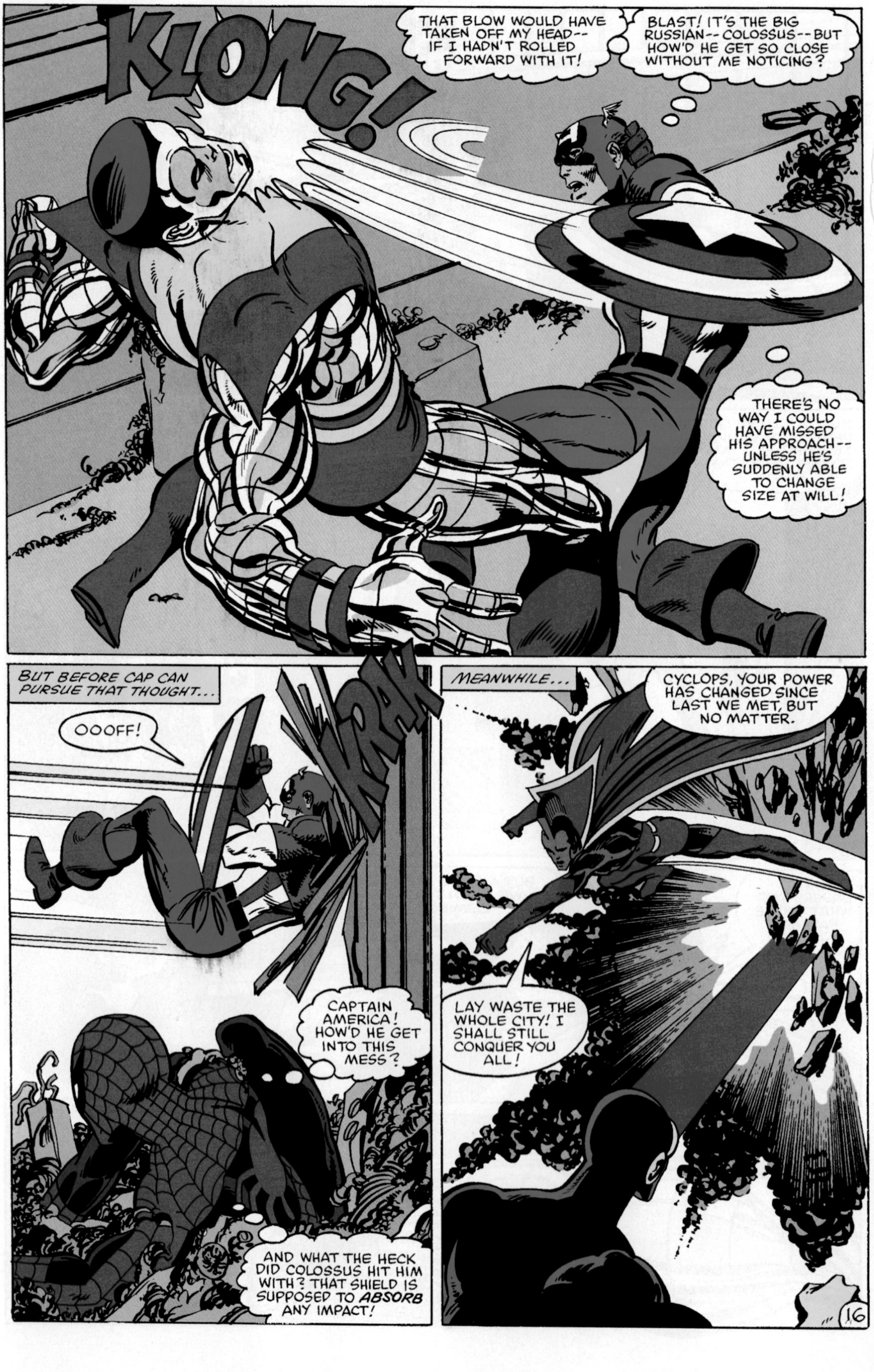
KLONG!
THAT BLOW WOULD HAVE TAKEN OFF MY HEAD-- IF I HADN'T ROLLED FORWARD WITH IT!
BLAST! IT'S THE BIG RUSSIAN-- COLOSSUS-- BUT HOW'D HE GET SO CLOSE WITHOUT ME NOTICING?
THERE'S NO WAY I COULD HAVE MISSED HIS APPROACH-- UNLESS HE'S SUDDENLY ABLE TO CHANGE SIZE AT WILL!
BUT BEFORE CAP CAN PURSUE THAT THOUGHT...
OOOFF!
KRAK
CAPTAIN AMERICA! HOW'D HE GET INTO THIS MESS?
AND WHAT THE HECK DID COLOSSUS HIT HIM WITH? THAT SHIELD IS SUPPOSED TO ABSORB ANY IMPACT!
MEANWHILE...
CYCLOPS, YOUR POWER HAS CHANGED SINCE LAST WE MET, BUT NO MATTER.
LAY WASTE THE WHOLE CITY! I SHALL STILL CONQUER YOU ALL!
16

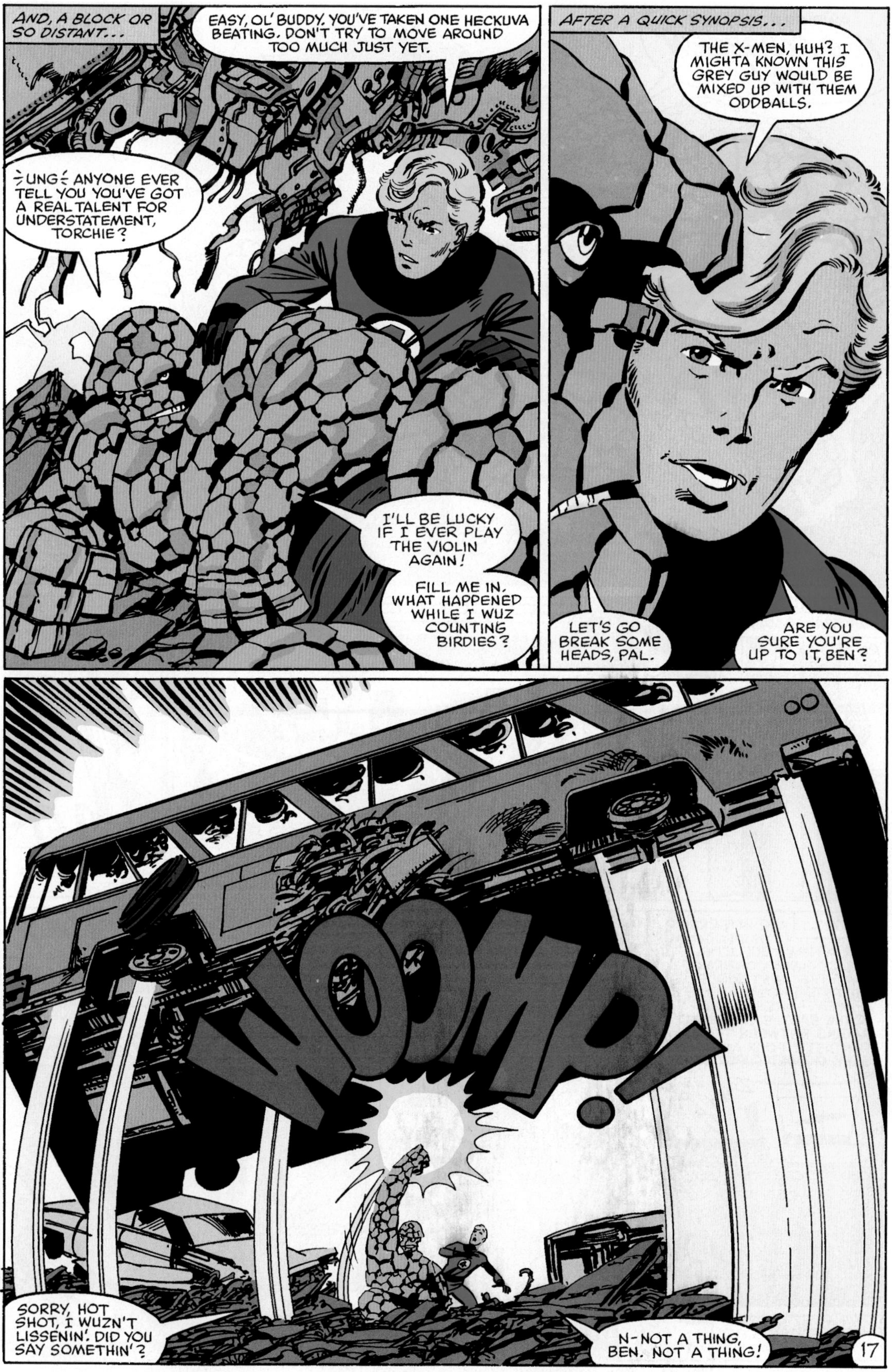
AND, A BLOCK OR SO DISTANT...
EASY, OL' BUDDY. YOU'VE TAKEN ONE HECKUVA BEATING. DON'T TRY TO MOVE AROUND TOO MUCH JUST YET.
-UNG- ANYONE EVER TELL YOU YOU'VE GOT A REAL TALENT FOR UNDERSTATEMENT, TORCHIE?
I'LL BE LUCKY IF I EVER PLAY THE VIOLIN AGAIN!
FILL ME IN. WHAT HAPPENED WHILE I WUZ COUNTING BIRDIES?
AFTER A QUICK SYNOPSIS...
THE X-MEN, HUH? I MIGHTA KNOWN THIS GREY GUY WOULD BE MIXED UP WITH THEM ODDBALLS.
LET'S GO BREAK SOME HEADS, PAL.
ARE YOU SURE YOU'RE UP TO IT, BEN?
WOOMP!
SORRY, HOT SHOT, I WUZN'T LISSENIN'. DID YOU SAY SOMETHIN'?
N-NOT A THING, BEN. NOT A THING!

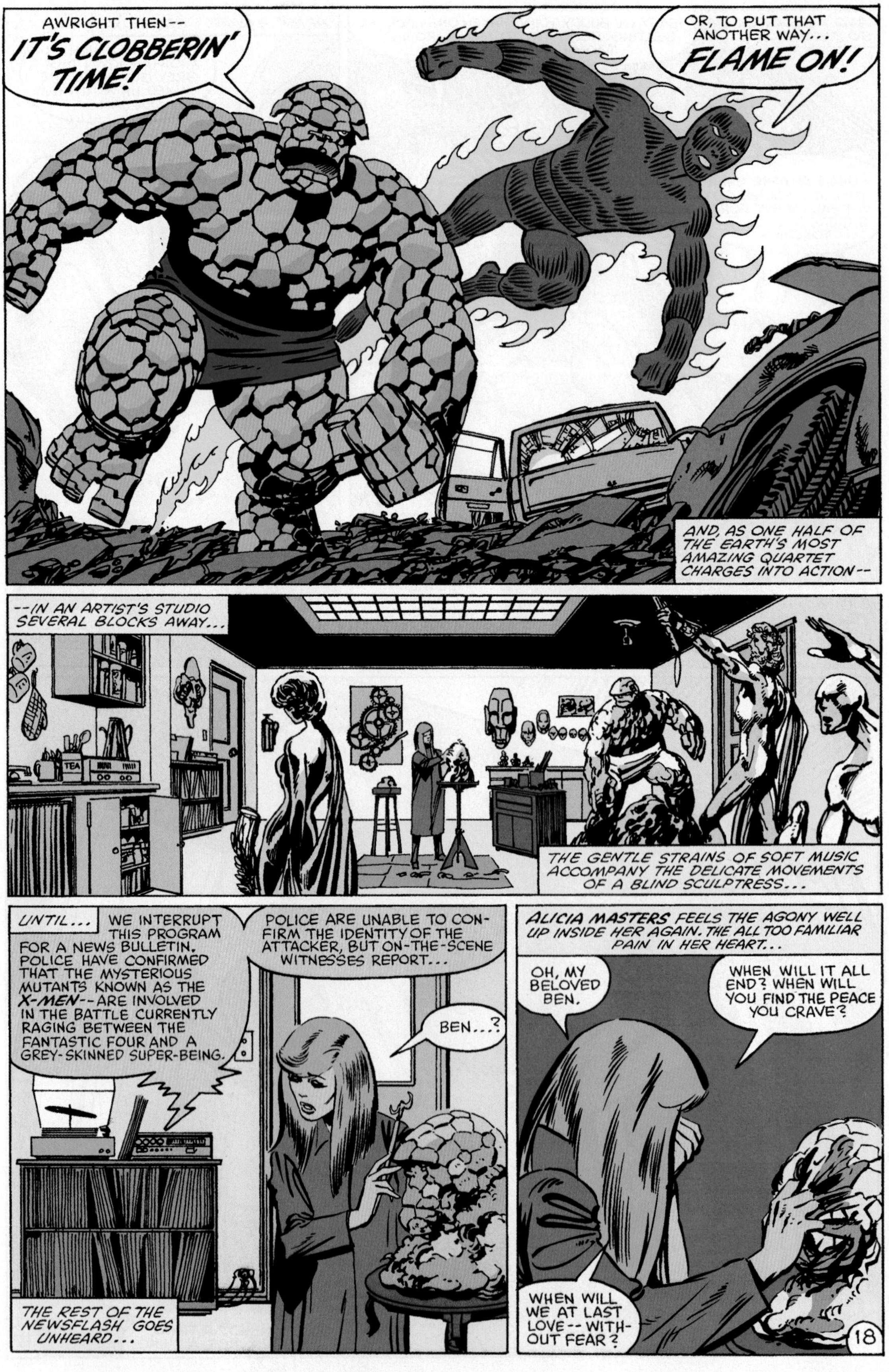
AWRIGHT THEN-- IT'S CLOBBERIN' TIME!
OR, TO PUT THAT ANOTHER WAY... FLAME ON!
AND, AS ONE HALF OF THE EARTH'S MOST AMAZING QUARTET CHARGES INTO ACTION--
--IN AN ARTIST'S STUDIO SEVERAL BLOCKS AWAY...
TEA
THE GENTLE STRAINS OF SOFT MUSIC ACCOMPANY THE DELICATE MOVEMENTS OF A BLIND SCULPTRESS...
UNTIL...
WE INTERRUPT THIS PROGRAM FOR A NEWS BULLETIN. POLICE HAVE CONFIRMED THAT THE MYSTERIOUS MUTANTS KNOWN AS THE X-MEN--ARE INVOLVED IN THE BATTLE CURRENTLY RAGING BETWEEN THE FANTASTIC FOUR AND A GREY-SKINNED SUPER-BEING.
POLICE ARE UNABLE TO CONFIRM THE IDENTITY OF THE ATTACKER, BUT ON-THE-SCENE WITNESSES REPORT...
BEN...?
THE REST OF THE NEWSFLASH GOES UNHEARD...
ALICIA MASTERS FEELS THE AGONY WELL UP INSIDE HER AGAIN. THE ALL TOO FAMILIAR PAIN IN HER HEART...
OH, MY BELOVED BEN.
WHEN WILL IT ALL END? WHEN WILL YOU FIND THE PEACE YOU CRAVE?
WHEN WILL WE AT LAST LOVE--WITHOUT FEAR?
18

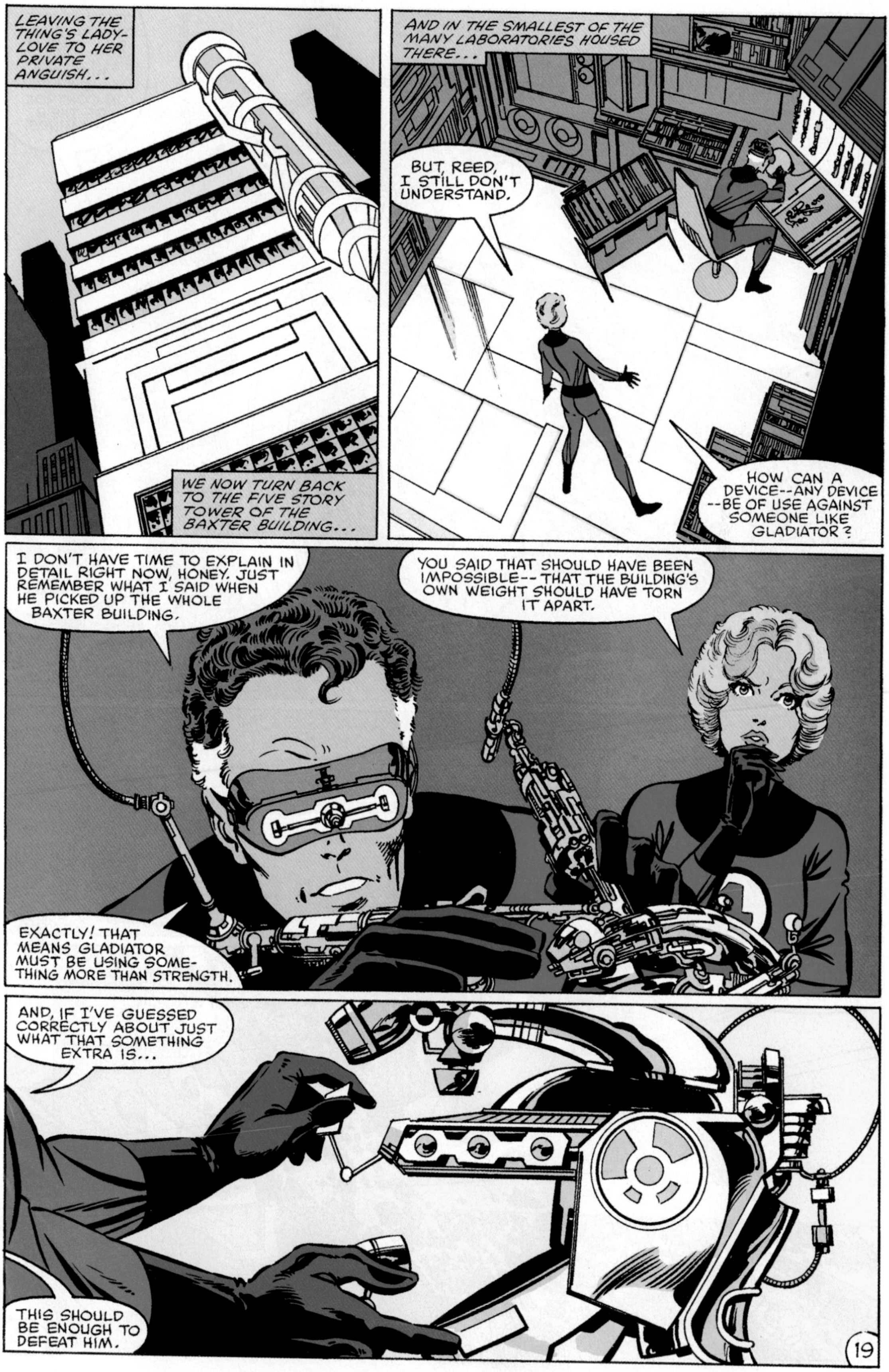
LEAVING THE THING'S LADY-LOVE TO HER PRIVATE ANGUISH...
WE NOW TURN BACK TO THE FIVE STORY TOWER OF THE BAXTER BUILDING...
AND IN THE SMALLEST OF THE MANY LABORATORIES HOUSED THERE...
BUT, REED, I STILL DON'T UNDERSTAND.
HOW CAN A DEVICE--ANY DEVICE--BE OF USE AGAINST SOMEONE LIKE GLADIATOR?
I DON'T HAVE TIME TO EXPLAIN IN DETAIL RIGHT NOW, HONEY. JUST REMEMBER WHAT I SAID WHEN HE PICKED UP THE WHOLE BAXTER BUILDING.
YOU SAID THAT SHOULD HAVE BEEN IMPOSSIBLE-- THAT THE BUILDING'S OWN WEIGHT SHOULD HAVE TORN IT APART.
EXACTLY! THAT MEANS GLADIATOR MUST BE USING SOMETHING MORE THAN STRENGTH.
AND, IF I'VE GUESSED CORRECTLY ABOUT JUST WHAT THAT SOMETHING EXTRA IS...
THIS SHOULD BE ENOUGH TO DEFEAT HIM.

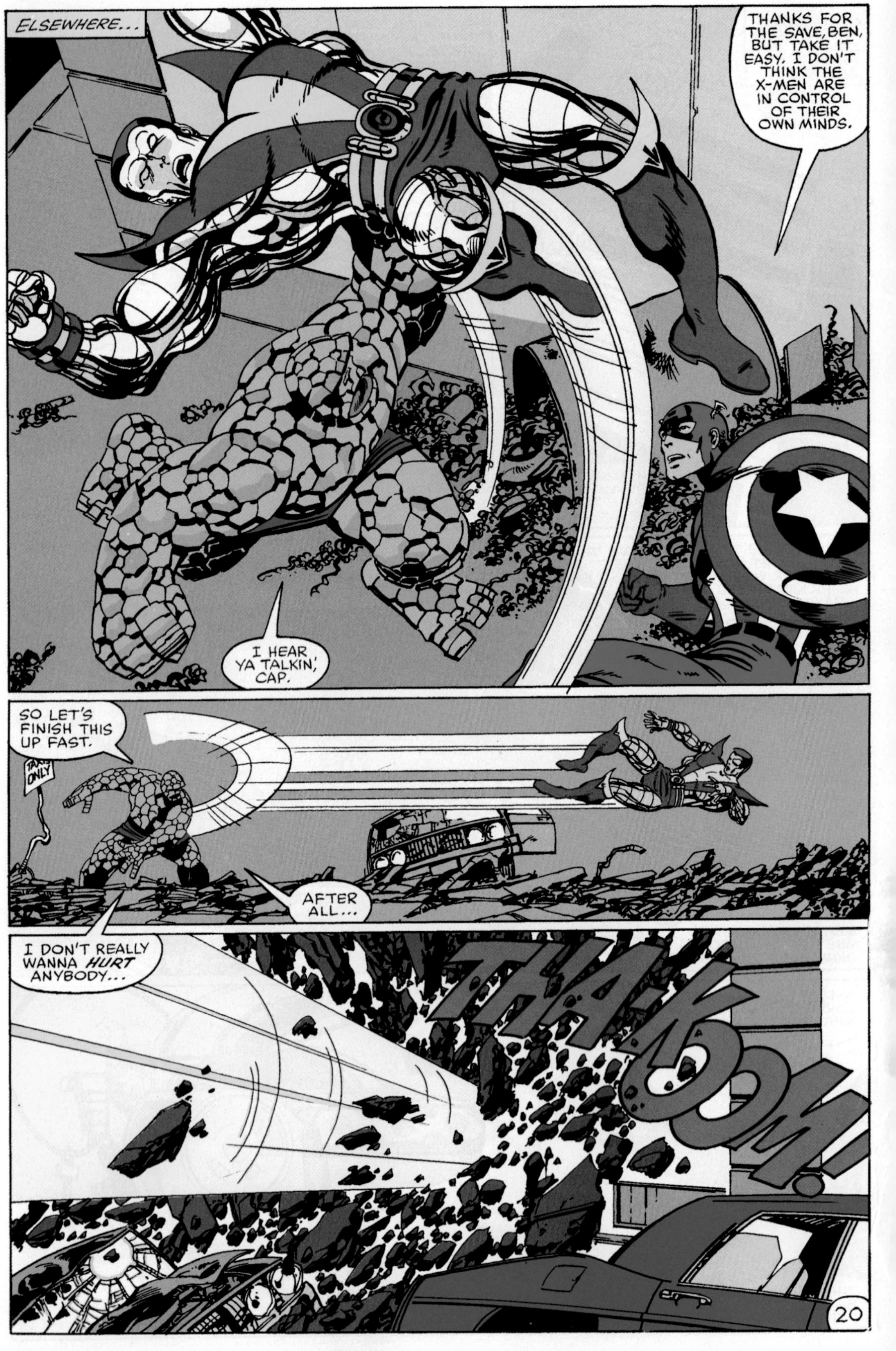
ELSEWHERE...
THANKS FOR THE SAVE, BEN, BUT TAKE IT EASY. I DON'T THINK THE X-MEN ARE IN CONTROL OF THEIR OWN MINDS.
I HEAR YA TALKIN', CAP.
SO LET'S FINISH THIS UP FAST.
AFTER ALL...
I DON'T REALLY WANNA HURT ANYBODY...
THA-KOOM!

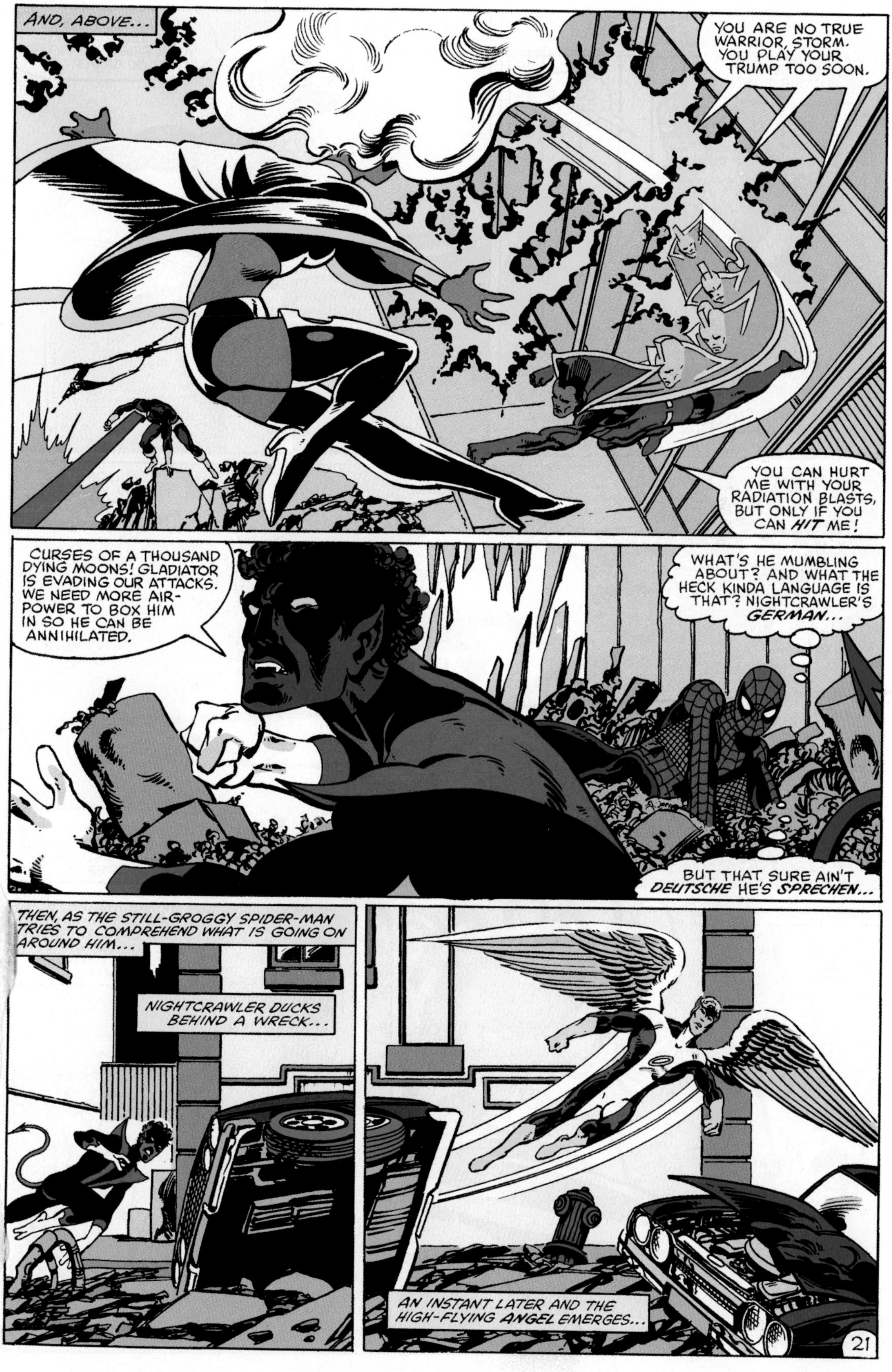
AND, ABOVE...
YOU ARE NO TRUE WARRIOR, STORM. YOU PLAY YOUR TRUMP TOO SOON.
YOU CAN HURT ME WITH YOUR RADIATION BLASTS, BUT ONLY IF YOU CAN HIT ME!
CURSES OF A THOUSAND DYING MOONS! GLADIATOR IS EVADING OUR ATTACKS. WE NEED MORE AIR-POWER TO BOX HIM IN SO HE CAN BE ANNIHILATED.
WHAT'S HE MUMBLING ABOUT? AND WHAT THE HECK KINDA LANGUAGE IS THAT? NIGHTCRAWLER'S GERMAN...
BUT THAT SURE AIN'T DEUTSCHE HE'S SPRECHEN...
THEN, AS THE STILL-GROGGY SPIDER-MAN TRIES TO COMPREHEND WHAT IS GOING ON AROUND HIM...
NIGHTCRAWLER DUCKS BEHIND A WRECK...
AN INSTANT LATER AND THE HIGH-FLYING ANGEL EMERGES...
21

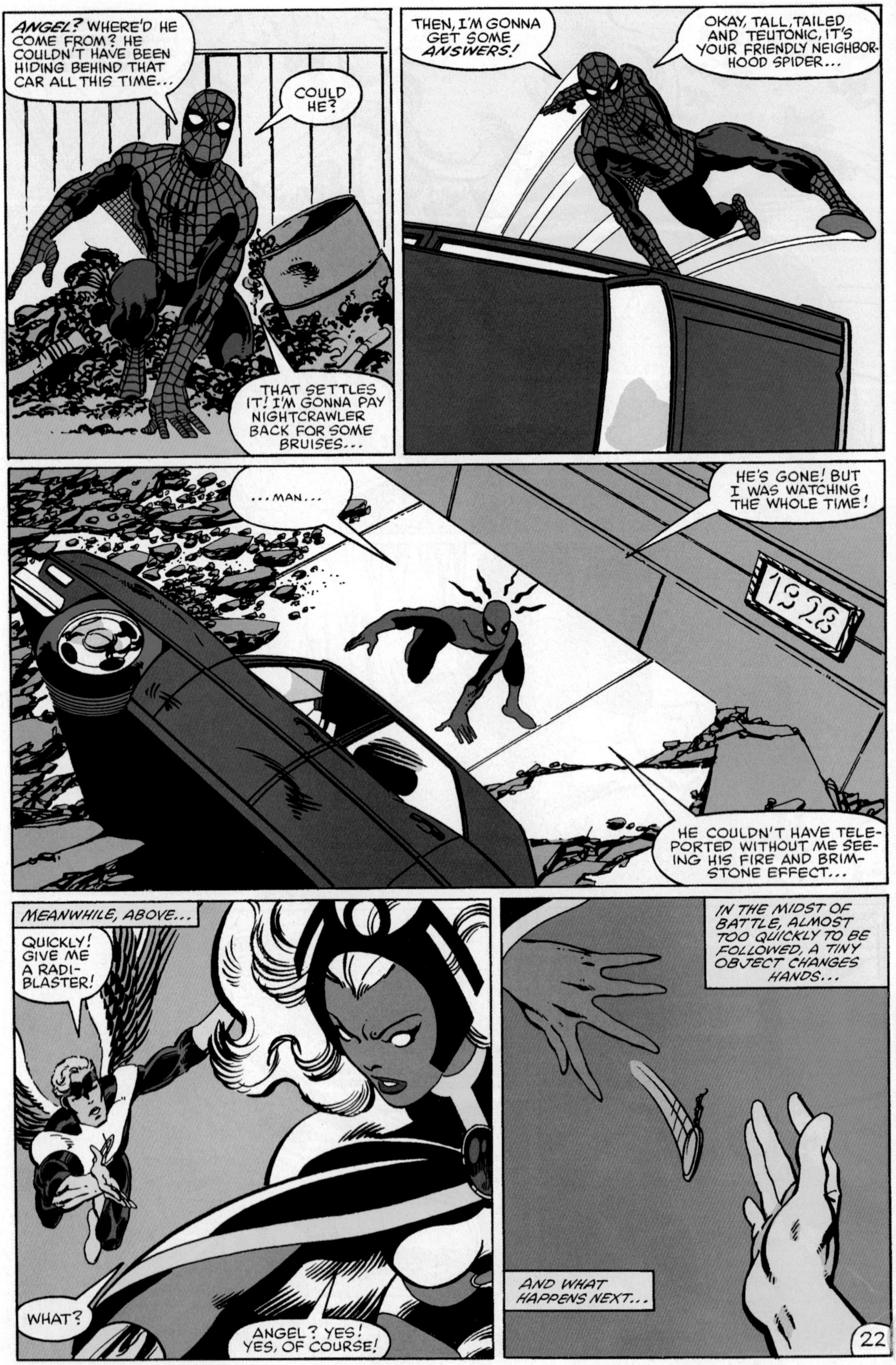
ANGEL? WHERE'D HE COME FROM? HE COULDN'T HAVE BEEN HIDING BEHIND THAT CAR ALL THIS TIME...
COULD HE?
THAT SETTLES IT! I'M GONNA PAY NIGHTCRAWLER BACK FOR SOME BRUISES...
THEN, I'M GONNA GET SOME ANSWERS!
OKAY, TALL, TAILED AND TEUTONIC, IT'S YOUR FRIENDLY NEIGHBORHOOD SPIDER...
...MAN...
HE'S GONE! BUT I WAS WATCHING THE WHOLE TIME!
1928
HE COULDN'T HAVE TELEPORTED WITHOUT ME SEEING HIS FIRE AND BRIMSTONE EFFECT...
MEANWHILE, ABOVE...
QUICKLY! GIVE ME A RADI-BLASTER!
WHAT?
ANGEL? YES! YES, OF COURSE!
IN THE MIDST OF BATTLE, ALMOST TOO QUICKLY TO BE FOLLOWED, A TINY OBJECT CHANGES HANDS...
AND WHAT HAPPENS NEXT...
22

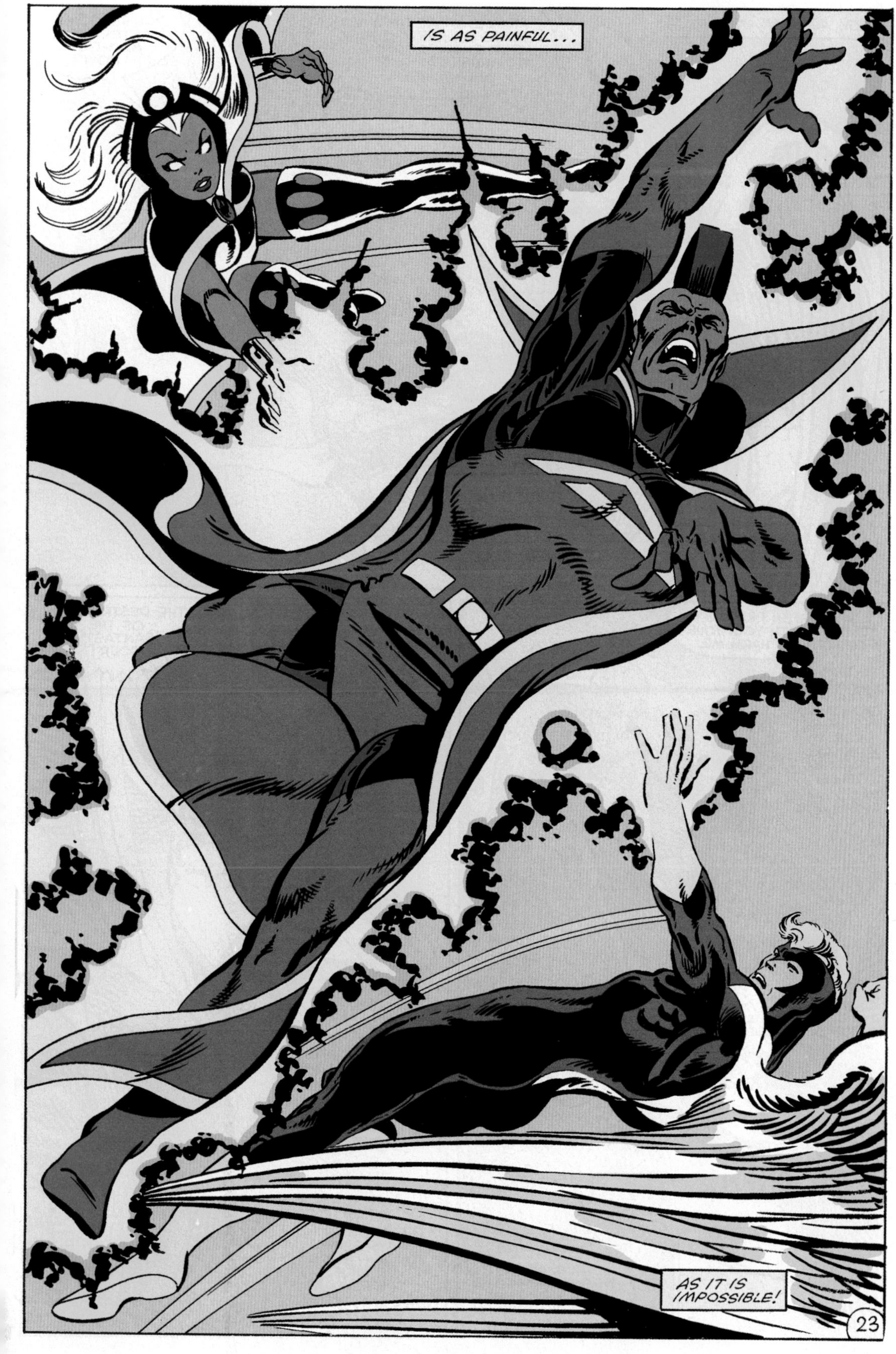
IS AS PAINFUL...
AS IT IS IMPOSSIBLE!

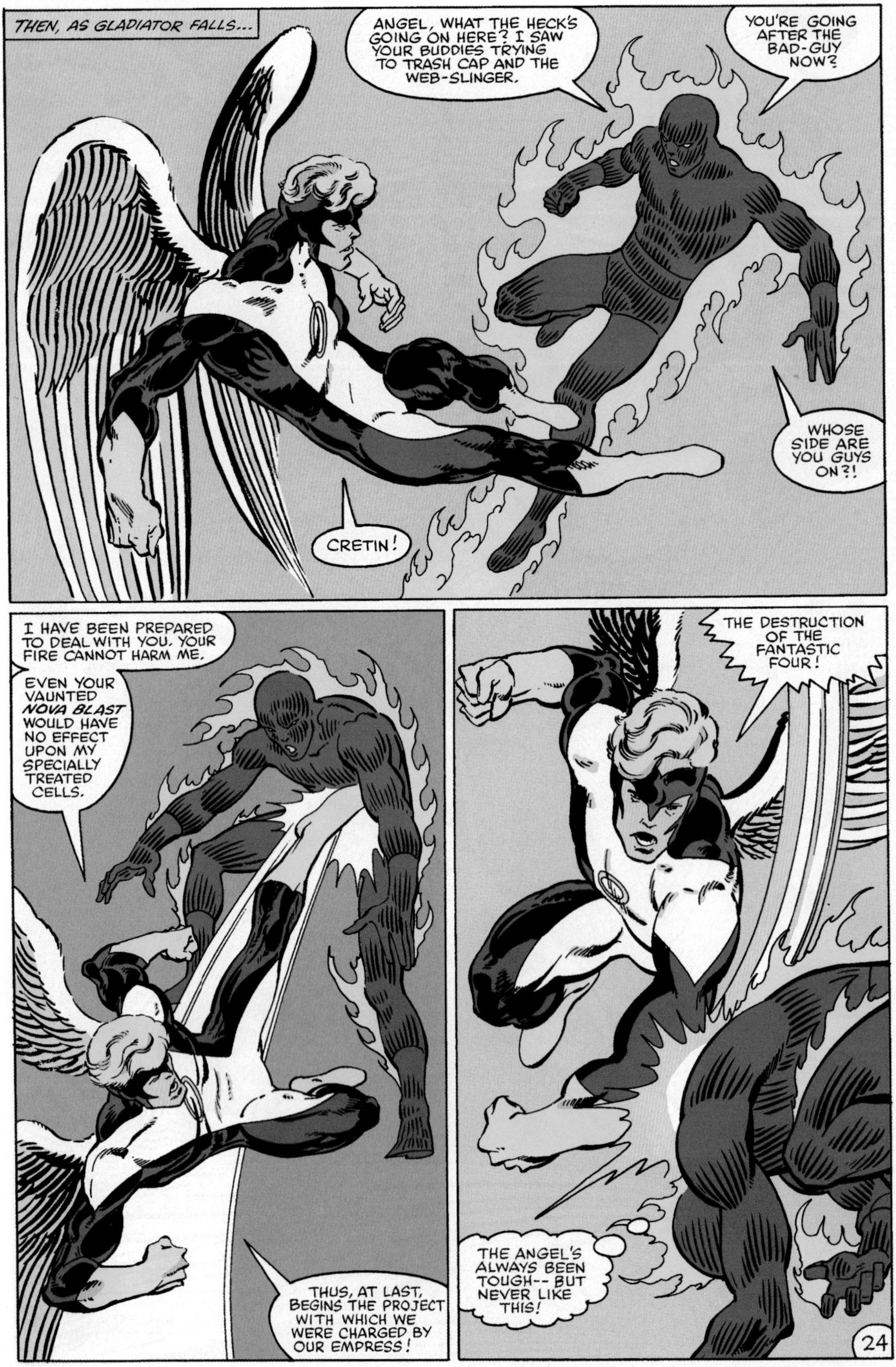
THEN, AS GLADIATOR FALLS...
ANGEL, WHAT THE HECK'S GOING ON HERE? I SAW YOUR BUDDIES TRYING TO TRASH CAP AND THE WEB-SLINGER.
YOU'RE GOING AFTER THE BAD-GUY NOW?
WHOSE SIDE ARE YOU GUYS ON?!
CRETIN!
I HAVE BEEN PREPARED TO DEAL WITH YOU. YOUR FIRE CANNOT HARM ME.
EVEN YOUR VAUNTED NOVA BLAST WOULD HAVE NO EFFECT UPON MY SPECIALLY TREATED CELLS.
THUS, AT LAST, BEGINS THE PROJECT WITH WHICH WE WERE CHARGED BY OUR EMPRESS!
THE DESTRUCTION OF THE FANTASTIC FOUR!
THE ANGEL'S ALWAYS BEEN TOUGH-- BUT NEVER LIKE THIS!

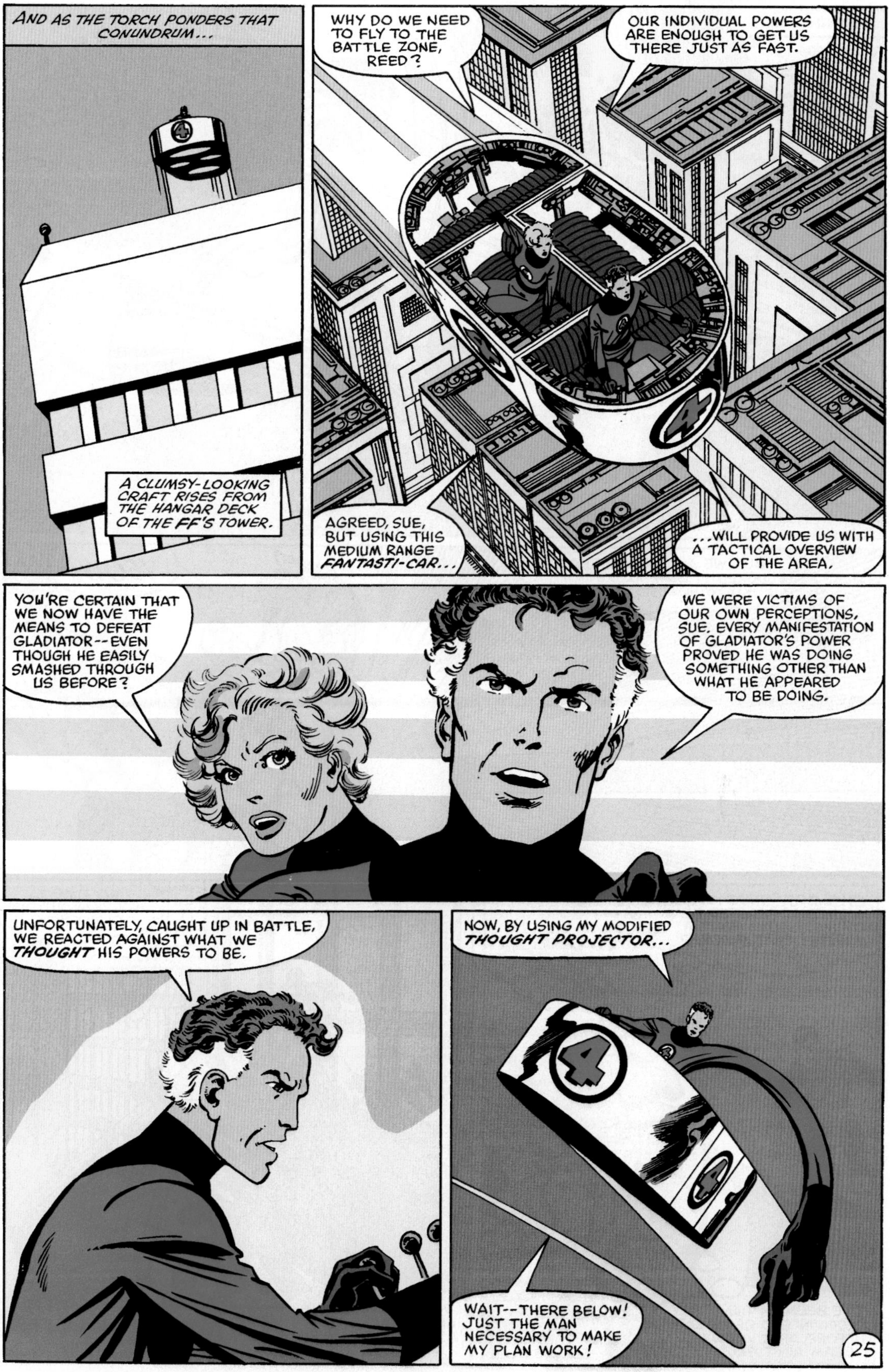
AND AS THE TORCH PONDERS THAT CONUNDRUM...
A CLUMSY-LOOKING CRAFT RISES FROM THE HANGAR DECK OF THE FF'S TOWER.
WHY DO WE NEED TO FLY TO THE BATTLE ZONE, REED?
OUR INDIVIDUAL POWERS ARE ENOUGH TO GET US THERE JUST AS FAST.
AGREED, SUE, BUT USING THIS MEDIUM RANGE FANTASTI-CAR...
...WILL PROVIDE US WITH A TACTICAL OVERVIEW OF THE AREA.
YOU'RE CERTAIN THAT WE NOW HAVE THE MEANS TO DEFEAT GLADIATOR--EVEN THOUGH HE EASILY SMASHED THROUGH US BEFORE?
WE WERE VICTIMS OF OUR OWN PERCEPTIONS, SUE. EVERY MANIFESTATION OF GLADIATOR'S POWER PROVED HE WAS DOING SOMETHING OTHER THAN WHAT HE APPEARED TO BE DOING.
UNFORTUNATELY, CAUGHT UP IN BATTLE, WE REACTED AGAINST WHAT WE THOUGHT HIS POWERS TO BE.
NOW, BY USING MY MODIFIED THOUGHT PROJECTOR...
WAIT--THERE BELOW! JUST THE MAN NECESSARY TO MAKE MY PLAN WORK!

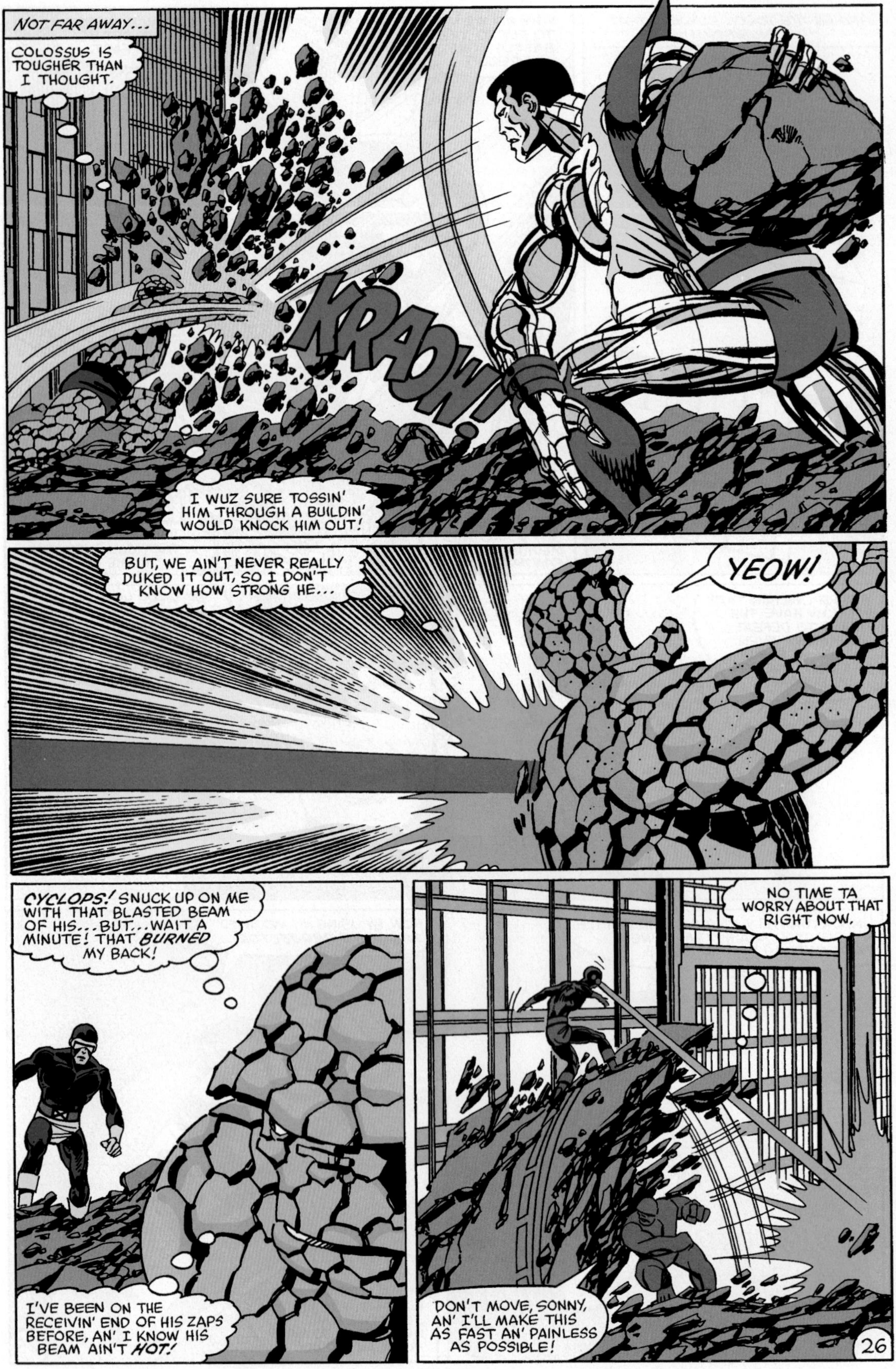
NOT FAR AWAY...
COLOSSUS IS TOUGHER THAN I THOUGHT.
KRAOW!
I WUZ SURE TOSSIN' HIM THROUGH A BUILDIN' WOULD KNOCK HIM OUT!
BUT, WE AIN'T NEVER REALLY DUKED IT OUT, SO I DON'T KNOW HOW STRONG HE...
YEOW!
CYCLOPS! SNUCK UP ON ME WITH THAT BLASTED BEAM OF HIS...BUT...WAIT A MINUTE! THAT BURNED MY BACK!
I'VE BEEN ON THE RECEIVIN' END OF HIS ZAPS BEFORE, AN' I KNOW HIS BEAM AIN'T HOT!
NO TIME TA WORRY ABOUT THAT RIGHT NOW.
DON'T MOVE, SONNY, AN' I'LL MAKE THIS AS FAST AN' PAINLESS AS POSSIBLE!

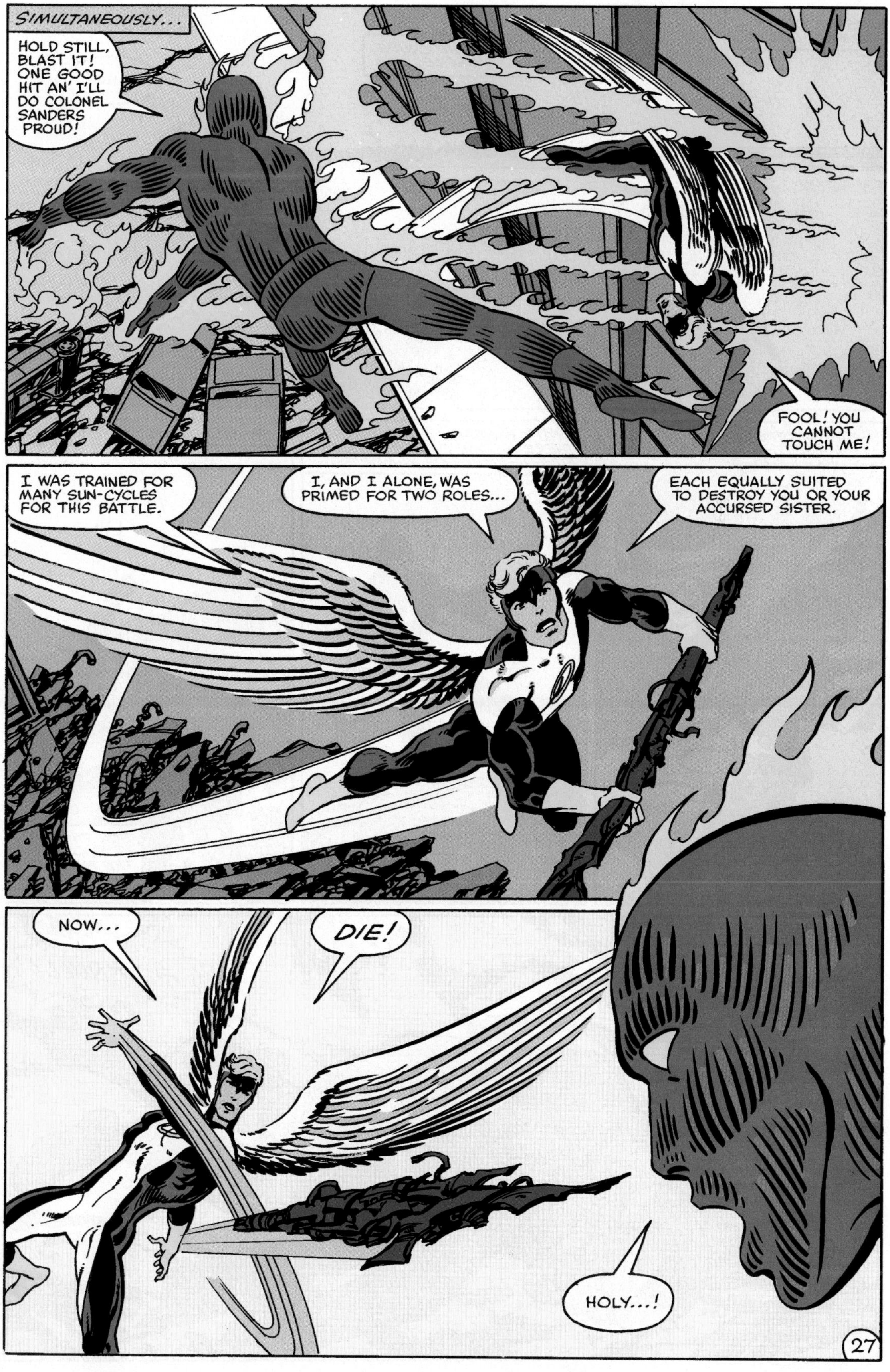
SIMULTANEOUSLY...
HOLD STILL, BLAST IT! ONE GOOD HIT AN' I'LL DO COLONEL SANDERS PROUD!
FOOL! YOU CANNOT TOUCH ME!
I WAS TRAINED FOR MANY SUN-CYCLES FOR THIS BATTLE.
I, AND I ALONE, WAS PRIMED FOR TWO ROLES...
EACH EQUALLY SUITED TO DESTROY YOU OR YOUR ACCURSED SISTER.
NOW...
DIE!
HOLY...!

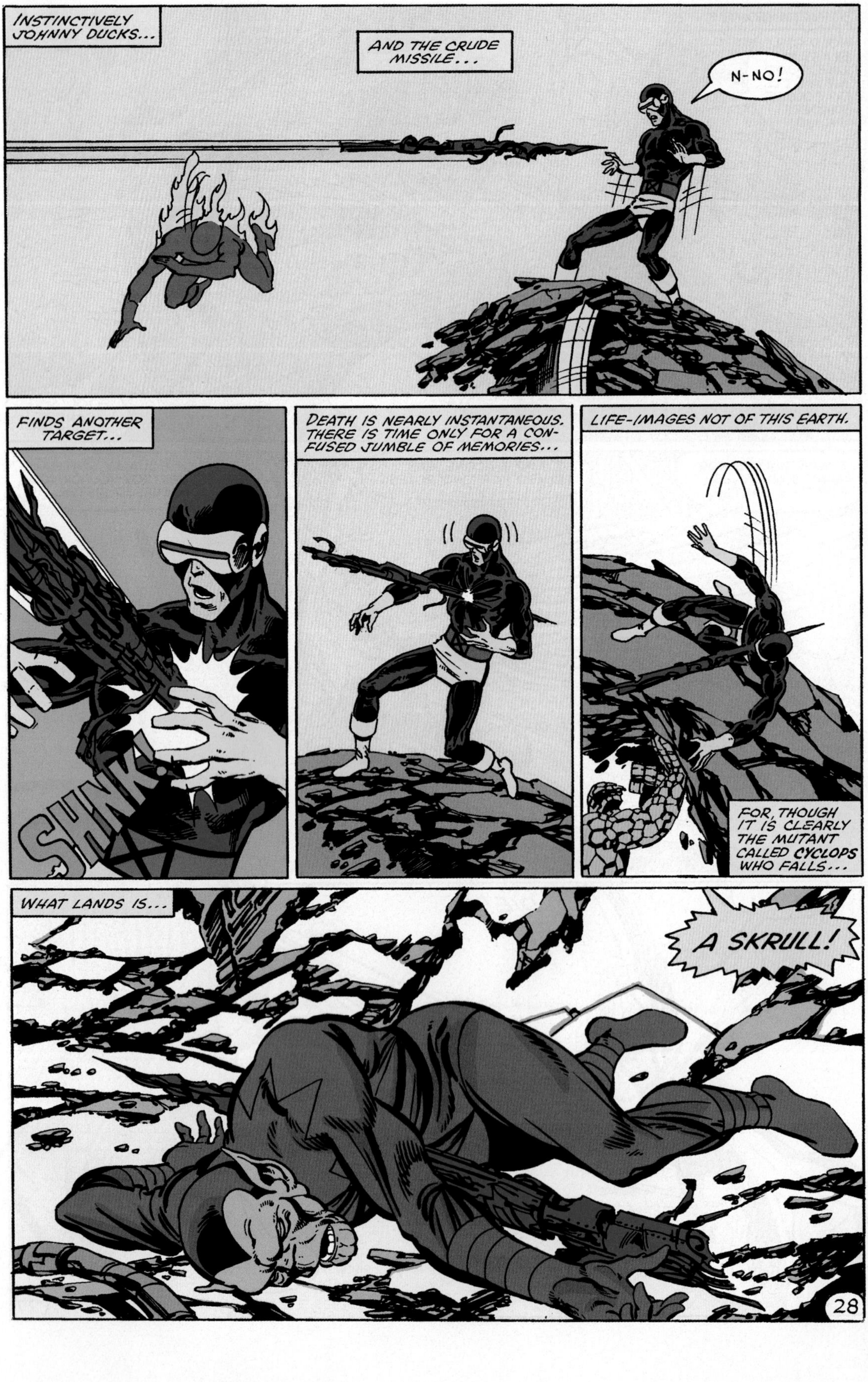

INSTINCTIVELY JOHNNY DUCKS...
AND THE CRUDE MISSILE...
N-NO!
FINDS ANOTHER TARGET...
SHNK
DEATH IS NEARLY INSTANTANEOUS. THERE IS TIME ONLY FOR A CONFUSED JUMBLE OF MEMORIES...
LIFE-IMAGES NOT OF THIS EARTH.
FOR, THOUGH IT IS CLEARLY THE MUTANT CALLED **CYCLOPS** WHO FALLS...
WHAT LANDS IS...
A SKRULL!

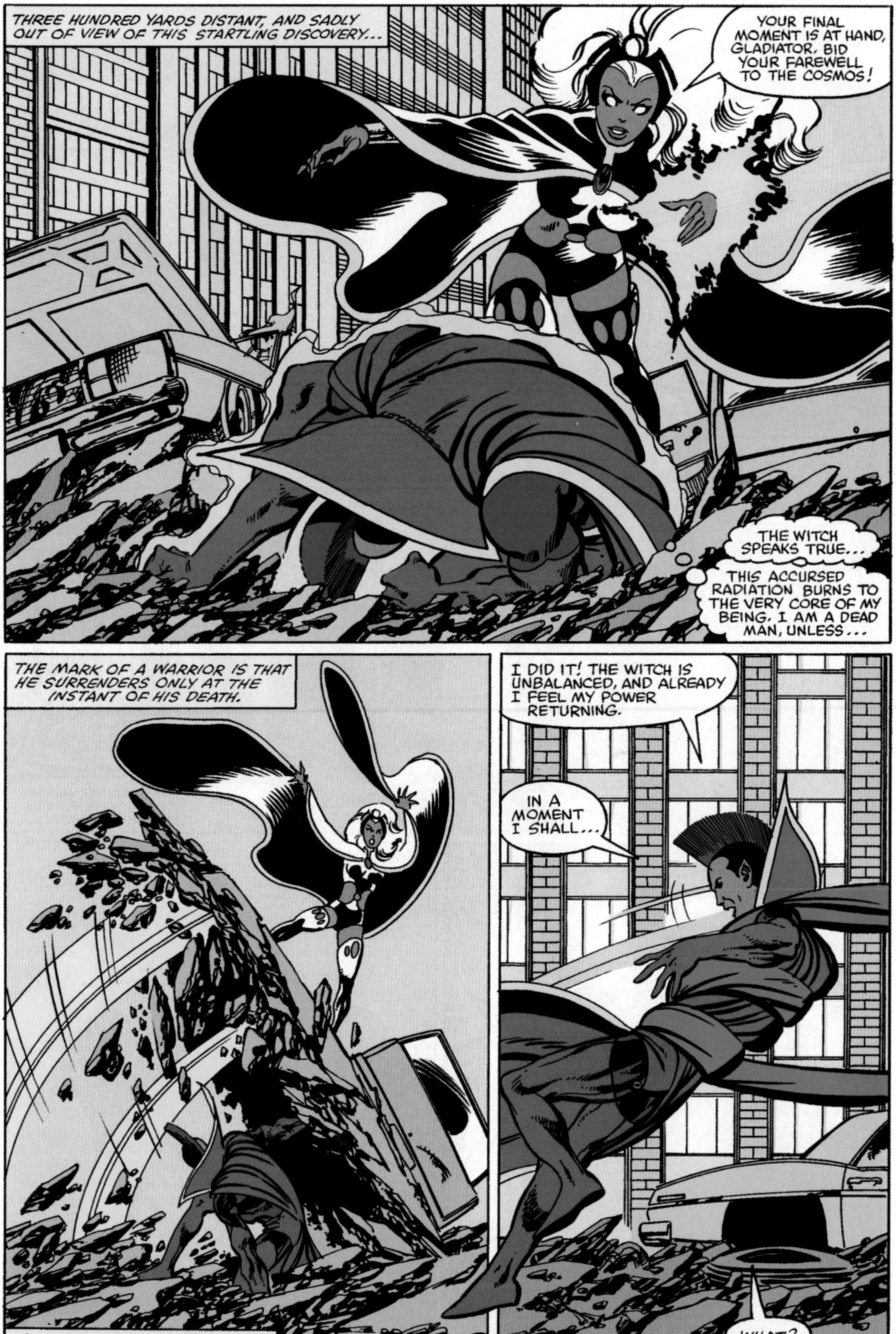
THREE HUNDRED YARDS DISTANT, AND SADLY OUT OF VIEW OF THIS STARTLING DISCOVERY...
YOUR FINAL MOMENT IS AT HAND, GLADIATOR. BID YOUR FAREWELL TO THE COSMOS!
THE WITCH SPEAKS TRUE...
THIS ACCURSED RADIATION BURNS TO THE VERY CORE OF MY BEING. I AM A DEAD MAN, UNLESS...
THE MARK OF A WARRIOR IS THAT HE SURRENDERS ONLY AT THE INSTANT OF HIS DEATH.
AND GLADIATOR IS A WARRIOR FIRST, LAST, AND ALWAYS!
I DID IT! THE WITCH IS UNBALANCED, AND ALREADY I FEEL MY POWER RETURNING.
IN A MOMENT I SHALL...
WHAT?
29

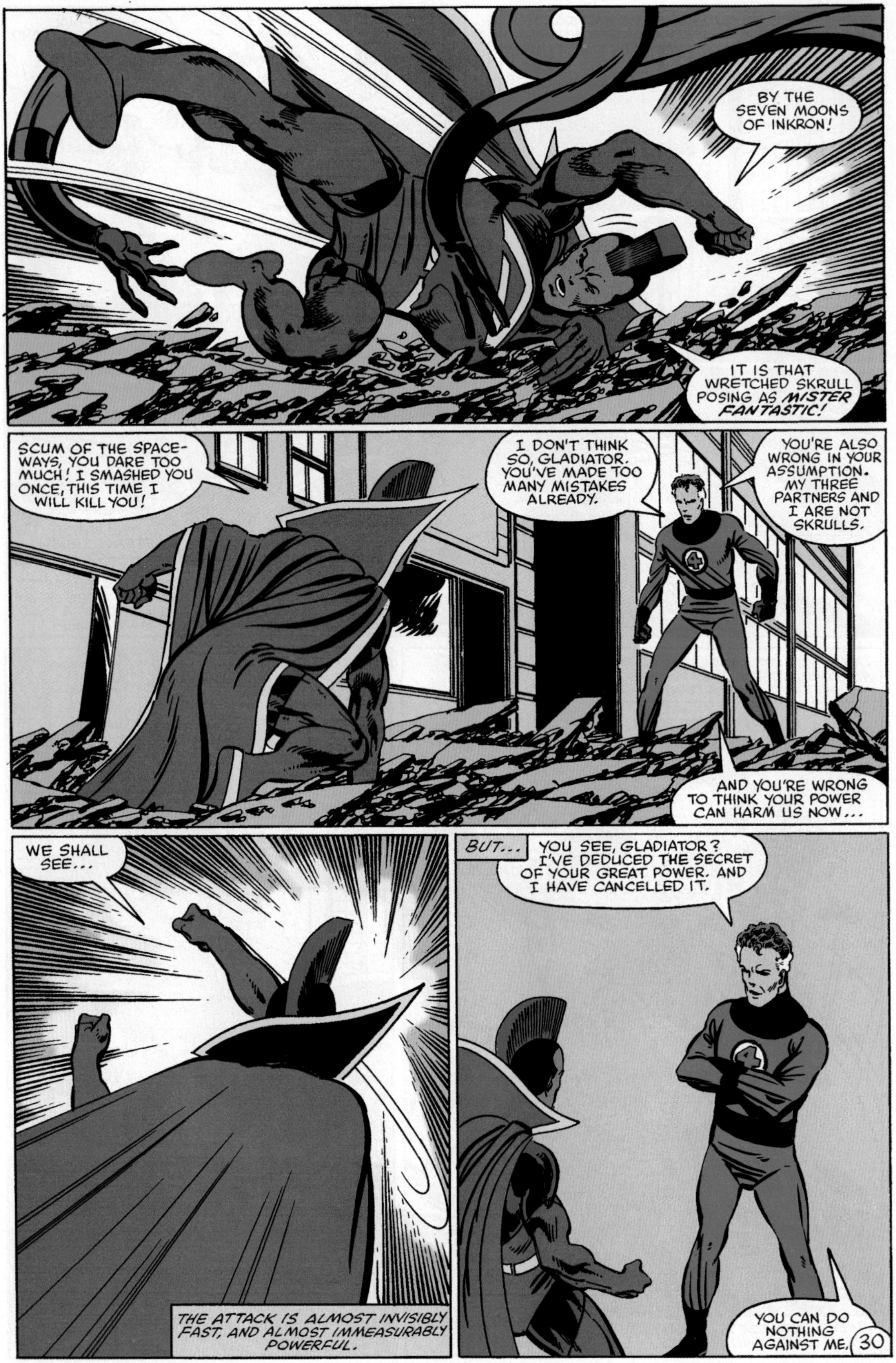

BY THE SEVEN MOONS OF INKRON!
IT IS THAT WRETCHED SKRULL POSING AS *MISTER FANTASTIC!*
SCUM OF THE SPACE-WAYS, YOU DARE TOO MUCH! I SMASHED YOU ONCE, THIS TIME I WILL KILL YOU!
I DON'T THINK SO, GLADIATOR. YOU'VE MADE TOO MANY MISTAKES ALREADY.
YOU'RE ALSO WRONG IN YOUR ASSUMPTION. MY THREE PARTNERS AND I ARE NOT SKRULLS.
AND YOU'RE WRONG TO THINK YOUR POWER CAN HARM US NOW...
WE SHALL SEE...
THE ATTACK IS ALMOST INVISIBLY FAST, AND ALMOST IMMEASURABLY POWERFUL.
BUT...
YOU SEE, GLADIATOR? I'VE DEDUCED THE SECRET OF YOUR GREAT POWER. AND I HAVE CANCELLED IT.
YOU CAN DO NOTHING AGAINST ME.

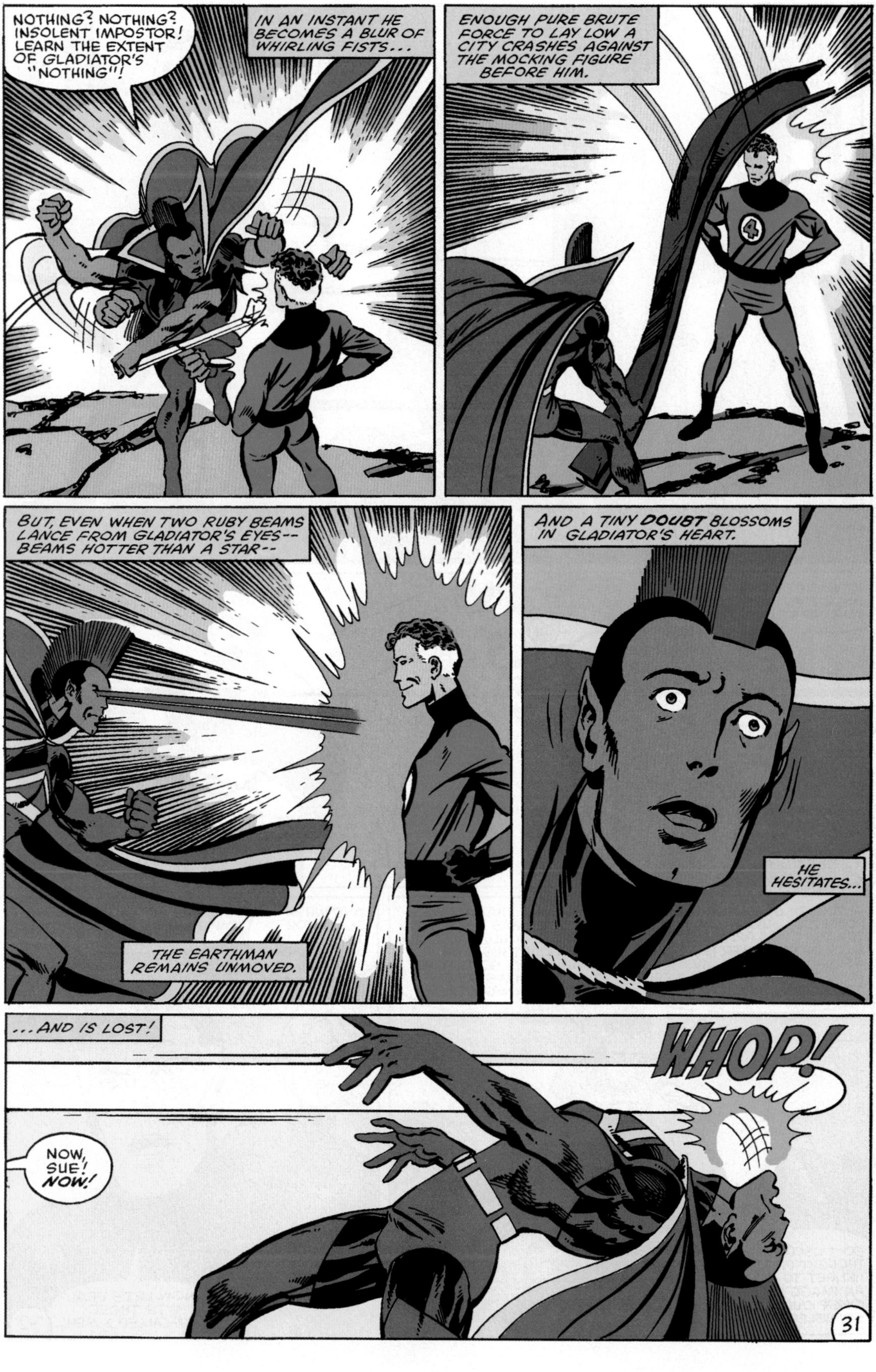
NOTHING? NOTHING? INSOLENT IMPOSTOR! LEARN THE EXTENT OF GLADIATOR'S "NOTHING"!
IN AN INSTANT HE BECOMES A BLUR OF WHIRLING FISTS...
ENOUGH PURE BRUTE FORCE TO LAY LOW A CITY CRASHES AGAINST THE MOCKING FIGURE BEFORE HIM.
BUT, EVEN WHEN TWO RUBY BEAMS LANCE FROM GLADIATOR'S EYES-- BEAMS HOTTER THAN A STAR--
THE EARTHMAN REMAINS UNMOVED.
AND A TINY DOUBT BLOSSOMS IN GLADIATOR'S HEART.
HE HESITATES...
...AND IS LOST!
WHOP!
NOW, SUE! NOW!

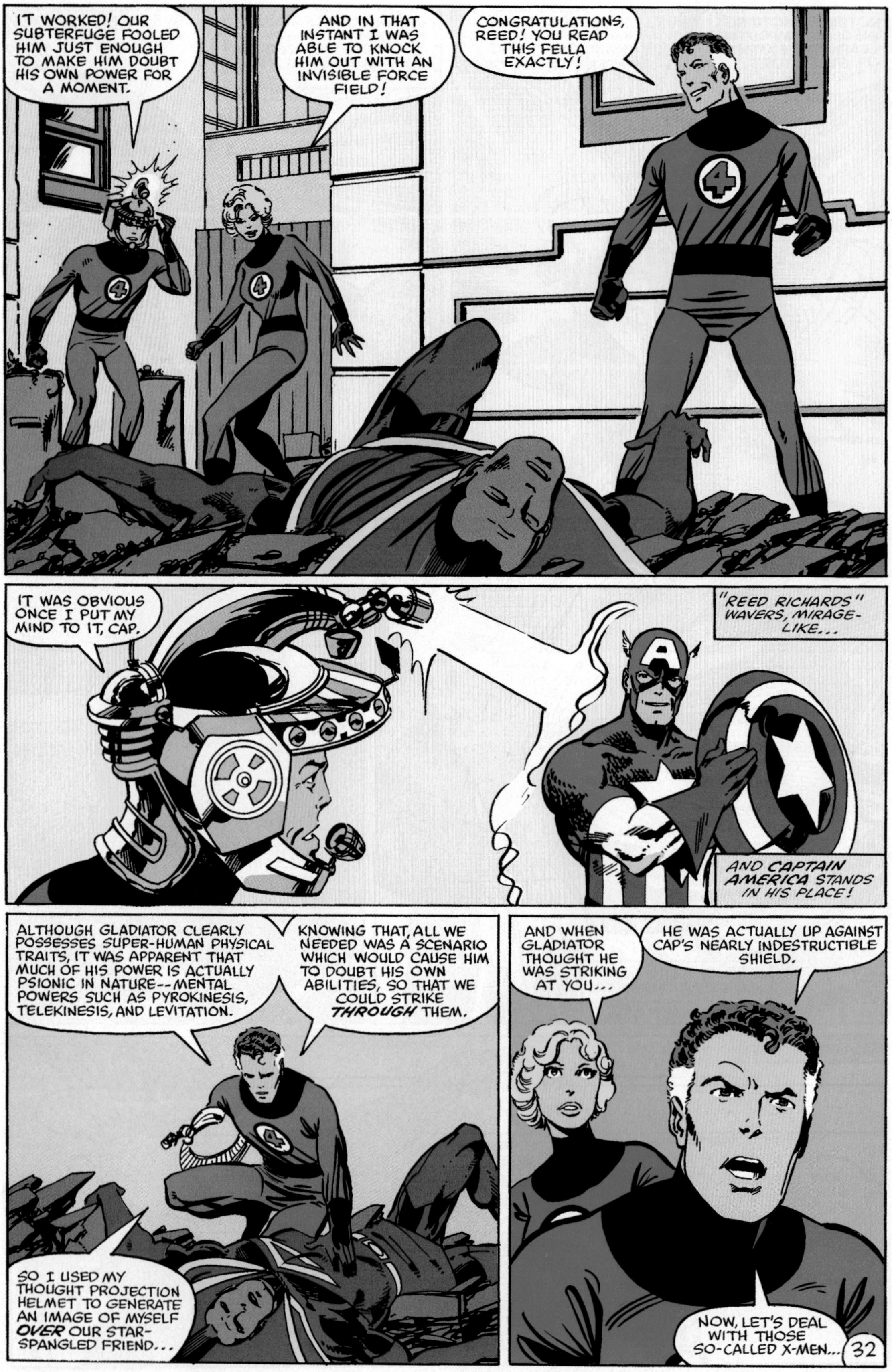
IT WORKED! OUR SUBTERFUGE FOOLED HIM JUST ENOUGH TO MAKE HIM DOUBT HIS OWN POWER FOR A MOMENT.
AND IN THAT INSTANT I WAS ABLE TO KNOCK HIM OUT WITH AN INVISIBLE FORCE FIELD!
CONGRATULATIONS, REED! YOU READ THIS FELLA EXACTLY!
IT WAS OBVIOUS ONCE I PUT MY MIND TO IT, CAP.
"REED RICHARDS" WAVERS, MIRAGE-LIKE...
AND CAPTAIN AMERICA STANDS IN HIS PLACE!
ALTHOUGH GLADIATOR CLEARLY POSSESSES SUPER-HUMAN PHYSICAL TRAITS, IT WAS APPARENT THAT MUCH OF HIS POWER IS ACTUALLY PSIONIC IN NATURE--MENTAL POWERS SUCH AS PYROKINESIS, TELEKINESIS, AND LEVITATION.
KNOWING THAT, ALL WE NEEDED WAS A SCENARIO WHICH WOULD CAUSE HIM TO DOUBT HIS OWN ABILITIES, SO THAT WE COULD STRIKE THROUGH THEM.
SO I USED MY THOUGHT PROJECTION HELMET TO GENERATE AN IMAGE OF MYSELF OVER OUR STAR-SPANGLED FRIEND...
AND WHEN GLADIATOR THOUGHT HE WAS STRIKING AT YOU...
HE WAS ACTUALLY UP AGAINST CAP'S NEARLY INDESTRUCTIBLE SHIELD.
NOW, LET'S DEAL WITH THOSE SO-CALLED X-MEN...
32

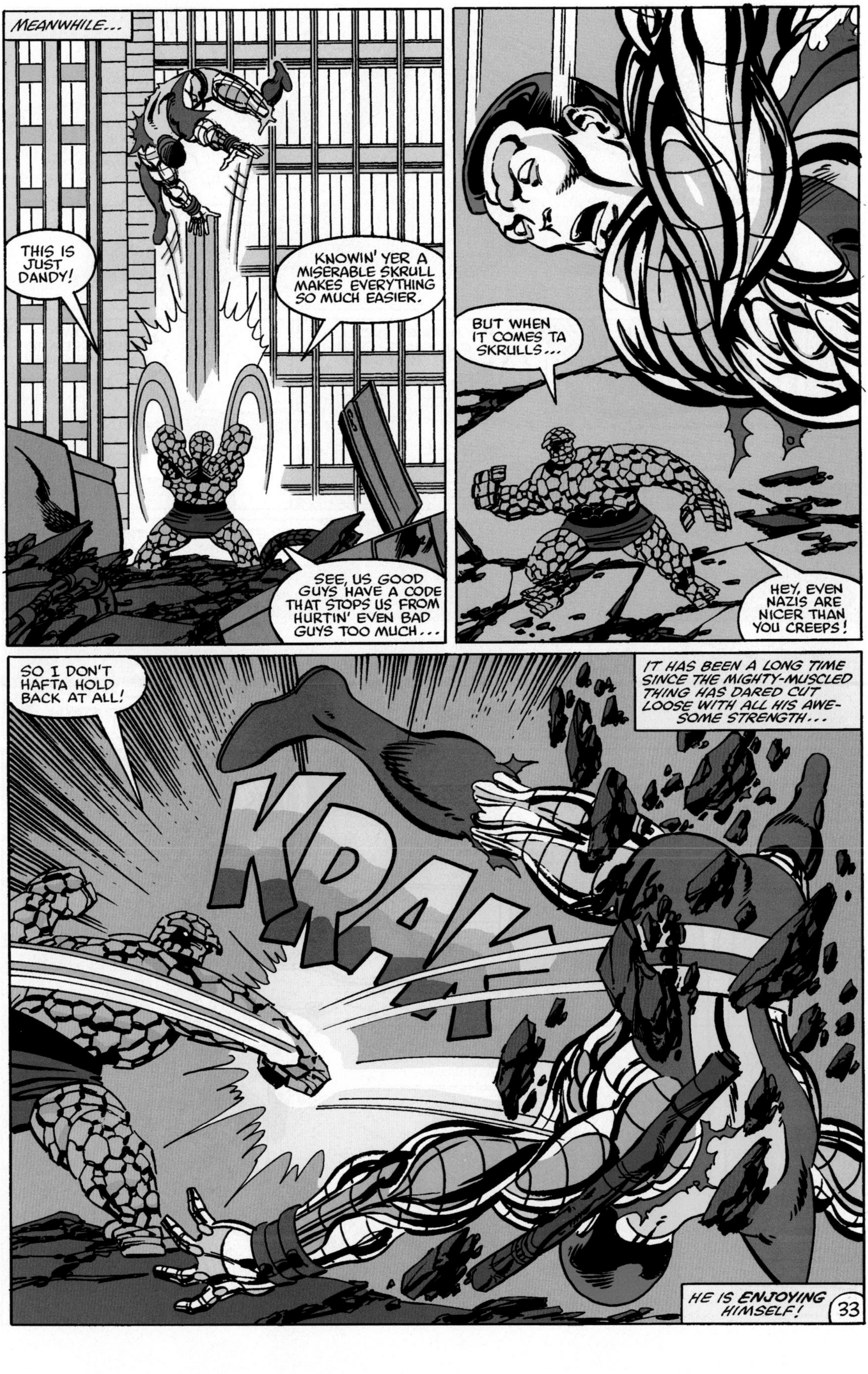
MEANWHILE...
THIS IS JUST DANDY!
KNOWIN' YER A MISERABLE SKRULL MAKES EVERYTHING SO MUCH EASIER.
SEE, US GOOD GUYS HAVE A CODE THAT STOPS US FROM HURTIN' EVEN BAD GUYS TOO MUCH...
BUT WHEN IT COMES TA SKRULLS...
HEY, EVEN NAZIS ARE NICER THAN YOU CREEPS!
SO I DON'T HAFTA HOLD BACK AT ALL!
IT HAS BEEN A LONG TIME SINCE THE MIGHTY-MUSCLED THING HAS DARED CUT LOOSE WITH ALL HIS AWESOME STRENGTH...
KRAK
HE IS ENJOYING HIMSELF!

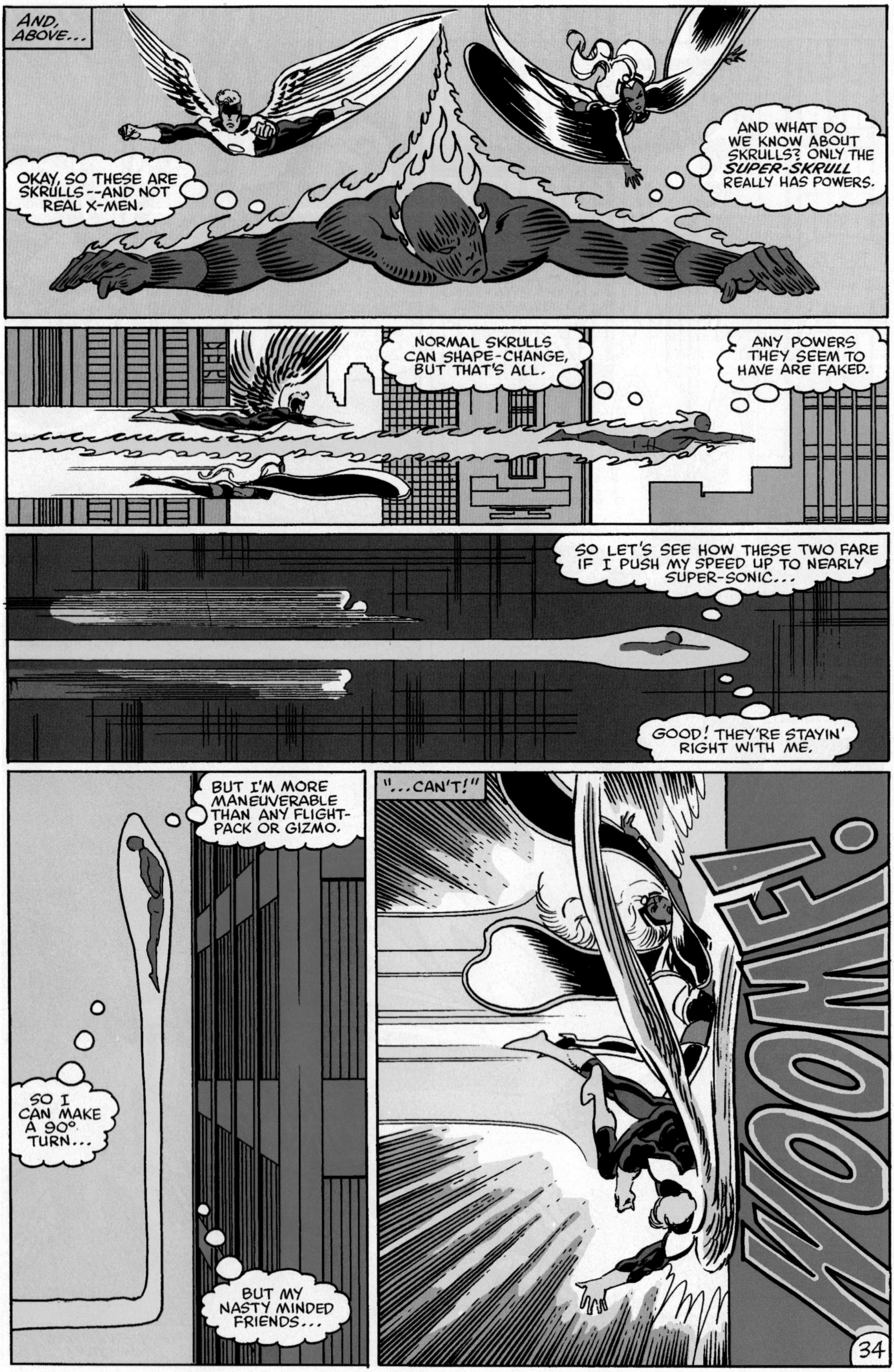
AND, ABOVE...
OKAY, SO THESE ARE SKRULLS--AND NOT REAL X-MEN.
AND WHAT DO WE KNOW ABOUT SKRULLS? ONLY THE SUPER-SKRULL REALLY HAS POWERS.
NORMAL SKRULLS CAN SHAPE-CHANGE, BUT THAT'S ALL.
ANY POWERS THEY SEEM TO HAVE ARE FAKED.
SO LET'S SEE HOW THESE TWO FARE IF I PUSH MY SPEED UP TO NEARLY SUPER-SONIC...
GOOD! THEY'RE STAYIN' RIGHT WITH ME.
BUT I'M MORE MANEUVERABLE THAN ANY FLIGHT-PACK OR GIZMO.
SO I CAN MAKE A 90° TURN...
BUT MY NASTY MINDED FRIENDS...
"...CAN'T!"
WHOOF!

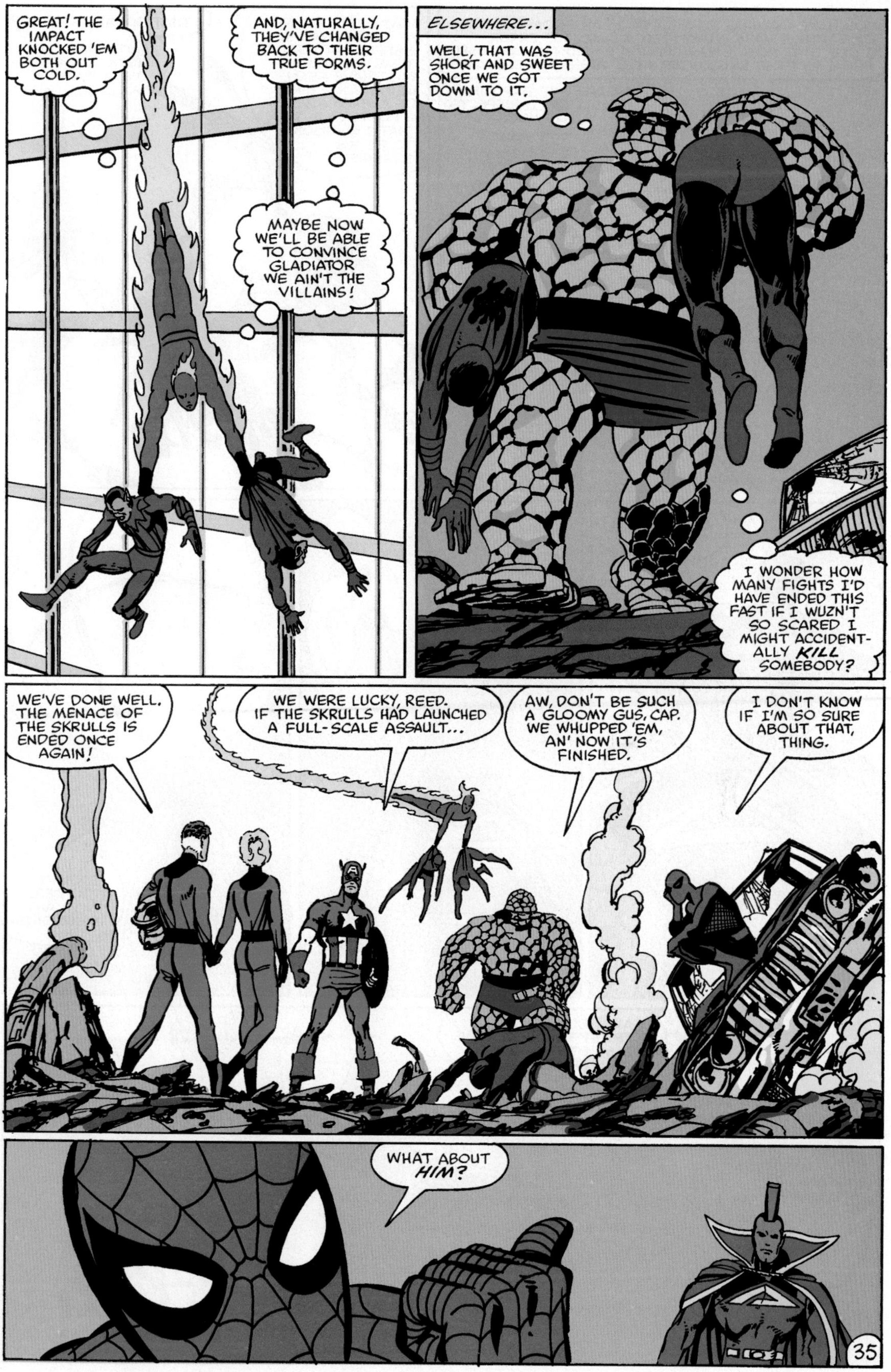
GREAT! THE IMPACT KNOCKED 'EM BOTH OUT COLD.
AND, NATURALLY, THEY'VE CHANGED BACK TO THEIR TRUE FORMS.
MAYBE NOW WE'LL BE ABLE TO CONVINCE GLADIATOR WE AIN'T THE VILLAINS!
ELSEWHERE...
WELL, THAT WAS SHORT AND SWEET ONCE WE GOT DOWN TO IT.
I WONDER HOW MANY FIGHTS I'D HAVE ENDED THIS FAST IF I WUZN'T SO SCARED I MIGHT ACCIDENTALLY KILL SOMEBODY?
WE'VE DONE WELL. THE MENACE OF THE SKRULLS IS ENDED ONCE AGAIN!
WE WERE LUCKY, REED. IF THE SKRULLS HAD LAUNCHED A FULL-SCALE ASSAULT...
AW, DON'T BE SUCH A GLOOMY GUS, CAP. WE WHUPPED 'EM, AN' NOW IT'S FINISHED.
I DON'T KNOW IF I'M SO SURE ABOUT THAT, THING.
WHAT ABOUT HIM?

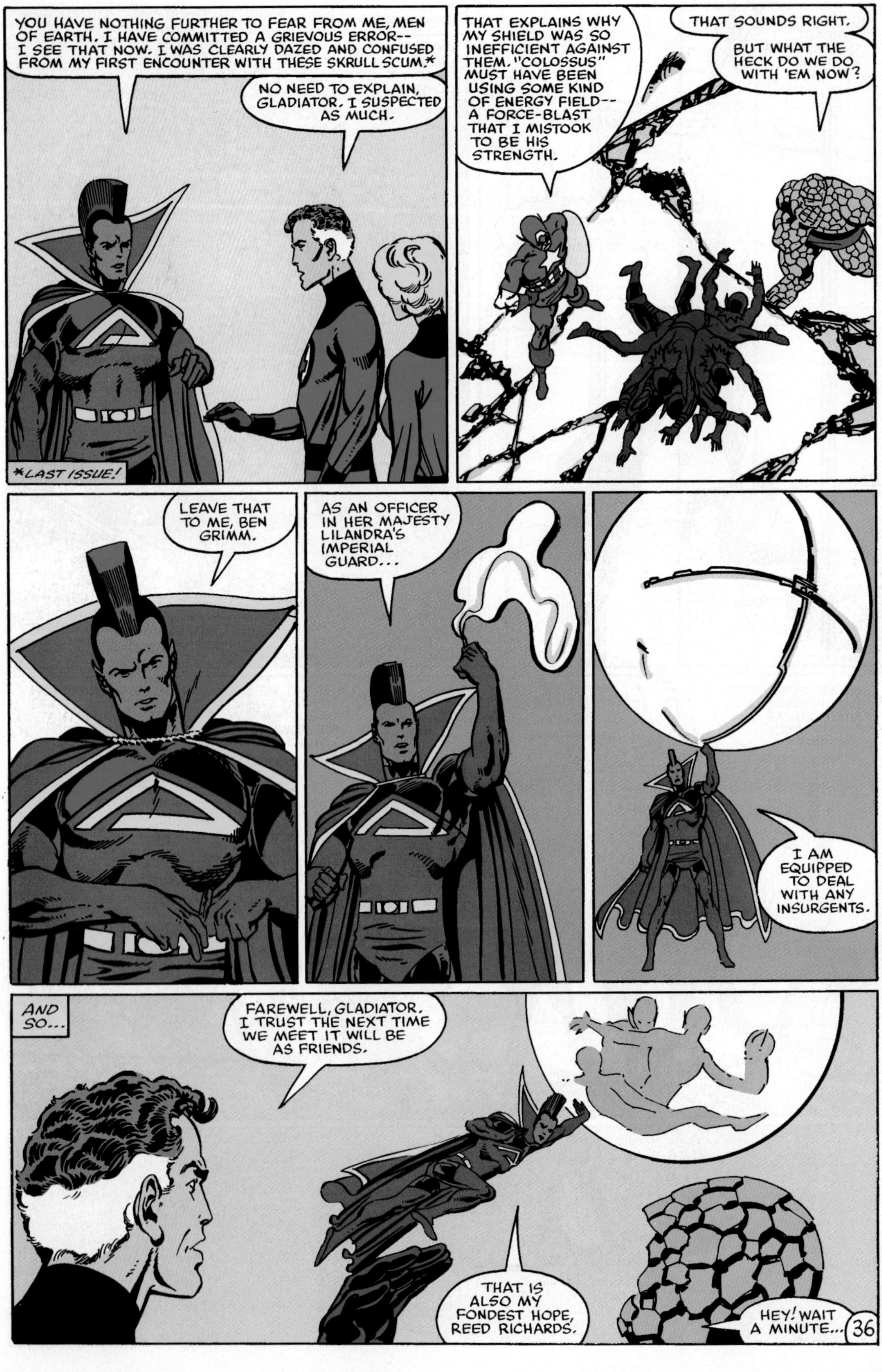
YOU HAVE NOTHING FURTHER TO FEAR FROM ME, MEN OF EARTH. I HAVE COMMITTED A GRIEVOUS ERROR-- I SEE THAT NOW. I WAS CLEARLY DAZED AND CONFUSED FROM MY FIRST ENCOUNTER WITH THESE SKRULL SCUM.*
NO NEED TO EXPLAIN, GLADIATOR. I SUSPECTED AS MUCH.
*LAST ISSUE!
THAT EXPLAINS WHY MY SHIELD WAS SO INEFFICIENT AGAINST THEM. "COLOSSUS" MUST HAVE BEEN USING SOME KIND OF ENERGY FIELD-- A FORCE-BLAST THAT I MISTOOK TO BE HIS STRENGTH.
THAT SOUNDS RIGHT.
BUT WHAT THE HECK DO WE DO WITH 'EM NOW?
LEAVE THAT TO ME, BEN GRIMM.
AS AN OFFICER IN HER MAJESTY LILANDRA'S IMPERIAL GUARD...
I AM EQUIPPED TO DEAL WITH ANY INSURGENTS.
AND SO...
FAREWELL, GLADIATOR. I TRUST THE NEXT TIME WE MEET IT WILL BE AS FRIENDS.
THAT IS ALSO MY FONDEST HOPE, REED RICHARDS.
HEY! WAIT A MINUTE...
36

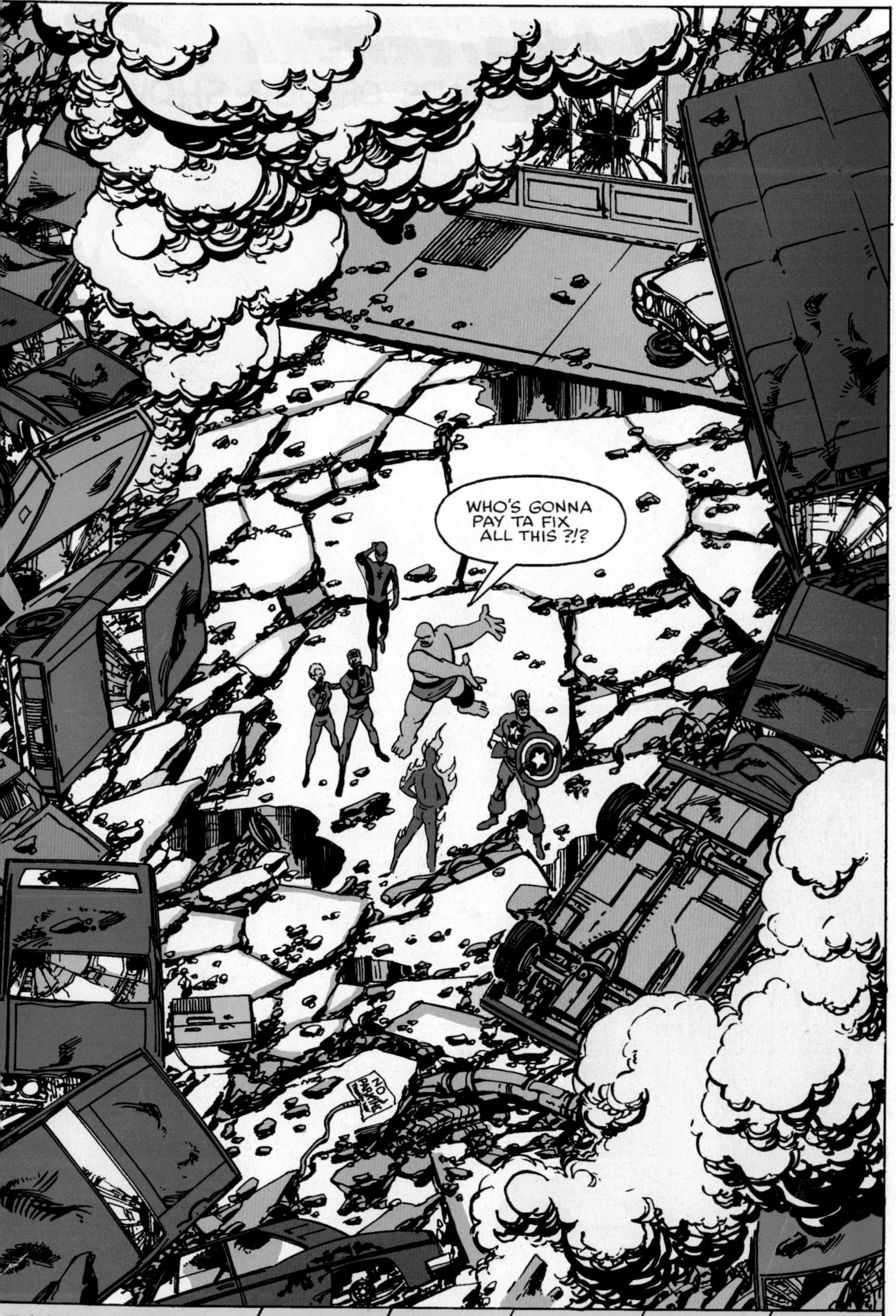
WHO'S GONNA PAY TA FIX ALL THIS ?!?

THIS
SSUE
ROUGHT
O YOU BY:

JOHN BYRNE
STORYTELLER

CHRISTIE SCHEELE
COLORIST

JOE ROSEN
LETTERER

TOM DeFALCO
SCRIPT EDITOR

JIM SALICRUP
PLOT EDITOR

JIM SHOOTER
EDITOR-IN-CHIEF

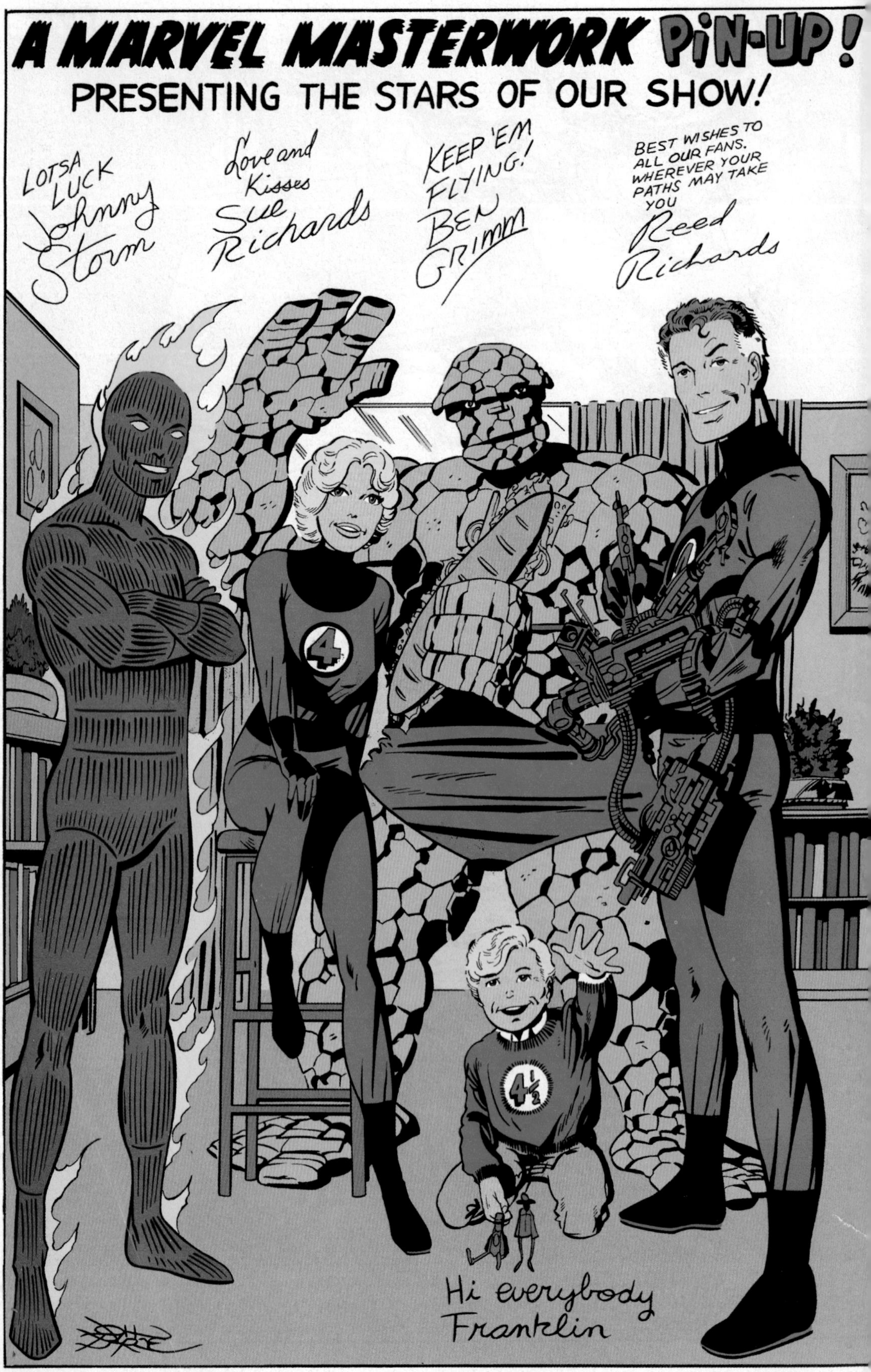
A MARVEL MASTERWORK PIN-UP!
PRESENTING THE STARS OF OUR SHOW!
LOTSA LUCK Johnny Storm
Love and Kisses Sue Richards
KEEP 'EM FLYING! BEN GRIMM
BEST WISHES TO ALL OUR FANS. WHEREVER YOUR PATHS MAY TAKE YOU Reed Richards
Hi everybody Franklin